NIGHT TRAIN TO NASHVILLE

NIGHT TRAIN TO NASHVILLE

THE GREATEST UNTOLD STORY OF MUSIC CITY

PAULA BLACKMAN

HARPER
HORIZON

Library of Congress Control Number: 2023932689

Printed in the United States of America
23 24 25 26 27 LBC 5 4 3 2 1

For my late mother, Anne, the talented wordsmith who nurtured me; my father, Ed, whose tough love gave me the perseverance necessary to turn a lofty dream into a reality; my Aunt Gayle; and my grandparents, Christine and Gab, whose love of life, family, and Southern storytelling inspired this book. I love you all.

CONTENTS

PART 3: THE 1960S

CHARACTERS

MAIN CHARACTERS

E. Gab "Blackie" Blackman	WLAC sales manager
Christine "Tee" Blackman	Gab's wife
Eddie Blackman	Gab and Christine's son
Susan "Gayle" Blackman	Gab and Christine's daughter
Anne Duff Blackman	Eddie's wife
William Sousa "Sou" Bridgeforth	New Era Club owner
Helen "Funny" Bridgeforth	Sou's wife
Harriett Gail Bridgeforth	Sou and Helen's daughter
James "Mister Jimmy" Stahlman	*Nashville Banner* newspaper owner
William "Hoss" Allen	WLAC disc jockey
Nancy Allen	Hoss's wife
Cecil Rogan Allen	Hoss's mother
Mamie Allen	Hoss's grandmother
Gene Nobles	WLAC disc jockey
John "John R" Richbourg	WLAC news announcer / disc jockey
Lillian "Lilli" Richbourg	John's first wife
Margaret Richbourg	John's second wife
Albert "Shorty" Banks	Sou's business partner
Katherine "Kat" Nuble	Sou's mistress / New Era Club waitress
Mayor Ben West	former *Nashville Banner* employee / Nashville mayor
Governor Frank Clement	Tennessee governor

Z. Alexander Looby	civil rights attorney/activist
J. Carlton Loser	district attorney
James Edwards	Tennessee State Prison warden

WLAC MINOR CHARACTERS

J. Truman Ward	station owner
F. C. Sowell	general manager
David Binns	station engineer
Paul Oliphant	program director
Tom Baker	former sales manager
Herman Grizzard	news and sports announcer/disc jockey
Jimmy Ward	Truman's son
Hugh "Baby" Jarrett	disc jockey
Guilford Dudley	L & C board member
Paul Mountcastle	L & C board member
Randy Wood	advertiser
Ernie Young	advertiser
John Cheek	car dealer advertiser
John Sloan	department store advertiser
Fred Harvey	department store advertiser
Sam Moore	Bible advertiser
Sam Phillips	record producer/former WLAC employee
Mary Elizabeth Hicks	staff musician/vocalist
Jordon Stokes	attorney
Don Whitehead	news announcer

NEW ERA CLUB MINOR CHARACTERS

Christine "Kitty" Kittrell	New Era Club vocalist
Ted Jarrett	New Era Club house musician/composer/producer
Edward "Skippy" Brooks	house band leader
Clarence "Gatemouth" Brown	house band leader
Nathan Bellamy	club manager
Wilma Jean	Kat Nuble's daughter

NASHVILLE BANNER CHARACTERS

Jack Phillips	salesman
Fritz Stahlman	assistant secretary
Dick Battle	reporter
Charlie Moss	managing editor
Robert Churchwell	reporter
John Malone	photographer
Ann Stahlman	Jimmy's daughter

STUDENT PROTEST MOVEMENT CHARACTERS

James Lawson	activist leader
Rev. Kelly Miller Smith	adviser
Rev. C. T. Vivian	adviser
Dr. Martin Luther King Jr.	adviser
Paul LaPrad	student protester
Diane Nash	student protester
John Lewis	student protester
Guy Carawan	musician

TIME LINE OF EVENTS

1922
Gab starts working full-time for the Castner-Knott department store
Truman Ward buys WLAC radio

1925
Sou moves to Nashville
The Grand Ole Opry broadcast debuts on WSM radio in Nashville
WLAC receives its radio broadcast license

1931
Gab goes to work at the *Nashville Banner*

1933
Nineteen-year-old Cordie Creek is lynched in Columbia, Tennessee

1934
Sou opens a pool hall on Charlotte Avenue

1936
Sou opens his first New Era Club adjacent to the pool hall

1941
Sou relocates the New Era Club to Fourth Avenue North

1943
Hoss Allen enlists in the army

1944

John Richbourg leaves WLAC temporarily for the navy

Sam Phillips is hired as John's temporary replacement

1945

Black caddies from the Richland, Woodmont, and Belle Meade country clubs build a golf course under the Cleveland Street viaduct

1946

John Richbourg returns from the navy

Columbia Race Riot—Black residents fight back after James Stephenson and his mother are victims of racism; this event becomes the opening salvo in the civil rights movement

Gab arrives at WLAC radio; Gene Nobles begins broadcasting race records

B.B. King leaves Indianola, Mississippi, for Beale Street in Memphis

Hoss Allen returns home from the army

Nashville civic leaders' proposal to build a city auditorium to replace the slums fails

1947

Sister Rosetta Tharp discovers Little Richard in Macon, Georgia

1948

Hoss Allen stars in the title role of *Othello* at Vanderbilt, resulting in his winning a scholarship to a prestigious summer stock theater in New England

WLAC radio applies for television broadcast license

Hoss gets part-time clerical job at new station WMAK

1949

Christine Blackman is elected head of the Nashville Council of Church Women

Gab hires Hoss Allen

City passes auditorium bond referendum

B.B. King debuts on Memphis station WDIA

1950

Sam Phillips opens a recording studio in Memphis
Robert Churchwell joins the *Nashville Banner*
Sixteen-year-old James Brown sent to prison
Eighteen-year-old Hal Hebb wounded in Korea

1951

B.B. King's "3 O'Clock Blues" reaches #1 on R & B chart
Sam Phillips records Ike Turner's masterpiece "Rocket 88"
Sou buys the Birmingham Black Barons
Ben West elected mayor of Nashville
Sou turns in his federal gambling tax stamp

1952

Thirty-two-year-old Frank Clement elected governor of Tennessee
Truman Ward sells WLAC back to Life and Casualty Insurance Company
James Brown is released from prison
Christine Kittrell records "Just Sittin' Here Drinkin'"
University of Mississippi students vote Gene Nobles favorite deejay
Big Mama Thornton records "Hound Dog"

1953

Sam Phillips records Johnny Bragg and the Prisonaires
Gab's nephew Buddy is killed in a plane crash
FCC awards WLAC a television broadcast license
Hoss Allen begins weekday *Top Five* broadcast

1954

Supreme Court issues *Brown v. Board* ruling
Sou hires Charley Pride as pitcher for Black Barons
Kitty Kittrell and Little Richard record "Lord Have Mercy" at the New Era
Frank Clement reelected governor
Sou indicted on federal gambling tax statute
Sam Phillips records Elvis Presley's first hit, "That's All Right"
Ray Charles records "I Got a Woman"

1955

City auditorium forces relocation of New Era Club to Twelfth and Charlotte
WLAC creates radio's first self-censorship board
Hall Hebb joins the Prisonaires
Hoss meets his mistress, Della Reese
John Richbourg's wife abandons her family
Sou is convicted on federal tax statutes, files appeal
Little Richard records "Tutti Frutti"
James Brown works as Little Richard's understudy/replacement singer
Rosa Parks is arrested for refusing to yield her bus seat

1956

Sou acquitted on appeal
Hoss Allen debuts James Brown's hit record, "Please, Please, Please"
Triple zero bet breaks numbers bankers
B.B. King performs 342 gigs during the calendar year
Little Richard, Fats Domino, and others perform at first interracial concert
    in Tennessee
Little Richard records Royal Crown Hairdressing commercial

1957

Court-ordered school integration brings violent protests
Hattie Cotton Elementary School bombed
Jewish Community Center bombed
Life and Casualty tower opens
John Lewis enters Nashville's American Baptist Theological Seminary

1958

James Lawson begins weekly civil rights lectures for college students

1959

Hoss takes over for Gene Nobles
Johnny Bragg pardoned by Governor Clement
Payola bribery scandal ensnares WLAC deejays

1960

Nashville college students protest segregation at downtown lunch counters

Hoss and John R charged in payola scandal

Z. Alexander Looby's home bombed

Confronted by student protestors, Mayor West capitulates

Nashville becomes first Southern city to desegregate its public spaces

Martin Luther King Jr. speaks to Nashville's student protestors

Johnny Bragg arrested

Gab fires Hoss for payola scandal misbehavior

1961

Hoss hired as southern sales representative for Chess Records

Gab hires Hugh Jarrett as Hoss's replacement

Kat Nuble's daughter's death causes fallout, breakup of Sou's marriage

Jimi Hendrix arrives at nearby Fort Campbell

1962

Gab advises John to create and sell a scrapbook to resolve financial issues; *Soul Book* sells one hundred thousand copies.

Gab is honored with sales award for implementing a strategy to correct payola issues

Jimi Hendrix meets New Era Club musicians at Clarksville's Pink Poodle Club

Student civil rights protests resume; fifteen-year-old Ella Bigham knocked unconscious by police

City auditorium attracts acts formerly seen at the New Era Club

1963

Nashville switches from city government to municipal government

Martin Luther King Jr. delivers "I Have a Dream" speech during the March on Washington

President Kennedy addresses civil rights during speech at Vanderbilt

Etta James records "Etta Rocks the House" at the New Era Club

Gab fires Hugh Jarrett, rehires Hoss; Gab implements a monitoring system known as "Blackie's Bible"

Gab advertises Bible created by door-to-door salesman Sam Moore

President Kennedy assassinated

Hal Hebb murdered; Hal's brother, Bobby, composes "Sunny"

1964

Noble Blackwell creates variety show *Night Train* for WLAC-TV; Jackie
Shane and Jimi Hendrix appear

Cassius Clay/Muhammad Ali holds court at New Era Club

1965

Nancy divorces Hoss

Hoss creates *Night Train*–type musical variety show, *The !!!! Beat*

1966

Otis Redding replaces Hoss as emcee of final *The !!!! Beat* after Hoss becomes
inebriated

After police crackdown on numbers runners, process server James Utley is
wounded and his four-year-old daughter, Antoinette, is murdered

1967

Police raid Sou's package store, confiscate his entire liquor inventory

Stahlman tries to prevent Martin Luther King Jr. and Stokely Carmichael
from speaking at Vanderbilt; riots follow

Nashville civic leaders reroute the planned construction of I-40 in order to
demolish Jefferson Street, home to 80 percent of the city's colored-owned
businesses

1968

Martin Luther King Jr. is assassinated

Gab hires first Black newscaster on a national network, Don Whitehead

James Brown records "Say It Loud—I'm Black and I'm Proud"

1969

Nashville's Black business district bulldozed to make way for a freeway

Former governor Frank Clement is killed in a car accident

Jimi Hendrix performs at Woodstock

John Richbourg discovers Joe Simon, produces Joe's #1 hit, "The Chokin' Kind"

James Brown performs at Nashville civic auditorium; John R honors him as
the bestselling R & B musician of 1969

1970

Hoss is charged with second-degree murder following a deadly car crash

Johnny Bragg sent to prison for third time

Hoss tapes his radio programs from a home studio

1971

Hoss enters Cumberland Heights rehab center

Judge dismisses Hoss's murder charges

B.B. King wins first Grammy award for "The Thrill Is Gone"

Aretha Franklin and Stevie Wonder perform in concert at Fisk University

Johnny Bragg receives third pardon

1972

Life and Casualty Insurance hires consultants who advise a switch to Top 40;
Gab and John R oppose the program change

Hoss changes his format to *Early Morning Gospel Hour*

1973

John Richbourg retires in protest to format change

Gab hires Spider Harrison, first Black deejay on WLAC as John R's
replacement

Gab retires in protest to Top 40 format change

PROLOGUE

SENTIMENTAL JOURNEY

> We started playing R & B with a definite
> purpose. We were trying to open up a new
> market, and we knew what we were doing.
>
> —JOHN RICHBOURG

My grandfather, E. Gab "Blackie" Blackman, kept a pair of well-worn, two-tone leather dance shoes in his closet. A cherished relic from another time, they stood apart from the wingtips, topsiders, golf shoes, and slippers he wore regularly. In the heaviness of their metal heel plates and stubbornness of the creases, the shoes seemed to boast of having taken him on a sentimental journey. When he was in his late eighties and walked with a cane, I asked if he planned to go dancing anytime soon. He laughed, blue eyes sparkling, and said, "I didn't keep those shoes for dancing. I've kept them for their *story*." *Night Train to Nashville* is that story.

I unknowingly began my research on the *Night Train* story in 1972. Each summer, I would spend many weeks at my grandparents' home on Old Hickory Lake near Nashville. However, the summer of '72 was special because it was the first time I'd had my grandparents to myself since my brothers were born. Mom was pregnant with my sister, and my brothers, involved in sports, couldn't leave Omaha, where we lived at the time. I was "fifteen going on thirty," according to my father, who was "thirty-five going on fifteen," according to my mother.

On the last night of the school year, I had slipped out of my bedroom window to attend a party my father had forbidden. When I came home in the wee hours, I discovered my window locked and my father waiting by the front door.

"Hopeless! You're grounded for life!" he yelled. Because my middle name is Hope, my father had nicknamed me Hopeless. He confined me to the house, where I sulked and whined and complained—as only a teenage girl can—until my very pregnant mother determined she was enduring the brunt of Dad's punishment. Exhausted from the constant tension between my father and me, my mother declared herself to be on the verge of a nervous breakdown. To keep the peace, Dad sent me to stay with his parents, Gab and Christine, whom I called Pop and Tee.

It was the greatest summer of my life!

I packed my suitcase with my summertime essentials: a church dress, two bikinis, Daisy Duke cutoffs, a pair of white Keds, and my favorite albums—mostly Motown, featuring Diana Ross, Stevie Wonder, and Marvin Gaye, supplemented by a few 45s from Carole King and James Taylor. I listened primarily to rhythm and blues (R & B), and while I had visited Pop's office and met the deejays, it wasn't until that summer I learned of the significant role WLAC played in the development of R & B. When I placed my beloved Supremes' *Farewell* album on the hi-fi, my grandfather said, "You know, Diana Ross gave us a lot of credit for her success."

"Gave who?"

"Us! WLAC." He told me stories of why he joined WLAC and how he and Gene Nobles pioneered R & B programming, long before Barry Gordy Jr. and Smokey Robinson came to the station to pitch him their new venture, Motown.

Pop was a master front-porch storyteller, pre-television-style. He had the gift Robert Penn Warren described as having "sprung from the pores of Southern society. Elaborate, winding, wandering creations that might never wear out, stories full of human perception and subtlety, told with a richness of laughter and expression. Not idle gossip, not diversions, mind you, but tales of wit and character, pathos and scope."[1]

I had the great fortune of hearing my grandfather tell his stories in that rich

---

1. John Egerton, *Nashville: The Faces of Two Centuries* (Nashville: PlusMedia, 1979), 214.

Southern style. They captivated me, and I couldn't get enough of them. Many nights after dinner, we would hop into his convertible Karmann Ghia and drive to the Tastee-Freez, where he'd order a vanilla cone and I'd get rainbow sherbet. The car's headlight dimmer switch had been rigged to tune the radio to WLAC. We'd cruise, top down, and as it was too early for WLAC's R & B broadcasts, I'd scan the stations for a Motown song I could sing along to. After my lyrical knowledge display, Pop would tap the dimmer, return to WLAC, and tell me a story related to the time, place, and musician we'd just heard. He didn't *love* the music. Not the way I did. However, he *loved* the musicians, especially B.B. King, and his deejays, particularly Hoss Allen.

Night Train to Nashville is a compilation of as many of those stories as I can recall. In addition to chronicling Pop's firsthand accounts of the legendary broadcasts, I have spent the better part of the last fifteen years verifying his tales, reading, researching, and interviewing the people who experienced these events with him—including B.B. King and Little Richard.

The *Night Train to Nashville* story was fairly well-known locally, following the Country Music Hall of Fame and Museum's exhibit of the same name. The museum's retrospective told a fascinating, although incomplete, story of the origin of rhythm and blues on WLAC. This book seeks to tell the rest of the story, the authentic lost history that was never revealed because it was not politically correct—that is, not the "Nashville Way." Instead, a "press release" version was circulated that omitted key details and led listeners to assume WLAC's extraordinary success happened accidentally. However, to anyone familiar with the Jim Crow South, the tale of two young Black men who entered the locked Third National Bank Building, bypassed security, rode an operator-manned elevator to the top floor, got past the locked lobby doors and then into a locked broadcast booth, where they interrupted an on-air announcer—who pleasantly asked the unwelcome intruders what he could do for them—sounded too fishy to be true. For sixty years folks have scratched their heads over how that had happened. The big hole in that story is obvious, isn't it? They had been invited and escorted.

What follows is the true, little-known account of how and *why* Gab Blackman launched the first national broadcast of what was then considered taboo race music. WLAC's foray into R & B was not accidental, nor was it done for socially progressive reasons. And make no mistake: neither Gab Blackman nor WLAC's owner, Truman Ward, was a white savior. The reality was the opposite—Black musicians saved radio. The prevailing thought at the time was television would kill radio. WLAC's revolutionary broadcast was created as a hedge against the anticipated catastrophe. What they hadn't anticipated was that this music—considered too low-class and dirty for the airwaves—would attract a mixed-race audience and inspire a cultural revolution.

While this story may seem like ancient history, what Gab experienced during this time of great societal change is relevant to understanding the nation's current racial tensions. When I first listened to my grandfather's stories, it was the music and musicians that interested me. However, as I dug deeper, through my research, I realized this story was about much more than the music, the broadcasts, and the musicians. It was historically significant because the broadcasts influenced a generation and inspired a cultural revolution.

At the time these events occurred, Nashville was segregated. Not into separate and equal halves but ruthlessly and inequitably, like a body beheaded. No interaction between the races existed beyond Blacks performing services for whites. When I started elementary school, three years *after* Nashville desegregated, the city still operated this way. And as I was born into this environment, it seemed normal. I went to school with other white children, in the same way I went to Sunday school with other Lutheran children. I never thought it odd—until I left the South.

I knew my viewpoints of those events were limited by my own and my grandfather's *white* perspective. To chronicle this story accurately, I needed a storytelling partner who could provide the *Black* perspective. My husband prayed about it. I meditated.

Even as I write this years later, I still find it hard to believe what happened. The next day, Dr. Kenneth Ulmer, a middle-aged Black man, walked into my home and changed my life.

Ken was about to purchase a home nearby, and when he saw my daughter put an Open House sign in our yard, he decided to come in for a peek. We enjoyed a pleasant conversation. Then something auspicious occurred: his wife came in and he called her Tee, the same nickname as my grandmother's. I felt a sense of déjà vu and asked Ken if he'd ever heard of Hoss Allen, John R, or Gene Nobles. His face lit up and he responded in a way only someone familiar with that broadcast could.

"Randy's? Do I know Randy's? Why, girl, they're the reason I changed my college major from music to radio broadcasting." Then a curious look crossed his face. "Better question is, how do *you* know Randy's?"

Randy's was the colloquial term the audience used to refer to the night-time R & B broadcasts after the program's first sponsor, Randy's Records. Dr. Ulmer had listened to the broadcast as a teenager. His perspective was precisely what I lacked.

My grandmother used to tell me coincidence was God's secret language, and if my daughter had placed that sign in the yard at any other moment, Dr. Ulmer and I might never have met. Just like that, I'd found my first story-telling partner.

To tell an authentic story of that time and place from the perspective of both races, I alternate narratives between my grandfather and William "Sou" Bridgeforth. Sou owned Nashville's legendary Chitlin' Circuit nightclub, the New Era. Sou's daughter, Harriett Bridgeforth Jordon, became my second story-telling partner, and she provided generous assistance to bring her father's story to life. Thus, *Night Train to Nashville* is as much Harriett's story as it is mine. Harriett and Dr. Ulmer were united in their belief that I should tell the true, unvarnished history. Where the record shows that characters used the N-word, they requested I not "whitewash" history to make these real-life people appear less offensive than they were.

Over the years it took to research and write this book, Harriett, Dr. Ulmer, and my princely mentor, the late Gregory Allen Howard, became some of my dearest friends. The gratitude I feel for their encouragement, advice, and assis-tance is unquantifiable.

In 1946, when Gene Nobles placed that first "race record" on the WLAC turntable, he transmitted sounds into the ionosphere that previously had been heard only in Black nightclubs. Those revolutionary vibrations received in homes throughout forty states marked the historic moment that the national

XXVI PROLOGUE

airwaves were integrated. Back when the only people who referred to Nashville as "Music City" were the country music fans who listened to WSM's Grand Ole Opry, WLAC's nighttime rhythm and blues signal served as a beacon that attracted an extraordinary array of musicians to Nashville: B.B. King, James Brown, Little Richard, Muddy Waters, Smokey Robinson, Etta James, Ella Fitzgerald, Jimi Hendrix, Ray Charles, Otis Redding, Diana Ross, Gladys Knight—the list goes on and on. When this music, with its thought-provoking lyrics and seductive beat, blanketed the Jim Crow South, a generation of previously divided people laced up their well-worn shoes and came together to dance, march, and ultimately change the world.

PART 1
THE 1940S

Before the internet and before the nightly TV shows, before Dr. King and Rosa Parks, there was *Jet* magazine, the national black newspapers, and WLAC Nashville, Tennessee.

—REV. JESSE JACKSON AT ARETHA FRANKLIN'S FUNERAL

1

AWAY DOWN SOUTH IN DIXIE

We had this guy nobody ever mentions. His name
was E. G. Blackman, and he was the sales manager.
He saw the great potential in this black music and in
this black audience that no one had ever tapped.

—WILLIAM "HOSS" ALLEN III

FEBRUARY 25, 1946

E. Gab "Blackie" Blackman waited for his ride on the corner of Woodmont Boulevard and McNairy Lane. His overcoat collar was turned up against the early morning wind, hiding the pinkish imprint of his wife's lipstick on his cheek. His belly was full of soft-scrambled eggs; his trouser pocket held index cards, a golf pencil, quarters, and a starched white handkerchief. For these and other reasons, he felt like the most fortunate man in Tennessee.

Gab enjoyed the carpool rides to the *Banner* newspaper with his coworkers, Fritz Stahlman and Jack Phillips. He was relieved they would soon no longer be necessary, though he knew he'd miss the camaraderie. It occurred to him that today would mark the first Monday in fifteen years his workweek wouldn't begin with a walk down Church Street to the department stores.

These Monday morning store visits weren't a requirement; rather, they were a sentimental gesture he'd established to honor his three mentors: his father, Eddie, who had been the building engineer of Castner-Knott department store; his uncle Carter, who held the same position at Cain-Sloan; and his uncle Finch Clark, who ran Castner-Knott's advertising department.

Gab was twelve years old when he'd started working as an errand runner for Finch. He would pick up ad proofs from the newspaper, distribute them for corrections, then take Finch's edited pages back to the paper. Afterward, he'd join his father and uncles at a lunch counter, where the men would regale Gab with funny mercantile tales. Gab enjoyed the Saturday tutorials for two years, until his father died unexpectedly. In an era prior to social security, Gab worked every available after-school hour to help his mother pay expenses. On Sunday afternoons, he tap-danced in local theater matinees, often in black-face. A year later, the family's financial pressures worsened when his sister's husband died, leaving the teenaged Gab with *two* heartbroken widows to support. He dropped out of school to work full-time. Eventually, his sister found a secretarial job, and Gab convinced Central High to let him return. He was a nineteen-year-old junior when the class voted him "happiest, wittiest, and best dancer."[1]

After high school, Gab worked as Castner's newsprint layout artist and copywriter. In 1931, James "Mister Jimmy" Stahlman, owner of the *Nashville Banner*, having noticed Gab's sunny disposition and work ethic, offered him an advertising sales position. Knowing the *Banner*'s staff were nearly all Vanderbilt University graduates, Gab realized he'd have to work harder and smarter than his coworkers. To compete with his erudite colleagues, Gab committed to becoming the newspaper's most well-informed employee.

Before long, Fritz's car pulled up. Gab climbed in and placed his bulging portfolio beside him. Jack pointed at the folder. "What'd you study this weekend, Blackie?"

"New cars," Gab said. "They should be rolling into town any day."

Since the automobile factories had been converted for the war effort, cars were hard to come by; gas, tires, and replacement parts were rationed. Gab,

---

1. Central High School Megaphone, 1927.

Jack, and Fritz economized by carpooling to save wear on their aging vehicles. The new postwar automobiles were expected any day, and Gab wanted to be one of the first to acquire one. After having researched the models, he'd decided on a 1946 Dodge sedan and was eager to visit the dealership.

Each morning, Fritz, Jack, and Gab tried to anticipate the subject of Mister Jimmy's editorial meeting and predict his most outlandish statement. On this day, they agreed his topic would be the city's newly proposed auditorium. It not only would be a great addition to downtown but would clear out a Negro shantytown of ramshackle shacks. The men favored the proposal and predicted Jimmy would be its most vocal supporter.[2]

Gab mimicked his prediction of Jimmy's outrageous statement: "Those Negro outhouses stink up the city to high heaven," he said in a perfect impersonation of Jimmy. "Nashville's supposed to look like Athens and smell like magnolias. Let's move 'em out!"

Fritz and Jack laughed. A gifted mimic, Gab could voice a conversation between four dialects so perfectly a blindfolded listener would think four individuals had spoken.

"That's good," Jack said. "But you left out what he thinks Nashville should sound like."

The men knew Jimmy shared the disdain most of the city's aristocrats had for the Grand Ole Opry crowd. They didn't appreciate the way the city sounded when hillbillies gathered at the Ryman and picked, plucked, and warbled about how great country life is when you're poor and in love. Or worse, the shrill reverberations that spilled from the juke joints a few blocks up the street, where gutbucket bluesmen touted a brokenhearted, down-on-your-luck misery.

Gab restated his prediction: "The stench of Negro outhouses is not what Nashville should smell like. It should look like Athens, smell like magnolias, and sound like an orchestra of songbirds chirping the 'Hallelujah' Chorus."

"That's it!" Fritz said. He pulled a quarter from his pocket. "My money's on that one."

"No," Jack said. "Jimmy's Nashville would sound like this." He whistled "Dixie."

---

2. Mary Jane Brooks, "City Auditorium Plaza Plans Announced," *Nashville Banner*, February 23, 1946, 1.

Fritz and Gab laughed. Jimmy was so hyper-Southern he often claimed he regretted being born fifty years too late to ride with prominent Confederate general Nathan Bedford Forrest.[3]

Gab enunciated: "Jimmy Stahlman's Nashville looks like Athens, smells like magnolias, and sounds like the Rebel Drum and Bugle Corps playing 'Dixie.'"

"With all the troops whistling along," Fritz added as he steered into the parking lot.

"And that ain't just whistling 'Dixie,'" Gab said. The three men whistled "Dixie" together.

Gab continued to whistle as he sprinted up the stairs to his desk on the third floor. His recent promotion hadn't come with an office or a raise—just a business card worded "*Banner Newspaper Sunday Magazine.* E. Galbreath Blackman, Publisher." Gab's primary responsibility was sales, and the pretentious title was simply Jimmy's idiom for top revenue producer.

The *Sunday Magazine* was a popular publication, short on narrative and long on photographs and ads. Gab had final content approval, which enabled him to take advantage of the power of the press. He hoped to use this to persuade his friend John Cheek to let him have one of the first new Dodges.

Gab kept a desk drawer stuffed with his quirky collection of index cards. For years, he had jotted onto cards snippets of data: quotes, statistics, and little-known trivia he thought might one day prove useful. He opened the drawer, tossed in the cards he'd created about cars, then dashed downstairs to attend the meeting employees called the Amen Chorus—the only acceptable responses were either "Amen" or "That's right, Mister Jimmy."[4]

The meetings were torturous because anything Jimmy said would later be refined and printed in his From the Shoulder column—required reading for the staff, who secretly called it From the Armpit. Gab and Fritz pulled out their index cards and golf pencils to finish their game. The men couldn't always predict Jimmy's speeches, yet they were more often right than wrong, as Jimmy had his favorites: the US Navy, Andrew Jackson, Vanderbilt, the Boy Scouts, Belle Meade Country Club, and the Old South lifestyle (Jim Crow

3. James G. Stahlman, "From the Shoulder," *Nashville Banner*, May 14, 1947.
4. David Halberstam, *The Children* (New York: Fawcett Books, 1998), 116.

segregation). And he also had his obvious foes: communists, Russians, radio, law violators, Negroes, the federal government, daylight saving time, and proponents of social equality (integration).[5]

Jimmy announced, "It won't be long before the Congress gets down to merging the army and the navy."

Gab scribbled: *Having served in both the army and the navy.* He showed the card to Fritz, who began a finger countdown. Fritz raised eight fingers before Jimmy said the words Gab predicted. Fritz slapped a quarter into Gab's hand. Gab slipped the coin into his pocket, turned the notecard over, and wrote, *Order new car! Red. Whitewall tires. 16" rims.*

Fritz tapped Gab's notecard with his golf pencil. "Yeah, ha! Good luck," he whispered.

Gab could envision his dream car: a four-door sedan, the same cherry-red shade as the Hupmobile Christine had when they met. He'd never forget how chic she looked whenever she chauffeured her father around town. He turned his attention back to Jimmy.

". . . The Hollywood pinks and reds under Welles and Douglas plied their propaganda. The films. The *radio*! The red press sustained the punks and pukes who love Moscow more than Washington. The outright red press has pooh-poohed the effort to awaken America to the danger from within. I'm not worried about Russia."[6]

Fritz elbowed Gab and pointed to what he'd written: *Because Russia has no navy.*

Gab began a countdown.

". . . She may have a big army. She may be ambitious. But Russia has no navy, *yet*!"

Gab had reached eight fingers when Jimmy pronounced Fritz's prediction—a tie.

". . . She can't control the world, except by infiltration of her political, economic, and social ideologies through a fifth column. We have that fifth column in America. You don't believe it? Keep on snoozing, and one of these days you'll wake up with your property confiscated by the government. Your

---

5. Halberstam, 116.
6. James G. Stahlman, "From the Shoulder," *Nashville Banner*, February 25, 1946.

liberties gone. Your throat slit, or your heart punctured by a purge pellet. You'd better come out of that coma, brother. Or it will be too late. Uncle Joe knows all the answers, and dead men tell no tales. Adjourned."[7]

"Amen!" Gab didn't buy into Jimmy's paranoia that there were secret communist agents lurking on every corner. Uttering "amen" celebrated the meeting's conclusion.

"I'm so happy I'm not a reporter," Fritz said.

Gab laughed because no one knew what Fritz did at the paper, including Fritz.

An hour later, Gab walked to Cumberland Motors. He recalled how his father had taken him to meet John Cheek after they'd become the first Dodge dealership in the country. Gab considered John and the dealership manager, Mac, personal friends.

"Blackie, I'm not buying an ad," Cheek told Gab as he entered.

"Not why I'm here, John. I came to offer you a feature story in the *Sunday Magazine*."

"Free advertising is the last thing I need," John said.

Mac sidled between Gab and John. "What Blackie really wants is a car, am I right?"

"Well, yeah," Gab agreed. "I'd love to get my hands on a four-door sedan."

"Come back next year," John said. "We'll have one by then."

"Next year?" Gab felt like he had when he'd asked Jimmy for a raise and Jimmy responded that Gab should be grateful he was promoted despite his lack of education.

"Thing is, we got hundreds of orders and no cars," John said. "Mac, take a deposit and add him to the list." He patted Gab on the shoulder and walked back to his office.

Gab followed Mac to his desk. "A year's the best you can do?"

Mac showed Gab the bulging file on his desk. "This here's orders from last week. We send 'em in but don't get nuthin'."

"Dad-gummit," Gab mumbled. "How can I get moved up on the list?"

"Wish I could. I'll call when you're close."

---

7. Stahlman, "From the Shoulder," *Nashville Banner*, February 25, 1946.

Gab didn't want to return to the office. He knew Fritz would ask how it went, and Gab didn't want to admit it hadn't gone well. Instead, he walked to Cain-Sloan and took the only vacant stool at the lunch counter near the takeout order pickup. A waitress greeted him with a steaming cup of coffee.

"Them men's fixin' to leave," she said with a nod toward the customers a few seats down. "You can scooch over where they's at if you don't wanna deal with the waitin' nigras."

"Nah, I'm fine. Just my usual," Gab muttered.

The waitress hollered at the cook: "Pimento cheese on a biscuit!" The cook nodded, then passed her a brown sack, which she handed to a Black man standing near Gab. The man opened the bag to check the contents.

"What you waitin' for? Out to the sidewalk with ya," the waitress instructed. She then turned to Gab. "Damn nigras. More trouble than they's worth, for no tip."

Gab ignored her comment and focused on how he might finesse a move up the Dodge wait list. Everyone needed something, and Mac was key. Gab needed to find out what Mac needed as badly as he wanted a car. After he finished his biscuit and coffee, Gab crossed the street to Cain-Sloan's longtime rival Castner-Knott. As soon as Gab stepped onto Castner's executive floor, he sensed something was off. Twenty years he'd been coming to this floor and it'd always felt the same—quietly busy. Now it sounded like the *Banner*'s newsroom.

"What's going on?" he asked the receptionist.

"Had an altercation at our Columbia outlet. A fistfight over a radio. They's trying to figure out what to tell the press."

"Why? Someone die?" Gab joked. "Fights don't make the news 'less someone dies."

"No, but it's bad. See, our repairman sold a radio belonging to a colored guy who'd been away in the navy. His momma'd brung it in, and when they come to get it, our guy told them he'd sold it, seein' as how it was past thirty days and therefore forfeit."

"What? The claim check may say that, but Castner's never sells customers' goods."

"Nope. Not even coloreds'."

"And radios are hard to get these days," Gab added. "I call on merchants

who sell 'em. What a low-down cheapjack your guy was. I hope he's been fired."
Gab understood it wouldn't be good if it got out that Castner's confiscated a
customer's property. Still, that didn't seem to warrant a frenzied meeting of
the executive staff.

"What's missing in this story? Besides the radio?"

She lowered her voice to a whisper. "When the customer argued with our
guy, he punched the customer in the face. Fists fly, next thing you know, customer throws our man through the display window! Manager calls the police;
they arrest the customer *and his mother!*"

"And the employee too?"

"No. Not him. He showed police the claim ticket proving he had the right
to keep the radio. Then he said what's a colored need with a radio anyway,
seein' as how no station nowheres broadcasts devil music. The police agreed
and arrested the customer *and* his mother. This got town colors riled up and
they's fixin' to protest."

Gab recognized a juicy front-page story when he heard one. "I'll be back
tomorrow," he said. Now it made sense why the executives were in crisis-
management mode. On his walk back to the paper, he wondered how Jimmy'd
handle it—if he'd downplay the story to protect a big advertiser or report it
accurately. Considering what Jimmy said about radio and colors, Gab would
bet his quarter Jimmy'd support the police. And the comment about how
Blacks didn't need radios because their music wasn't broadcast was a typical
incendiary statement Jimmy'd preach to the Amen Chorus. Gab couldn't count
how many times Jimmy'd told him not to bother calling on merchants with
Negro clientele as "most of 'em couldn't read anyway."

As Gab neared the Maxwell House Hotel, it dawned on him that this
story was significant, in part because it happened in Columbia, which was
near the birthplace of the Ku Klux Klan—and where it was still active. Gab
remembered how, when he joined the *Banner*, the old-time reporters said on
their first day, they'd been given a gun and instructions how to kill a Negro
and get away with it. Gab felt a knot form at the back of his neck. A warning
that a "sick" headache was imminent.

Later, after two doses of Goody's Headache Powder, a copyboy handed
him a tear sheet:

"2 NEGROES HELD IN ATTACK ON COLUMBIA MAN"

Two Negroes are in jail on temporary charges in connection with an attack this morning on William Fleming, 28, who was in King's Daughter's Hospital suffering from injuries, which were believed not serious. According to witnesses the Negroes, who gave their names as Gladys Stephenson and her son, James Stephenson, pushed Fleming through a plate glass window of the Castner-Knott store here and then slashed him with pieces of broken glass. The alleged attack took place during an argument over a radio, witnesses said. Chief of Police J. W. Griffen said the Negroes admitted pushing Fleming through the window but declared that they did not stab him. The argument started inside the store where Fleming, a veteran of two years in the Pacific Theater of war, works as a radio repairman, and continued on the street in front of the store. A large crowd gathered and witnesses said that Fleming continued trying to ward off his assailants until police arrived. The Negroes were taken into custody with some difficulty, observers reported. The extent of Fleming's injuries had not been determined shortly before noon. The brother of Flo Fleming of the State Highway Patrol, who is the democratic nominee for sheriff of Maury County, the injured man is one of seven sons of John Fleming of Culleoka, who served in World War II.[8]

Gab noted what was left out. There was no reference to Stephenson's military service or that he'd just returned from the Pacific. Nothing about the stolen radio or the snide remark that a Negro didn't need one, and most importantly, no mention of the repairman having thrown the first punch. The tidbit about the repairman's six brothers' military service with one now a sheriff nominee was classic Stahlman creative journalism—an oxymoron if there ever was one.

"Hey! Old man!" Gab looked up. One of his oldest friends, Ben West, had dropped by Gab's desk. They had first worked together on the Central High

---

8. "2 Negros Held in Attack on Columbia Man," *Nashville Banner*, February 25, 1946.

School newspaper, before moving on to the same positions at the *Banner*. Old Man was the nickname Ben had given Gab at Central, because at the time, Gab was nineteen while Ben was fifteen.[9] Ben had since gone to Vanderbilt and was now Nashville's deputy district attorney and head of Tennessee's Democratic Party. He'd lost his bid for mayor several years ago but planned to run again—hence his frequent visits to the *Banner*.

"How do, Ben?" Gab said.

"Say, Blackie. Heard you told Jimmy about the fight at Castner's."

"Yep. Overheard 'em flappin' their lips on my sales call. You got a political angle on it?"

"Nah, but Columbia's Momma's hometown. I know it well. Been years since they had a lynchin'. We were here in '33 when Cordie Cheek was lynched and sheriff said nobody was sorry, remember?"[10]

"Oh, yeah. The sheriff wouldn't arrest the guilty cause he said he didn't want his best citizens in jail." Gab felt a wave of nausea hit as he recalled the poor boy had been tortured, castrated, and lynched after someone paid a white girl a dollar to lie and say he'd assaulted her.

"If they're lookin' for an excuse to lynch another Maury County Negro . . ."

"Over a radio?" Gab put his head between his knees and breathed deeply. After the nausea passed, he looked up at Ben and sighed.

"Still getting them migraines?" Ben asked.

"Yeah. Doc said they're triggered by stress and I should avoid it."

"In this place?" Ben said. "He know you work at the *Banner*?"

"Hey, Blackie!" Jack interrupted. "Fritz and me's fixin' to leave." He waved the *Banner*'s front page as he approached Gab's desk. "Guess we know the topic of tomorrow's Amen Chorus. I'll tell ya right now, Jimmy's gonna ask why a colored needs a radio."

"I sure don't miss those meetings," Ben said.

"Jimmy's gonna blame the communists," Fritz said as he joined the men at Gab's desk.

"Nah. He'll blame the radio itself," Gab opined.

---

9. Central High School Megaphone, 1927.

10. "Atkinson and Bauman Go To Columbia," *Nashville Banner*, December 20, 1933, 1.

"I'm thinkin' the bellicose soundwaves coming outta Jimmy's mouth's givin' all y'all brain damage," Ben said.

"Brain damage," Gab repeated. "Your best yet." He took a quarter from his pocket and handed it to Ben. Jack and Fritz followed suit.

Although Gab laughed at Ben's comment, he wondered if Jimmy was the cause of his migraines. Headaches ran in the family, but he'd never gotten one while Jimmy was away in the navy. Christine speculated the headaches would end if Gab had a different boss—meaning a different job. He would always be grateful to Jimmy for having listed him as essential to the press, which kept Gab from being drafted, and for helping his beloved nephew, Buddy, get a Vanderbilt scholarship. However, Gab had decided it was time to move on.

Advertising's future was in television, and he was an adman, not a newsman, so that's where he belonged. *Advertising Age* magazine had reported that radio manufacturers planned to produce between 250,000 and one million television sets by year-end. Unfortunately, sales would be limited to four cities: New York, Chicago, Philadelphia, and Los Angeles.[11] When television might arrive in Nashville was anyone's guess, but for Gab, it couldn't come soon enough.

On Saturday morning, Gab and his eight-year-old son, Eddie, visited the Dodge showroom. While Eddie explored the new models, Gab positioned himself within earshot of Mac's desk. When he overheard Mac complain he couldn't find a new refrigerator, Gab had exactly what he needed. Since Christine's best friend had recently married the manager of Sterchi's Furniture, Gab was confident he could acquire a new refrigerator before Mac could.

Days later, two delivery men rolled the new, hundred-pound-capacity refrigerator toward Gab's front door. "Hold up," he said. "That goes on my back porch."

"You sure? New icebox's mighty hard to find."

"I'm sure."

---

11. "Television This Year, Newspaper Reports," *Tennessean* February 25, 1946, 2.

As soon as the fridge was plugged in, Gab invited Mac over for drinks and their favorite snack, rat trap cheese.

After their second drink, Gab said, "Step out here. Got something to show ya."

When Mac saw the refrigerator, he gasped. "Where'd you find that? I've been looking everywhere, without a bit of luck. How much you want for it?"

"It's not for sale."

"Not for sale? What do you need with a porch icebox?"

"Don't need it. What I need is a new car. Lemme pick one from your next shipment and you can have the fridge."

Mac's eyes twinkled. "Throw in some rat trap cheese and it's a deal."

Two weeks later, Gab and Eddie walked along the railroad tracks, where the new cars were stacked atop an autorack. "There she is," Gab said, pointing to a bright-red four-door sedan. "Wait till your mother sees this. She's gonna love it."

"Heck yeah!" Eddie said. "You still gonna carpool to work?"

"Absolutely. Can't wait to pick up the guys. They won't believe it."

Gab had *needed* a new car so he could leave the *Banner*. The Federal Communications Commission had just announced one television license would be issued for each of the twenty largest broadcast markets. Nashville was the final city to make the list. Gab planned to break into television early by first working at a radio station, as only radio station owners could apply for television licenses. He'd carefully studied the three stations in town and concluded his best opportunity was at WLAC. Getting hired wouldn't be a problem because the owner, Truman Ward, had tried repeatedly to recruit him. Gab intended to persuade Ward to launch a television station and let him run it.

Before that could happen, Gab needed to prove himself. WLAC's ranking third in a three-station market provided the ideal scenario for him to turn things around. And thanks to a random comment repeated by the receptionist at Castner's, he now had an idea how he'd do it.

2

A BOY NAMED SOU

Sou Bridgeforth commands the respect of a community elder, his entry into a room changing nearby conversations and inspiring a litany of sincere inquiries as to his health and well-being.

—DANIEL COOPER, *SCUFFLING: THE LOST HISTORY OF NASHVILLE RHYTHM & BLUES*

FEBRUARY 26, 1946

It was a rare occurrence when William Sousa "Sou" Bridgeforth came home before midnight. He walked into the bedroom at sunset, surprised to find his wife, Helen, seated at her vanity.

"Funny, why aren't you ready?" Sou asked, using the pet name he'd given her after she made him laugh so much during their first encounter. "You're funny," he'd told her. In her witty way, she'd replied, "No. I'm Helen." At that moment Sou decided he'd call her Funny forever after. Since then, they'd married, divorced, and remarried, but throughout it all, she stayed his funny little sweetheart. He'd never met another woman like her and knew he never would.

"I thought you wanted me to get you to the club before the crowd arrived."

"I do, Bridgy, but all the gossip at the beauty parlor slowed things up. All the gals was yappin' and speculatin' rather than snippin' and rollin'." She spun around. "You heard about the skirmish at Castner's in Columbia?"

"Just bits and pieces," he replied. He watched her clip on her pearl button earrings and realized her hair was shorter. "I like the new shorter do," he said. "Shows off your pretty face."

Helen's hairstyle may have taken longer than expected, but it was worth it. The modern, sexy-short cut highlighted her warm chestnut skin and pretty features. Sou loved showing off his wife—nearly ten years his junior—at his nightclub, the New Era. As good-looking as Helen was, her beauty wasn't what Sou loved most about her. She was smart and well-read. More well-read than not only most colored women in Nashville but most white women too. He knew she'd be pleased he'd donated to the legal fund for the colored protestors arrested in Columbia.

"Teddy came by collecting for the legal bills of them arrested," he said.

"You gave him good money, I hope." She placed her lipstick into her pocketbook.

"Hundred dollars," he said proudly.

"A hundred? Bridgy, why not five?"

"Five hundred? Woman! That's more money than the club took in. Numbers is slow too. And I still gotta pay the musicians."

"You musta not heard what happened, or you'd know a hundred's not near enough."

"I said I hadn't. I was plannin' to read the *Banner* at the club."

"I *hate* that you read that damn paper."

"If the *Globe* was daily, I'd read it daily. Anyway, it's good to know your enemy."

"*Banner*'s the enemy, alright! And that James Stahlman's the devil hisself! Don't think anything he reports is anywhere near to true."

"So tell me what you heard while I change." He pulled a fresh dress shirt from the closet.

"You know about the radio? And them it was stolen from got arrested, rather than that thieving repairman, right?"

"Yes. I heard a Castner's employee stole a radio from a colored customer, then started a fight and the customer was arrested."

"And his mother! Now local coloreds are protesting, so they're arresting them too. A group of crackers gathered on the city square last night. They was passin' 'round whiskey and weapons and callin' for a lynchin'. The veterans in Mink Slide—that's what they call the colored section of Columbia—sensed danger. They shot out the lampposts and set armed lookouts 'round the neighborhood. Then half the local police surrounded Mink Slide. The colored lookouts fired warnin' shots, but police didn't halt. Shots was fired. Four officers wounded. Then near on all the white men in town surrounded Mink Slide. Tennessee Guard was called in; then police and soldiers went through Mink Slide with machine guns, destroyin' folks' property, ransackin' homes. They cleaned out the coloreds' businesses' cash drawers, took their valuables, includin' their weapons. They arrested *one hundred coloreds* when only four did anything and all were denied bail *and* counsel! Your hundred-dollar donation works out to a dollar a person, and ninety-six of 'em's innocent! A hundred helps, but it's nuthin' compared to what's needed."[1]

"I'll see what more I can do."

The most significant detail Sou learned was the besieged colored people of Columbia had stood up for themselves, fought back, and lived to tell about it—albeit from jail—in a town less than thirty miles from the birthplace of the Ku Klux Klan.

"Can you believe this catastrophe started over a radio?" she asked.

"Of course I believe it. Plenty colored men been lynched down there for a lot less. What I don't get is why he thought a radio was worth fightin' over. All they broadcast is white folks doing minstrel shows makin' us out to be fools. If we're not played as buffoons, then we're made out to be lazy, shiftless, superstitious, or criminals.[2] No self-respecting colored should support an industry that promotes that stereotype. It's the same way Hitler fostered hatred of Jews. They wanna classify us as less than—oh, woman, don't get me started." Sou bunched up his work shirt and tossed it to the floor.

"Of course, you're right," Helen said. "As usual." She attached his cuff link

---

1. Leslie T. Hart, "Long Distance Calls to Riot Scene Traced," *Nashville Banner*, February 26, 1946.
2. William Tymous, letter to FCC director, March 1946. Federal Communications Commission. (1946a). *Public Service Responsibility of Broadcast Licensees* [The Blue Book], Washington, DC: FCC.

and kissed his cheek. "Let's get us some supper and listen to the band. Who's playing tonight?"

"Louis Brooks. Should be a great show."

Helen loved being at the New Era when Louis Brooks played his saxophone. Especially when he covered Erskine Hawkins's "Don't Cry Baby," her favorite. Listening to boogie-woogie while dining on greens, cornbread, and barbeque from Harlem's would be just what she needed to stop her ruminations about the tragedy in Columbia.

She held out Sou's suit jacket. He slipped it on, then reached for her hand. Her husband was such a handsome man, Helen thought. And a hardworking, ambitious one too. She had to look out for him to ensure he didn't wind up in jail. He said the profit from running numbers was worth the risk because he had the police chief on his payroll, so she shouldn't worry.

But Helen couldn't help it. Worrying about your man getting arrested was what colored women did. He could be a banker, a schoolteacher, or just walkin' down the street mindin' his own business, and she'd be anxious until he crossed the threshold of their home. Now with the mess in Columbia, there was no telling what impact that might have on local law enforcement. Add the worry that on any day that devil Stahlman might get up on the wrong side of his throne and decide to declare war on Sou, as he'd done to Bill James, Sou's mentor. The way Stahlman had gone after James, setting him up and then sending him to jail, would make for one hell of a Hollywood film—if Hollywood ever decided to tell the truth about life in the Jim Crow South. *As if* that *would ever happen*, she thought.

When they arrived at the corner of Fourth Avenue where Charlotte became Cedar, Helen heard Louis warming up his sax. She loved how jazz could raise her spirits. For Sou's sake, she'd try to hide her anguish over the Columbia mess and enjoy their evening together. Then she remembered that it was on this historic corner where downtown gave way to the original Black business district, where city leaders had proposed to build a new auditorium. The local powers that be didn't just want a new venue—they intended to destroy the thriving Black-owned businesses here.

While Helen went next door to order dinner from Harlem Barbeque, Sou took his favored seat to the right of the door and settled in to read as the vocalist warmed up. The *Banner* headline read, "Order Restored in Columbia; Officers Probe Arms Source; Outside Contacts." Beneath the headline: "Long-Distance Calls to Riot Scene Traced; Ten Injured." Sou scanned the article, befuddled as to why long-distance calls warranted a front-page mention:

> Meanwhile, authorities have begun checking several long-distance telephone calls intended for leaders of Columbia. Among the calls which are being investigated include one from a man who gave his name as Charles Stuart of Columbus, Ga.; Joe Booker of Chicago; a man who identified himself as Witherspoon of Nashville; besides other calls from Detroit and numerous calls from local Negroes. All of these calls, according to reliable information, were received this morning at the A. J. Morton and Son Funeral Home operated by Negroes.[3]

Sou wasn't much of a writer, as his love letters to Funny could attest, but this much he knew—buried midway on the second page was a line that *should* have been the headline: "Wrecked by machine gun fire from patrolmen," followed by the list of Mink Slide businesses destroyed: "Silver Top Café, I Buy and Sell New and Used Clothes, Tunnel's Café, Guy Hamlet's Café, Charlie Harris' Café, Blair's Place, and The Twilight Inn."

Instead of law enforcement's gunfire destroying businesses, Stahlman thought long-distance calls to a funeral home were the most significant detail in a lengthy article that also included the undertaker's statement: "The Negroes that came to my home believed there was going to be a lynching and one of them said, 'We are aiming to stop it.'"

Sou took a deep breath and willed himself to subdue his anger. Helen was right. He could give more than a dollar per person. What happened in Columbia was unconscionable. Seven colored businesses destroyed *with machine guns*, while here city leaders plotted to bulldoze his business and others nearby. Once again, the "genteel Nashville Way" was being deployed to disguise their true intent. The auditorium's location disguised a strategy to remove colored

---

3. Hart, *Nashville Banner*, February 26, 1946.

folks from an area they'd inhabited since they'd been freed from slavery. If the aristocrats had their way, this town would wipe out any evidence Negroes ever flourished here.

He tossed the paper in the trash and forced himself to focus on preparations for the evening's entertainment.

"Gotcha all your favorites, Bridgy," Helen said sweetly as she returned with two steaming plates. By God, he loved that woman.

Saturday morning, Sou watched his assistant, Nathan, double-check the lottery ticket sales ledger while dozens of numbers runners waited for their commissions. After Nathan paid the beat cop and police chief to look the other way, the employees, Louis Brooks and his band, the winning payout, and the runners their percentage, Sou told Nathan to deliver whatever was left to Z. Alexander Looby, the attorney representing those arrested in Columbia. Helen suggested they ask each runner to contribute. Knowing some of them were illiterate, Sou read the news aloud from the *Banner*: "'Long-Distance Calls to Columbia After Riot Being Checked. Outside influences may have been directly connected with the racial discord in Columbia this week and a high official said this morning that arrests may soon be made as an investigation of long-distance telephone calls to local Negroes continues.'"[4]

"Why're you readin' that bullshit?" Nathan exclaimed.

Sou ignored Nathan: "Says here radio station WLAC is set to broadcast an address from Columbia's mayor on the situation following the race riot."

"Maybe that mayor can explain why the onliest thing they's investigatin' is whose far-off relatives called to check on 'em," a runner shouted.

Sou continued: "'An informant, who requested that his name not be used, admitted that authorities have spent a considerable amount of time during the past week delving into the ramifications of telephone calls received here from Chicago, Detroit, Columbus, and several from Nashville. The calls, it is known, were received at the local Negro funeral home a few

---

4. "Long Distance Calls to Columbia After Riot Being Checked," *Nashville Banner*, March 2, 1946.

hours after the raid by Tennessee Highway Patrol on the Mink Slide section of Columbia.'"

Nathan stopped counting. "Who the hell else you call but the undertaker when your kin got no phone and you worryin' your daddy done been gunned down by a police machine gun?"

"Or worse, lynched by an angry mob," Sou added.

"Why's it matter who's calling who from whereabouts?" Nathan asked.

Sou scanned the paper for an answer and read, "Forty-two Negroes were returned about five-thirty o'clock yesterday afternoon from the Davidson County Jail where they were taken Thursday afternoon following a shooting affray that took the lives of two Negroes."

"They even bother to name them two was killed?" a runner asked.

Sou searched. "They named one. William A. Gordon. Says just before he was taken from the cellblock Gordon said, 'Somebody's going down if I get killed or hung.'"

"Two dead Negroes and all's they's worryin' about's who called the undertaker," Nathan said with disgust.

Silence filled the room. *Without* comment, Sou walked to the coat rack, removed his fedora, turned it upside down, and placed it on the security guard's stool. He wadded up the newspaper and tossed it into the garbage.

After the money had been tallied, the runners paid and gone, Sou picked up the collection hat. From the looks of the donations, it appeared the runners had given more money to the legal fund than they kept for themselves.

"Take it next door to Looby," Sou instructed Nathan.

"Every penny?" Nathan said. "You sure?"

"Yeah. Hopefully when Louis Jordon comes next month, we'll get back in the black."

Two months later, on Friday evening, April 25, Sou escorted Helen into the opulent Jubilee Hall at Fisk University. Friday payday nights were often the rowdiest at the New Era, and he hated to leave his club to the care of his partner, Shorty Banks; Nathan; and a security guard. He had forgone his responsibility to his business and would miss one of the best live boogie-woogie performances of the year to escort his wife to an Italian opera. It wasn't something he could have imagined when he worked the plow on his grandparents' farm. Nor could he have imagined then the small fortune he'd paid for the dress Helen wore.

This was the price one paid for having married the most beautiful and brilliant woman in Nashville. As reticent as Sou was to attend the opera, he knew Helen was right when she'd said there was triumph in an entire Negro performance—conductor, orchestra, vocalists, audience—of an Italian opera. She insisted that they support the arts at every opportunity. "If we don't pay to see it," she said, "who will? Because we can, we must."

As Sou waited for the velvet curtain to rise, he scanned the leaflet he'd been handed, the NAACP's explanation of what happened in Columbia: "State troopers went to work 'restoring order' by robbing Negro homes, wrecking their business establishments, and arresting them wholesale. Restitution is sought for this damage. There must be no future Columbias."

He smiled as he read the chairperson's name: *Mrs. Franklin D. Roosevelt.* If Eleanor Roosevelt could see to it that the aggrieved victims received justice, it would signal a new era in Tennessee. The lights flickered and Helen elbowed him.

"What's the name of this again?" he whispered. Helen held up the program: *The Marriage of Figaro.* Sou had never listened to opera, but the music sounded familiar. The lusty couple began their duet, in English, while the man measured the floor.

"What makes you there so busy measuring?" the woman caroled.

"I'm seeing if the bed, a gift from our generous master, is suited well for this corner."

Sou closed his eyes. *Generous* and *master* were two words his grandparents had used frequently, but never together. His thoughts drifted from the gothic theater to the cotton farm deep in Limestone County, Alabama, where his grandparents, Henry and Mary Stuart, reared him after his mother and baby sister died of tuberculosis. Both former slaves, Henry and Mary had endured more trauma than Sou cared to imagine. Mary had been separated from her own mother at such a young age she couldn't even recall her full name. Family meant everything to Mary.

From Henry, Sou learned the value of hard work and the importance of determining your own destiny. Henry survived the Civil War and afterward worked years to obtain his own land. He toiled long, hard hours in the field every day to provide for Sou and Mary. After Henry died, Sou's uncle Nick brought Sou to Nashville so he could teach him the masonry trade.[5]

As the music filled his senses, Sou was transported from the opera to his first glimpse of Nashville as a boy of eighteen. Coming from a rural community, Sou had never known a place like this existed. He remembered how Mary had asked him to read her the *Nashville Negro City Business Directory*. Henry had never learned to read or write, and Mary could write little beyond her own name.[6] Sou explained that the directory was a phone book, not a storybook. Mary had known that; she'd just wanted to hear the names of all the occupations local coloreds enjoyed. He enumerated: doctors, lawyers, dentists, insurance agents, undertakers, grocers, butchers, pharmacists, barbers, bakers, mechanics, architects, contractors, blacksmiths, ministers, real estate agents, bankers, college professors.[7]

"And each a Negro," she had said with pride.

Sou thought of how the seats here were filled with people whose lives had been incomprehensible to Mary when she'd been enslaved. Even the thought of Fisk, considered by many to be the Black version of Vanderbilt, would have been unimaginable.

Helen squeezed Sou's hand. It pulled him out of his sentimental journey.

The character of the master onstage crooned: "The scoundrels, I'll requite them."

The slave girl: "He merits not pardon who cannot forgive."

Her mistress: "The proverb holds good here, to live and let live."

The master: "To all who've offended, then grace be extended."

Sou wondered what his grandparents would think of the proverb. They survived slavery, the Civil War, Reconstruction, and the terror of the KKK, yet he was sure they met their maker with hearts full of grace and gratitude. A wave of tenderness consumed him. Neither Mary nor Henry had been able to

5. William Bridgeforth, personal story pamphlet, July 2001.
6. Bridgeforth, personal story pamphlet, July 2001.
7. Nashville Colored Business Directory, 1929.

read the Bible, but they had faith in God and the rich, stern words contained in the Good Book. Sou's blessings today stemmed from their faith, good works, and lack of bitterness. He'd been raised with loving-kindness.

Sou considered the depth and breadth of the collective knowledge represented here. The people who surrounded him could match their wisdom and expertise with Vanderbilt's elites. Here were scholars, scientists, businessmen, craftsmen, artists, athletes, and soldiers. People of countless talents, who'd proven that brilliance, success, bravery, and patriotism were *not* the monopoly of Caucasians. Sou's great-grandfathers had known little beyond the boundaries of an Alabama plantation, yet here—at Fisk's library—all the wisdom of the world was at one's fingertips. Compare the men here, Sou thought, to the ignorant boll weevil bigots who hid beneath white hoods, whose malicious and degenerate caricatures of humanity displayed their sense of inadequacy.

Helen tapped his arm. He opened his eyes and noted the lights had brightened.

"It's intermission. I'm thirsty," she said. "Can you get me some lemonade?"

Sou welcomed the excuse to stretch his legs, call the club, and check in. Before he made it to the pay phones, the lawyer, Z. Alexander Looby, called out to him.

"Hey, Sou," Looby said. "I'd like to convey the gratitude of all my clients."

Sou shook hands with Looby and the two professors with him. "How's it going?"

"I'm optimistic," Looby said. "I intend to prove no Negro's been called for jury duty in Maury County in fifty years. I'll call all ten thousand colored residents to testify if I have to."

"That's brilliant," Sou said.

"Can't wait to hear what the *Damn Banner* says about that!" a professor said.

"Stahlman'll label me a communist operative, for sure," Looby replied. "It's his go-to explanation for anyone he doesn't agree with."

The lights flickered, a signal to return to the auditorium. Just in time, Sou remembered Helen's lemonade. When the lights dimmed, Helen leaned against his shoulder.

"Don't sleep through this half," she whispered.

"I didn't sleep. I just hear the music better with my eyes closed."

"But you miss the gorgeous scenery."

"I'm here, Funny. Let that be enough."

She kissed him on the cheek. "You're right, Bridgy. Like Aunt Lottie used to say, that ain't nuthin'."

3

MAKING A WAY

The DJs always knew that black music was out
there, but they didn't dare play it for fear criticism
might sink them. They were only waiting for
someone to open the door so they could walk in.

—TED JARRETT, *YOU CAN MAKE IT IF YOU TRY*

Gab pulled into the Woodmont Country Club an hour before the season's first blind bogey tournament was scheduled to begin. Jewish community leaders had founded the club after the Belle Meade and Richland country clubs denied Jews membership. Since the majority of Woodmont's members honored the Sabbath, the club made the course available for citywide events on Saturdays. Gab loved the course and played in as many Saturday morning golf events as time—and Christine—would allow.

He recognized one of the two caddies who waited near the curb. Both men were dressed in the requisite white linen shirts and slacks, still as crisp as the morning's early spring air. Like most Southern golf clubs, Woodmont exclusively employed young colored men as caddies. During the war, many caddies had left to serve in the military. Now recently returned, most attended Fisk University or Tennessee A&I on the G.I. Bill.

The caddy Gab recognized was the taller of the two, nearly the same height as Gab—five feet eight—yet whereas Gab was lean, the caddy had bulked up and was built like a professional boxer. Gab took pride in remembering the name of nearly every person he ever met, so it vexed him that he couldn't remember this caddy's name. "I'm glad to see you returned from the war in one piece," he said.

"Thank you, sir," the caddy said. He caressed the hood of Gab's car. "Looks like you done good. Brand new, ain't she?"

"Yep. The newest. It's the 1946 model."

The shorter caddy pulled Gab's clubs from the car. "Bet she rides smooth as chess pie."

"She sure does. Y'all students now?"

"I am," the shorter one answered. "I'm Willie. I'm over to Fisk. Staff Sergeant Malcolm here, he's waiting for his G.I. Bill to come through."

"They ain't makin' it easy on me neither," Malcolm said.

"Want your sticks over to the practice green?" Willie asked. "Or you fixin' to eat first?"

"I brought breakfast," Gab said. He opened the passenger door and retrieved a box of Krispy Kreme donuts. "Thought I'd eat while I hit a few at the range."

"Range's closed on account of they's building a pool and tennis courts."

"Dang!" Gab eyed the table beside the caddy stand. "Y'all mind if I sit there? I don't want to carry donuts inside. You know they frown on outside food comin' in."

"You ain't wanna set at the caddy's table, Mister Blackie," Malcolm said.

Gab knew that even though there was no sign, it was assumed one would know that a caddy table was for coloreds. Gab placed the donuts on the table, took one out of the box, pulled a chair off to the side so it was near but not *at* the table. "Y'all help yourselves. They're still warm."

Each caddy took a donut, but they stood at a distance and eyed Gab suspiciously.

"Y'all both cartin' today?" Gab asked between bites.

"Yes, Mister Blackie," Malcolm said. "Now you got that nice ride, you joined up anywheres, Richland or Belle Meade?"

"Heck no," Gab said. "Even if I could afford it, I wouldn't care to spend my days with those uppity farts. I do play Richland some since my soon-to-be brother-in-law's a member. Joe Warren. You know him?"

Willie smirked. "Carted for him a few times. Next time you play Mister Warren, ask for me, Little Willie. Guarantee you'll wallop him with me pulling your sticks."

"Which of you's the better caddy?" Gab asked.

"Willie's best at readin' a course. I'm the better golfer," Malcolm said.

Willie laughed. "Look where we at. This ain't Douglass."

"What's Douglass?" Gab asked.

"Our course. We done built six holes under the Cleveland viaduct," Malcolm offered.

"Six *golf* holes?" Gab said, astonished. "On the riverbank?"

"Yeah. Where else we gonna play? You know they ain't gonna let us on no golf course hereabouts. Not even this Jew one we at. We done did our own," Willie said proudly. "Play 'em six holes three times to make regulation. Even got us a league."

Gab was flabbergasted. "You built a regulation golf course outta riverbank swampland? By yourselves? That took some real genius ingenuity."

"Genius ingenuity," Willie repeated. "I likes it. Whites like to say it's 'nigga-rigged.' To us it's makin' a way outta no way." He smiled wide.

"Making a way outta no way's same as ingenious, ain't it? He pulled a pencil and index card from his pocket and scribbled: "Make a way outta no way. Malcolm and Willie—Woodmont C.C."

"Make a way outta no way" was exactly what Gab intended to do at WLAC. If these enterprising young men could build a golf course under a bypass, anything was possible. He took another bite and let the donut's airy sugar melt on his tongue. "If the angels created a food, then Krispy Kreme is it," he said. "I'll leave the rest for the caddies."

"Mister Blackie, you know Landon Cheek?" Malcolm asked, taking another donut.

"Sure, caddy master at Richland."

"Landon runs our league," Malcolm said. "Got us twenty-four players, including till just recent, Rags Rhodes hisself."

"*The* Ted Rhodes?" Gab said. "Heard he's the first Negro professional golfer."

"Yep," Willie said. "Rags was back last month and got Richland to agree to host our championship. Winner gets a trip to the Joe Louis tourney."

"Richland's gonna let coloreds play their course?" Gab said.

"Once. For the tourney," Malcolm clarified.

"Good for y'all," Gab said.

The sudden bleep of a horn diverted the men's attention. A white Cadillac pulled up to the caddy stand. "We got to work, Mister Blackie, but thanks for the donuts."

Malcolm gave Gab a playful salute. "See ya greenside."

Gab calculated the distance from the fairway to the green at 140 yards—a perfect six-iron shot. "Hand me that spade, Willie."

Willie pulled the mashie instead. "Wanna beat Fritz, use this'n and aim left."

Gab lined up his shot as Willie advised. The ball sailed past the flag to the left edge of the green and landed with a thud. It rolled toward the hole and stopped inches from the pin. He gave Willie a thumbs-up. "I'm calling Joe soon as I get home. Good news is, Joe'll only play for money. Whatever I win, I'll split with you!"

"Then bet the house, Mister Blackman," Willie said.

"Say, Willie. Can I ask your opinion about a business idea?"

"Don't know nuthin' 'bout business, but you can ask."

"You listen to the radio?"

"Not really."

"Read the newspaper?"

"Only *Banner*'s sport page for the winning numbers."

"Where do you get your news?"

Willie laughed. "Obvious you ain't been in a caddy shack. Wanna know anything—I's sayin' anything—from what the president's doin' to who's doin' your laundress, there's a caddy what knows. White mens put all they's business on the course, 'specially when they's drinking. And us caddies? We's silent as the grave—till we's back at the shack, that is."

"So if I wanna know something about someone, you're saying I should ask a caddy."

Willie smiled. "Well, I is and I ain't."

"You ever hear tales about Fritz's kin, Jimmy?"

"That's like askin' a saint he ever heard tales of the devil."

"You're up, Blackie!" Fritz yelled.

Gab placed his ball where his marker had been. He tapped the ball softly and sank the putt. "Three," he announced.

"You're on fire, Blackie," Fritz said. "I've never seen you play this good."

"Willie's my good luck charm," Gab said.

As they made their way to the tee box, Gab resumed his conversation with Willie. "You get your news in the caddy shack. Is there a radio or music in the shack?"

"No. Only music's when a caddy sings. Caddies sing a lot though."

"Like what?"

"Spirituals, some, but mostly stuff from the clubs. Member of our league, Sou Bridgeforth, owns the best club. Former caddy here, Ted Jarrett, plays piano there and here too."

"Gab!" Fritz yelled. "Stop gabbing and golf!"

Willie handed Gab a driver. "Dogleg left. Three quarters swing."

Gab hit to the middle of the fairway and turned back to Willie. "Lemme ask you. If the music Jarrett plays at Bridgeforth's club was played on the radio, would you listen?"

Willie burst into laughter. "Ain't nobody puttin' no race music on the radio."

"But if they did?"

"If they done did, no colored person 'cept maybe the preacher *wouldn't* listen."

"Why wouldn't the preacher?"

"'Cuz preacher be thinkin' race music's devil's music. Why you askin'?" Willie traded a midiron for the driver.

"What if I wanted to hear music like what's played at Bridgeforth's club?"

Willie pointed toward the green. "Aim for them trees over yonder."

Gab swung but didn't watch where his ball landed. "Where could a white man like me hear music played in colored nightclubs?"

"From records." Willie sighed. "They's in jukeboxes and on Victrolas."

"What if I could get your records played on the radio? Would you bring some by the station?"

Willie gave Gab a shrewd look. "I's startin' to think you ain't come here with Krispie Kremes just for practice."

"You're smart, Willie. What about it? Wanna visit a radio station with me?"

"Okay. Me and Malcolm'll come, but if we bring our records, you gotta bring us somethin' better'n donuts. Somethin' good to eat and somethin' better to drink."

"You like fried chicken?" Gab asked.

"Depends on who's doing the frying."

"I know the best chicken fry cook in all of Tennessee."

"Fried chicken tastes mighty fine with cold beer. Bring it and I'll bring records."

"Blackie!" Fritz yelled. "If you don't stop running your mouth, your tongue's gonna get sunburnt! Hit the damn ball already!"

The next afternoon, Gab drove through the idyllic rolling hills of Brentwood to Maryland Farms, Truman Ward's famed equestrian breeding stables. As he steered toward the manor home, Gab felt confident that Ward was the type of visionary who would grasp the significance of what he planned. After all, Ward's foresight was legendary. He had acquired WLAC from Life and Casualty Insurance Company after the firm's executives sent him to New York City to sell the station. On the train ride, Ward fell for his own sales pitch and, instead of selling the station, borrowed the money to purchase it himself.

Prior to Pearl Harbor, Ward anticipated the catastrophic events in Europe, predicted a building-material shortage, and stockpiled supplies. He even bought old bricks salvaged from razed houses. The Federalist brick home Gab pulled up to looked as if it had stood there a century, although it was only five years old. Gab parked, grabbed his briefcase, and walked toward the porch. A lanky teenage boy met him.

"Hi, I'm Jimmy. Father asked me to bring you to the stables. Thought you might like a tour before drinks."

Gab left his briefcase in the entry and followed Jimmy to the stables. He marveled at the simplistic beauty of the building with its roomy, immaculate stalls. The thought crossed his mind that Ward's horses lived better than most Negroes on Capitol Hill.

"Come say hello to American Ace," Jimmy said. "Father's pride and joy."

Truman greeted him and introduced Gab to each of his American saddle-bred and Tennessee walking horses. By the time they returned to the house, Gab had reached his quota of equine introductions and needed a stiff drink. He sipped the bourbon Truman offered and then pulled out the maps and statistics from his briefcase. "Before I explain why I've brought these," Gab said, "would you mind sharing with me your future plans for WLAC?"

"First, Blackie, I want to confirm you're here to discuss you joining the station and this isn't some Stahlman scheme to trick me into commenting on the demise of radio."

"Stahlman knows nothing about this, Mr. Ward."

"Well, great. Although I'm curious why you'd leave your prestigious position *now*. You've been at the *Banner* how long?"

"Fifteen years."

"You get what, three, four weeks' vacation?"

"And a Thanksgiving turkey. Plus, some fish Jimmy catches in Florida."

Truman laughed. He took a swallow of bourbon then came to the point. "I can provide a turkey, even horseback riding lessons for your kids, but no fish. Let's cut to the chase: I'd love to have you at WLAC. Our top salesman passed away last month and I'm short-staffed, but all I got open's a sales position. F. C. Sowell's general manager and Tom Baker's sales manager. I can match your salary, but ad solicitor is a big step down in title and responsibility."

"I don't care about titles. I have a wife, two children, a widowed mother, mother-in-law, and sister to support. They're the only responsibility that matters. I'm motivated to build a future with greater earnings potential, and I expect to be compensated for any *new* revenue I bring in. I'm confident I can increase your profitability exponentially with a new late-night program."

Truman lifted his glass in salute. "You're hired. But be forewarned you're swimming upstream. Radio's facing serious threats on two fronts. Now that the FCC has granted our biggest competitor a television license, many have predicted we won't survive. You got a strategy to bring in revenue late nights when nobody's listening? Late night's yours. That you're willing to come aboard without a title or managerial responsibility—for a percentage of new revenue—says you're sure it'll work. When can you start?"

Gab circled back. "You said two threats. Besides television, what's the other?"

"Come. I'll show you." Gab followed Ward into his wood-paneled study. Truman handed Gab a blue booklet titled *Public Service Responsibility of Broadcast Licensees.* "It's the FCC's new regulations. They're trying to BBC-ize us. Did you read *Hucksters?*"

"I did. It's partly why I've reconsidered radio." The novel helped clarify Gab's thinking that radio had a future, *if* a new audience could be identified to replace those lost to television. Gab believed that audience existed and could bring radio back from the brink. He'd determined that WLAC's directional signal reached 80 percent of the country's Negro population. The way he saw it, radio would soon be Lazarus and the colored musicians, its savior.

"May I take this?" he asked, referring to the FCC booklet.

"Sure. Blackie, I want you on board, but you need to leave the *Banner* with your eyes wide open. We've encountered criticism for letting advertisers determine our programming. Right now, you've got clout around town. Work for us and you'll likely be called a huckster. Not as prestigious as publisher."

"I've been called worse," Gab said. He wanted to get home and read the guidelines. "I'll read this and get back to you tomorrow."

"Excellent."

Gab slipped the booklet into his briefcase and said a quick goodbye. Whether his plan would work—or not—could depend on the FCC's new regulations. He was relieved Ward hadn't asked him to disclose his strategy, and he'd learned something valuable: Ward was both a visionary and an honorable man. If anyone possessed the acumen and the strength of character to put Gab's revolutionary idea into motion, it was Truman.

After Christine and the children had gone to bed, Gab studied the FCC report. Christine was in favor of him leaving the *Banner*; however, she wouldn't be if she knew his plan was to launch a race music program. He'd checked.

The repairman at Castner's had been right about one thing: no Negro music was broadcast anywhere. In reviewing the FCC report, Gab learned that complaints had skyrocketed; public discontent of radio had reached an all-time high. Criticism of radio's oligopolistic structure portrayed station owners as robber barons who prostituted the airwaves, while listeners believed the airwaves were public and should be obligated to perform public services.[1]

After reading the booklet, Gab realized that a race music program would address some of the FCC's concerns. He reviewed their list: (1) undue influence from advertisers, (2) overly sensationalistic programs, (3) lack of minority representation, (4) negative effects of propriety, (5) lack of programs intended to serve minority tastes and interests, (6) lack of programs devoted to nonprofit organizations.[2] Gab circled points 3 and 5.

When he crawled into bed, Christine stirred. "What time is it?" she asked.

"Time for me to resign from the *Banner*." He glanced at the clock. "Nearly two."

"Goodness, Gab! What have you been doing?"

"Plotting how I'm gonna make a penny-a-chicken at my new job."

Christine propped herself up. "We're not going into the chicken business. My frying pan is for your personal use only."

"What if I was to sell Mrs. Jones's chicks over the radio?"

"Sounds like a nightmare—especially for the chickens." She pulled the covers over her head. "Lemme sleep 'fore you have me dreaming of plucking feathers and frying hearts."

Christine was out instantly, but Gab was too excited to sleep. He planned to use the penny-a-chicken commission metaphor when he accepted the sales job, provided he had total control of the late-night broadcasts. Gab didn't intend to actually sell chickens, yet the audacity of the idea inspired him. Rather than count sheep, Gab counted products that might make good sponsors of a race music program. Whatever Negroes needed but couldn't find easily where they lived was what he'd plan to sell. This would be his next question for Willie. First thing in the morning, he'd call Joe Warren and schedule a golf game. He intended to take Willie's advice and "bet the house" that an underserved radio audience was out there, waiting for someone to find it.

---

1. *Public Responsibility of Broadcasters Licensees* (Federal Communications Commission, March 7, 1946).
2. *Public Responsibility of Broadcasters Licensees.*

Two weeks later, on his second day at WLAC, Gab informed the Third National Bank building's late-night watchman that he'd invited two guests to the studio. The guard unlocked the elevator. Gab worked the controls himself, closed the iron gate, and moved the lever to the notch for the top floor. He unlocked the station's lobby door, placed the basket of Christine's fried chicken on the counter, then dialed the number Willie had given him.

"Tell Willie I'm waiting in the lobby," he told the woman who answered.

Gab then walked down the long corridor until he reached the broadcast booth. A red sign above the booth flashed "On Air," an indication the door would be locked and the announcer was not to be disturbed. Gab knew on the other side of the door was Gene Nobles. He could hear Gene's voice through the broadcast speaker. When music replaced Gene's voice, Gab knocked. Skull Schulman peeked out.

"Heavens to Betsy, Skull," Gab exclaimed. "Why're you here?"

Gab had known Skull since he was a boy, hawking the *Banner* in Printers Alley. He remembered having visited Skull in the hospital after the car accident that cracked the young man's head and provided his memorable nickname.

"Keeping Gene company," Skull said. "Why're you here, Blackie?"

Gene pointed to the "On Air" sign and motioned for Skull and Gab to step out.

In the hallway, Gab told Skull, "I left the *Banner* and work here now. Tell Gene I'm bringing two visitors by. One's a sergeant recently returned."

"Gene don't like visitors."

"Well, what're you?"

"He don't like visitors 'cause it interrupts our gin game."

"Gene's gonna meet these fellas. Ward put me in charge at night and I'm doing my job. Tell Gene I said put the cards away and say hello."

Gab returned to the lobby and chatted with the security guard until Willie and Malcolm arrived. When they approached the front door, the guard shot Gab a suspicious look. "You didn't say they was colored. Mr. Ward know about this?"

"He does," Gab said. The guard grunted his discontent and begrudgingly unlocked the door. "Anything goes wrong, it's on you."

When Gab knocked at the booth again, Skull opened the door and stated the obvious: "Blackie's here with two coloreds."

Gene was unfazed. He put the needle on a Jo Stafford record and switched off the microphone. "Hello, fellas," he replied good-naturedly. "Whatcha doing up here so late?"

"Mister Nobles," Malcolm started, "when I's in the navy, wherever we was, we listened at you. Could tune you in from anywheres, and feel we was near to home. Would you play some of our records? Play 'em for them what's homesick, and all us coloreds? Nobody nowhere plays music for us to listen at."

"Show me whatcha got, soldier," Gene said. He scanned the stack of 78 vinyl records: Erskine Hawkins, Big Joe Turner, Roosevelt Sykes, Louis Jordan and the Tympany Five, Wynonie Harris. "Heard of Jordan. 'Choo-Choo-Ch'-Boogie' is a fine tune. Don't know the others."

"Jordan done played here month ago," Willie said. "Mr. Blackie asked we bring some records of what's played over to the New Era."

Gene placed Louis Jordan's record on the second turntable. He fixed himself a glass of VO whiskey and cola, handed the bottle to Malcolm, and pointed to his makeshift bar on a bookshelf. The men drank in silent appreciation as they listened to Jordan's song.

"Sounds a bit hillbilly," Gene said, "but better. I like it."

"Ted Jarrett, the pianist at the Era, calls it 'jump blues.' Says makes folks wanna jump and jitter."

Gene read the record labels. "These other guys play there too?"

"Yeah," Willie answered. "Hawkins and Roosevelt was there recent."

"I'll give 'em a spin. See what my jerks and fillies think of jump blues."

No one that night—not Gene, Gab, Skull, Malcolm, or Willie in the station; not Mr. Ward, who listened from home; not even Sou Bridgeforth, who listened to a similar live performance in his club—had any idea of the effect this music was about to have on Gene's audience, the late-night lonely hearts, shift workers, college students, and insomniacs, his "jerks and fillies."

Among the veterans who tuned in to Gene's broadcast that night was a twenty-three-year-old jazz drummer who had played in USO shows. He had just returned to his hometown of Gallatin, twenty miles north of Nashville, with plans to continue his education at Vanderbilt. His name was William "Bill" Trousdale Allen III, but his childhood friends called him Hoss.

4

AIN'T NOBODY HERE
BUT US CHICKENS

For every 100,000 orders of baby chicks, we received
approximately 99,999 complaints, or thereabouts.

—GENE NOBLES

MAY 7, 1946

James Stahlman tinkled a silver-plated fork against his champagne flute to alert
the Belle Meade Country Club socialites it was time to take their seats. Nearly
every woman present eyed the tuxedo-clad William "Bill" Trousdale Allen III
as he sauntered across the room. Bill was every debutant's—and her mother's
and grandmother's—dream man. He had it all: charm, looks, a prestigious
lineage, a Webb preparatory school and Vanderbilt University education. Bill
was an athlete, actor, musician, and scholar who towered over the other men
of Belle Meade. Bill's drop-the-cast-iron-skillet gorgeousness came from his
mother, Cecil Rogan Allen, a woman *Banner* readers voted "the most beautiful
matron in Tennessee." Bill inherited not only beauty from Cecil but also charisma. She had groomed Bill to help woo her clients—the well-heeled society
matrons who collected Cecil's pricey, imported *objets de vertu*.

When Bill was a child, neither Cecil nor her mother, Mamie, had much interest in him. They were too preoccupied with international social climbing and rare trinket collecting. Cecil divorced Bill's father when the boy was a toddler. Soon thereafter she departed on a worldwide collectibles quest and abandoned Bill to the care of Mamie's Black domestic, Anna Day. A few years later, after Mamie's husband died, she joined Cecil on the treasure hunt.

The *Banner*'s society pages detailed Mamie and Cecil's escapades in swanky European resorts, at opulent parties, and on chic shopping trips. They summered in Paris and London and wintered in Palm Beach and on Coronado Island. Meanwhile, in Gallatin, Bill became better known as Hoss, Anna's light-skinned colored boy. He ran wild with his colored friends and ate his black-eyed peas, salt-pork greens, and buttermilk biscuits at Anna's table in the shack behind his grandmother's home. At night, Bill slept alone with only rare porcelain figurines to keep him company. A stone's throw from his bedroom the railroad groaned a staccato pattern beneath the gospel sounds that soared from the Black Baptist church where he worshipped with Anna on Sundays. In his loneliness, he'd lie awake listening to the random rhythm of life: train whistles, animal cries, lively spirituals and elegiac blues blasting from front-porch Victrolas.

When Bill was twelve, he'd spent so little time with his mother and grand-mother that when he arrived for a holiday in Palm Beach, they were appalled by his coarse table manners, preference for soul food, and crude, backstreet expres-sions. Cecil realized that despite having been born with a platinum spoon in his mouth, Bill had no clue how to use one. In her mind, he had the mannerisms of a colored child from shantytown. And with his swarthy complexion, full lips, hazel eyes, dark brows, and wavy black hair, Cecil feared her son might be mistaken for a mulatto. She contacted Bill's father, a pharmaceutical executive in Ohio, and demanded he pay for his son to attend Webb, the prestigious preparatory boarding school, as an antidote to the boy's feral upbringing.

Heads turned when Bill took his seat at the lavishly decorated head table of the Steeplechase Gala. He apologized for his tardiness, nodded first to the widow on his left, Mrs. Bingham of the *Louisville Courier-Journal* Binghams, then to the maiden on his right, Ann Stahlman of the *Nashville Banner* Stahlmans. Both women looked at him with unabashed admiration, something to which Bill was accustomed. He glanced at his mother, knowing she'd schemed to place him between the debutant turned Navy WAVE and the empress of Louisville. How did she expect him to engage them, when anything he said was likely to be reported in a newspaper? Bill wished he could retreat to the comfort of Anna's kitchen table. Unfortunately, she'd passed away while he was serving overseas. The pain of losing her was still raw.

James Stahlman introduced himself as the master of ceremonies: "Honored guests, welcome to the celebration of the Iroquois Steeplechase," he announced. "This race commemorates one of the greatest horses that ever ran a race. And there have been millions of them, but Iroquois was that one in a million. So, it is only fitting that tomorrow is set aside for a running in his memory. And there's the Truxton purse in memory of another great horse, also owned and raced by Andrew Jackson, who is the greatest American developed in our history."[1]

At the mention of Andrew Jackson's name, the crowd stood and clapped enthusiastically.

Jimmy continued. "When the bugle blows for the Iroquois, as the hedge-hoppers sweep past the starter's flag, and our hearts thrill with love for the game of kings, and for our horses, let's remember they give us some of the greatest joys in our collective thrill-filled lives. Let's lift our glasses to General Jackson and to his devoted friends, Iroquois and Truxton, as well as to all the owners, riders, trainers, and, especially, the horses. To our beloved friends."[2]

Following protocol learned at Webb—age before beauty for greetings, toasts, and conversation—Bill touched his glass first to Mrs. Bingham's then to Ann's. He would play the part of a gentleman because that's what this society expected. But for him, it was a thespian performance. Unlike his mother, Bill didn't enjoy the pretentiousness of Belle Meade. He was happiest as Hoss, the ruffian from Gallatin's backstreets, who preferred butter beans and collard greens, along with vodka in a jelly jar, to playing William Trousdale Allen III, who dined on lobster and drank champagne from crystal goblets.

---

1. James G. Stahlman, "From the Shoulder," *Nashville Banner*, May 10, 1946.
2. Stahlman, "From the Shoulder," *Nashville Banner*, May 10, 1946.

"Have you thought about what you're going to do next?" Ann asked.

"Have you?" he replied, with a flirtatious lift of his left brow. He turned to Mrs. Bingham. "Given your unique experience, what advice might you offer Ann and me?"

Across the table, Cecil beamed. Her son had seamlessly redirected the spotlight to the guest of honor. Because Mrs. Bingham's late husband had been Roosevelt's ambassador to the United Kingdom, everyone wanted to hear what she thought about the monarchy, the abdication, and the events of war. And while Bill appeared to be captivated by Mrs. Bingham, Cecil alone noticed how he kept time to the music with his fingers. As Mrs. Bingham entertained with tales of His Majesty George V, President and Mrs. Roosevelt, Neville Chamberlain, Joe Kennedy, Wallis Simpson, Winston and Mrs. Churchill—people she quoted directly—everyone listened with rapt attention. Bill heard only the music.[3]

Earlier that day, Bill had informed his mother and grandmother he intended to study drama and become an actor. They insisted it was time for him to do something serious.[4] Bill argued that television would soon create a world of new opportunities for actors. They didn't care. The women felt there was little difference between an actor and a gigolo; one couldn't become the former without first becoming the latter.

Bill felt a blunt kick to his calf, his mother's age-old signal to pay attention. He realized Mrs. Bingham had an answer for the question he'd forgotten he asked.

"My advice is do what you love. At my age, one realizes our days are too few to squander. Dream big. But start small. And local. What is it you most enjoy?" she asked.

"Music," he answered. "I was a drummer in the USO and play with a small orchestra now, but I'm not interested in becoming a musician."

"What about radio? You could start now. If it's right, you'll know soon enough."

---

3. "Nashville Society Turns Out For Steeplechase Today," *Nashville Banner*, May 11, 1946.

4. Gilbert A. Williams, *Legendary Pioneers of Black Radio* (Westport, CT: Prager, 1998), 30.

The following afternoon, Bill escorted his mother down the sloping hills of Percy Warner Park to her VIP box at the horse track. Cecil waved to Ann Stahlman in the adjoining box.

"I'm sure you'll have more fun with her."

Bill dutifully followed his mother's cue to sit beside Ann. A colored woman dressed in a white maid's uniform handed him a wrapped sandwich and a glass of ice.

"What you wanna drink with this pimento cheese?" the maid asked. She motioned to the array of liquor bottles displayed on a nearby table.

Bill pointed to the bourbon. "Some first-class service you got," he told Ann.

"Not me. That's Mrs. Sloan's maid. You know, the department store Sloans. Heaven forbid they'd have to unpack a picnic basket or pour liquor themselves."

"You haven't been back long either, I see," he teased.

"Well, kinda defeats the point of a picnic, don't you think?" she said. "Actually, I think one of her boys is in the mule race."

Ann pointed to where Negro jockeys, dressed in vibrant multicolored silks, led mules draped in matching colors toward the starting post.[5]

"What is this? A Shakespearean comedy?" Bill asked. "Jesters at a jousting match?" He pulled the brim of Ann's blue and white derby hat. "Don't look. It's too disturbing."

She pushed the brim up. "It's silly, right? The Monkey Simon Mule Race?"

"Monkey Simon? That's what they call colored jockeys on mules?" he said with contempt. "It's worse than silly!" He stood up. "Hey, what do y'all give the winner?" he yelled to the owner's box below. "A lawn jockey statue? Of themselves?"

Ann yanked Bill's sleeve. "You're making a spectacle of yourself. Sit down."

"Those sons of—" Bill noticed his mother's horror-struck expression and replaced the swear word with Nashville's moniker for the old-moneyed sect. "The Bourbon Aristocracy!" He directed his ire toward the men below, who'd inherited their roles as puppet masters of the city's politicians: Stahlman; John and Paul Sloan, owners of Cain-Sloan; Newman and John Cheek, the Maxwell

5. James G. Stahlman, "From the Shoulder," *Nashville Banner*, May 10, 1946.

House coffee heirs; and Edwin Craig and Guilford Dudley, insurance company kingpins.

"Look around," Bill said to Ann. "See any colored spectators? Other than the few working as domestics? I can't stay and be a part of this farce."

"Why?"

Bill couldn't explain how he felt in a way Ann could understand. The woman a few seats over had given birth to him; however, to sit here felt like a betrayal of Anna, the mother who'd raised him. Anna's oldest boy, Jim, had worked at a horse track and taught Bill to ride. Had Anna birthed Bill, rather than having raised him, he could be out there, forced to act the fool for men too pompous to carry their own picnic baskets.

"Give my mother a ride to Belle Meade, would you, Ann?"

"Copy that, sir," Ann said with a playful salute.

Bill returned to Vanderbilt in the fall. At Cecil's insistence, he'd switched his major from drama to English. In early December, he followed Mrs. Bingham's advice and took a part-time job at WKDA, a new radio station started by Tom Baker, the former advertising director of WLAC. Mrs. Bingham had advised Bill to start small and local. No station was smaller or more local than WKDA. Yet it allowed Bill to dream big because it was mere steps from the two 50,000-watt powerhouses, WLAC and WSM, where legendary careers were launched.

Rumors swirled that Tom Baker left WLAC in protest after Truman Ward gave Gab Blackman—an ad solicitor—control of the nighttime air. Many department managers weren't happy that Gab had turned WLAC into a "nigger station."[6] Businessmen were kidding them about it on the golf course and at the country clubs.[7] When they complained, Gab refused to back down. When asked how this happened, Gab told them that one night a couple of veterans attending Fisk asked Gene to play some of their records. Next thing you know, Gene's getting mail from Detroit to the Bahamas and everywhere in between.

---

6. John Broven, *Record Makers and Breakers* (Champaign: University of Illinois Press, 2009), 99.
7. Broven, 99.

So, Gab told Gene, "Well, gosh, why don't you play some more of that?"[8] Gene got more records from Louis Buckley, a jukebox operator with boxes in Black nightclubs. And the more race music Gene played, the more mail poured in, which sent Gab on a search for advertisers and sponsors that would sell what Gene's audience wanted to buy.

Gab hadn't socialized with his former coworkers since he'd left the *Banner*. Stahlman had tried to convince Gab that going into radio was a huge mistake since television was about to kill radio. Gab missed Fritz and Jack and their carpool banter, yet he enjoyed being the master of his own fate. When he received an invitation to the 22nd annual Gridiron Dinner at the Maxwell House Hotel on Tuesday, December 2, 1946, Gab decided this was the perfect opportunity to reconnect with his former coworkers. Modeled after the National Press Club event in Washington, DC, the event lampooned both national and local politicians.

As Gab and Christine made their way through the ballroom, they overheard several snide whispers about how Gab had turned WLAC into a "nigger station."[9] When they reached the table where Jack and Melba Phillips waited, everyone nearby heard someone proclaim, "Who else but Blackie Blackman could've put a Black face on WLAC?"

Gab turned around but couldn't identify the heckler. The thought crossed his mind that he stood precisely where the founders of the Ku Klux Klan had first elected Nathan Bedford Forrest as Grand Wizard. He couldn't help but wonder if the blackface comment had come from one of Forrest's modern-day successors. Gab muttered his frustration. Jack confided that Gab's late-night broadcasts had become the brunt of racist jokes all over town.

"It's your name," Jack said. "If we hadn't all called you Blackie, Blackie Blackman, since elementary school, they wouldn't have a punch line."

The lights dimmed and the curtain opened to the tune of "Smoke Gets in Your Eyes." A parody of Mayor Cummings's failed auditorium proposal opened with the mayor asking Pie Hardison, his blackface porter, "Do you think the voters will ever find out what really happened?"

8. Williams, *Legendary Pioneers*, 30.
9. Williams, 30.

"Wal, sah," Pie responded, "I's spect by time people finds out about that you'll be outta office anyhow!"[10]

Gab raised his glass in salute to his Ben West. "From Pie's lips to God's ears," Gab said. He and Jack had encouraged Ben to run for mayor. At present, Ben was focused on changing city council elections from at-large to districts, which, if successful, would enable the colored population to elect one of their own.

Despite the hecklers, Gab enjoyed his evening with his former cohorts. "Let's not wait so long to get together again," he told them at the conclusion of the show.

Ben lifted his glass to Gab. "Here's to you, Blackie. What you did took courage."

The following week, musician Louis Jordan strolled down Charlotte Avenue. He was certainly back in the South, he thought, as everyone he passed on the street was colored and polite. In Los Angeles, where he now lived, or in New York, where he'd lived previously, coloreds and whites interacted, though rarely was anyone polite. When he reached Fourth, he asked the doorman if Sou was around.

"Who be askin'?" the guard asked.

"Louie Jordan. Don't ya recognize me without the brass?"

The guard escorted Louis to the second-floor gambling parlor. Sou and his partner, Albert "Shorty" Banks, were seated at a poker table laden with ledgers. When Sou opened his first pool hall, Shorty had owned the adjacent liquor store, Dixie Liquor. Since alcohol by the drink was illegal in Nashville, Shorty became Sou's package liquor supplier. Eventually the two men became partners. Sou handled the gambling and entertainment side of the business; Shorty handled the food and beverage side.

"We wondered if you was gonna stop by," Shorty said.

"Came to ask after a fella, Gene Nobles. Folks say he broadcasts my music. Know him?"

10. "Annual Gridiron Dinner Revived By Lions Club," *Nashville Banner*, December 4, 1946.

"Of him," Sou answered. "He's a gambler. Horses mostly. Station's just three blocks down Fourth. Want me to call 'em for ya?" Sou said.

"Yeah. I'm thinking they could help fill the auditorium, maybe sell some records."

Gab listened politely to Bridgeforth's request that Gab invite Louis Jordan to the station as he had Malcolm. Gab had heard all about Bridgeforth from his time at the *Banner*. He wondered if the newsroom rumors were true: that Sou made more money than any white man in town. Knowing how much that irked Jimmy, Gab hoped it was true.

"Gene'll be thrilled to meet Jordan," Gab said. "He usually arrives a few hours before his show. If Jordan wants to be live on the broadcast, we'd be honored."

Sou confirmed Jordan would be there. Gab stayed late to tell Gene personally.

"Why're you still here, Blackie?" Gene asked.

"You won't believe it! Louis Jordan's in town and wants to come meet you. He's on his way. He thinks you can help 'em sell some tickets and records."

"I can. Us playin' race music's gonna be great for the coloreds' business."

"Yeah, but we're playin' it to make *us* money. We need to find a way to profit off Jordan's records."

Gene set up the large studio to accommodate Jordan going live. He tapped John Richbourg, the station's news announcer, to help.

Twenty minutes after Gene signed on and played his cohort's Tarzan yell, he made the announcement: "Here with me tonight live in studio is Louis Jordan himself."

Jordan took the microphone: "I love chickens. You know that leg, I just lay on that. Name of this tune is 'Ain't Nobody Here but Us Chickens.'" He played the horn, then sang.

"Well done, Louis," Gab said at the conclusion of the song. "That's not just gonna sell a lot of records—might sell a few chickens too."

"Because everybody loves fried chicken, right?" John added.

"I'll say," Gab said. "Makes my mouth water just thinkin' about them wings."

"You writin' me another verse?" Jordan asked.

"Nah, commercials are more my thing," Gab replied. "Wish I'd thought to invite Agnes Jones up tonight. She'd likely've sponsored this program."

"And just how're we 'spose to sell chickens over the air?" Gene asked.

Gab repeated for John and Jordan a story he'd already shared with Gene. "Back when I first worked at the *Banner*, I was given a referral from classified sales to call on Agnes Jones. She had this nice house on Main Street in Gallatin. When she opened the door and I stepped into her parlor, what did I see? Two fancy antique chairs and a three-thousand-egg incubator!"

The men laughed. Gab continued, "See now, a few years earlier, Agnes had pioneered the sale of baby chicks via parcel post. Said she discovered newly hatched chicks could survive forty-eight hours with no food or water, and since she'd won numerous blue ribbons, people wanted her chicks. She started mail-ordering them to anywhere they could be delivered in two days. Each year I buy baby chicks from her for my kids' Easter baskets. I pick 'em up, though. I wonder how many of our listeners live within two days of Agnes's place?"

Gene laughed. "Hell, if she can ship 'em, I can sell 'em!"

The following Monday, Gab visited Agnes's hatchery. The business had outgrown her home and now operated from a three-story building that contained thirteen two-thousand-egg-capacity incubators. Gab decided to test shipping baby chicks. He ordered ten chicks mailed to Christine and each of her three sisters. The chicks grew into plump hens who later had their necks snapped, feathers plucked, and parts fried. By the time Gab nibbled on that first drumstick, Gene had sold hundreds of thousands of what would be called the "infamous WLAC baby chicks."

Gene recorded numerous versions of the baby chicks commercial, including: "Friends, raise your own fryers and broilers. Cut down on your grocery bill. Have chickens and eggs to sell to friends and neighbors for the low, low price of one dollar and ninety-eight cents . . ."

Having determined Agnes's blue-ribbon chicks were too expensive for his audience, Gab went in search of a hatchery that could provide a hundred baby chicks for a dollar. Eventually, he settled on the Carter Hatchery in Eldorado, Illinois. He wrote the huckster spiel himself: "One hundred of the finest baby chicks you ever saw . . ." The commercial was perfect. The baby chicks, not quite, considering most were scrub roosters that would have otherwise been drowned.

The "red-topped baby chicks" that survived became "bantam-type roosters that grew to fly like eagles, and in gangs of twenty-five or thirty, sweep out of trees to attack dogs, cats and unwary human beings."[11] Having anticipated his customers wouldn't be satisfied with their vicious poultry, Gab devised a strategy to profit from their dissatisfaction. Gene recorded the offer: "We will replace at half-price any of your baby chicks that fail to survive."

Within the first few months of baby chick sales, Gab realized he'd created a money-making bonanza. His plan to earn a penny-a-chicken had come true. Thus motivated, he went in search of additional products he could sell per inquiry or, in laymen's terms, per product sold, as opposed to selling airtime.

The station's mailroom, which had been a one-desk, closet-sized repository for press releases and political announcements, morphed into a room-sized cash till. Months earlier, a lone postman had delivered mail from his over-the-shoulder satchel; now he lugged overstuffed burlap sacks in daily. Because the station didn't have a fully staffed mailroom, the hallway quickly became a burlap sack obstacle course.

Gene's wife, Eleanor, replied to all his fan mail. She was the first to recognize most of the correspondence Gene received came from barely literate, rural people. Gab and Truman deemed Eleanor's findings confirmation their plan to create an audience where none previously existed—a colored audience—had worked. With a Negro high school graduation rate of about 10 percent, the illegibility of the letters indicated they'd hit their target. In addition, the baby-chick sales hinted at something else: Gene's audience was gullible. It brought to mind an expression Gab had learned from his three mentors:

"Sell to the rich, you'll dine with the poor. Sell to the poor, you'll dine with the rich."

On Gab's first day at WLAC he had illustrated for Ward how WSM generated millions in profit from hillbilly music whose lyrics celebrated the joys of a poor country life. And there was only one group larger and more economically challenged than hillbillies, he'd told Truman:

---

11. Wes Smith, *The Pied Pipers of Rock 'n' Roll* (Marietta, GA: Longstreet Press, 1989), 95.

"Negroes. Their music is mostly broken hearts and despair. No station broadcasts that, yet broken hearts and despair's universal. 'It's gone and started rainin', I'm as lonely as a man can be.' Who can't relate to that? No one escapes life without experiencing some loneliness. We play that, advertise what coloreds want to buy, and we'll own a massive untapped market."

Because Truman was bold enough to approve Gab's strategy, and Gene had the audacity to implement it, they made broadcast history and more money than any of them anticipated. Although not as much as they helped a young, recently returned army veteran earn.

Randy Wood had opened an electrical appliance repair shop down the road from Agnes's chicken hatchery. Whenever he repaired an amplifier, the customer would ask Randy to demonstrate that it worked. Randy surmised this could become a good add-on sales opportunity. He called Louis Buckley, a jukebox distributor who advertised used records. Since most of Buckley's boxes were in colored juke joints and billiard halls, his inventory was heavy with jazz, blues, and boogie-woogie records. Buckley offered Randy a deal on a hundred-record mélange featuring race, hillbilly, and gospel. Randy put a speaker outside his store to advertise the records and sold out in a day. After that, Randy ordered his records from national record companies.

In February 1947, when a salesman for Capitol Records, Bob Holmes, visited Randy's store, he invited Randy to tag along with him to WLAC. There, Randy and Gene got along well. Gene told Randy how many baby chicks he'd sold through the mail, and since it worked for chicks, it'd probably work for records. Gab sold Randy five one-minute midnight spots for five dollars each. They ran for five consecutive nights. After the fifth night, having received only one order, Randy canceled the ads. The following week, Randy's mail arrived, not by satchel but by cartload.

Randy called Gene at home and exclaimed, "Put that ad back on!"

Randy's first commercial featured records by Johnny Mercer, Nat "King" Cole, Ella Mae Morse, and Eddy Arnold. However, the orders Randy received weren't for the advertised records. Instead, they were requests for Wynonie Harris, T-Bone Walker, Cecil Gant, and other names Randy didn't recognize.

"Who are these people? And what's 'Who Threw the Whiskey in the Well'?" Randy asked Gene. They quickly realized whatever Gene played, his audience would buy. Gene expanded his playlist to a wider variety of artists. Gab sold Randy a sponsorship for Gene's show, and Gene kept Randy apprised of what he played.

"Send no money, friends, just your name and address," Gene pitched. Each day thereafter, orders flooded in by the thousands. Gene and Randy had stumbled upon a way they could directly profit off race records like Louis Jordon's. The mailman delivered the records and collected the money. Before long, the lowly mailroom expanded into a frenzied office that reminded Gab of the newsroom of the *Banner*. Randy's appliance repair shop was rebranded as Randy's Record Mart, and millions of Gene's fans forever after called WLAC "Randy's."

5

WHO THREW THE
WHISKEY IN THE WELL?

Things were wrong, and they're still wrong and when
you see it, it's important to say it right then and there.
This is wrong and I'm not going to be a part of it.

—NASHVILLE CITY COUNCILWOMAN BETTY CHILES NIXON

Sou noticed his golf buddy, Malcolm, come into the club with Ted Jarrett. Ted had left Nashville an overweight, starry-eyed student poet at Fisk and, after two years in the navy, had returned a lean, hardened, restless man. Sou considered how different Ted was from Malcolm's other veteran friends, men who primarily drank, boxed, and gambled. Ted, however, worked multiple jobs to support himself, his mother, and his sister while he struggled to complete his education at Fisk. When Sou discovered Ted was also a talented pianist, he hired him to accompany a few of his guest vocalists. The New Era exposure led Ted to pick up gigs in other clubs: the Del Morocco, Maceo's, Brown's Supper Club, Club Baron, Sugar Hill, and the Pink Elephant. Recently, Ted had secured a weekly gig at Woodmont Country Club.

Bill Allen had met Ted Jarrett at Woodmont. At first blush one might think Bill "Hoss" Allen and Theodore "Ted" Jarrett had little in common. But like Bill, Ted had been born into a wealthy family with a nanny/cook/house-keeper, and a chauffeur who would drive little Ted around in a big Cadillac. Ted's life was upended in 1927, when his father was murdered. And like Bill, Ted was abandoned by his mother. Ted was raised by his grandmother, Sally Ann Tillman, and her abusive sharecropper husband. He endured eight years of physical abuse from his step-grandfather before Ted was finally returned to his mother. Ted's rescue, however, wasn't for his benefit—it was because he was old enough to help support her financially. While Ted attended Pearl High, he worked numerous jobs: at the Belle Meade Bowling Alley, Tennessee Chemical, and Loveman's apparel store. In addition, he side-hustled as a shoeshine man and caddy so he could pay the thirteen-dollar monthly rent for a dilapidated shack with no electricity, plumbing, or heat. Ted's family relied on an outdoor privy, kerosene lamps, a coal stove for heat, and a fire hydrant for water.

After Ted's stint in the navy, he returned to the same shack he'd shared with his family and reenrolled in Fisk. They never acquired running water, yet he eventually got electricity so he and his sister could study at night. Ted rarely had time to study. He'd start his day at a shoeshine stand in Printers Alley. After school, he'd bus tables; then he played piano for the supper crowd at Woodmont; and finally, he'd accompany a vocalist at the Era or another nightclub. Ted was allowed to bus tables and play the piano in white clubs, but he wasn't permitted to use the front door or fraternize with guests.

Segregation was supposed to work both ways, with whites barred from colored venues. Yet there had long existed a certain class of whites who wanted to fraternize with coloreds. Some simply loved the music, and a few clubs made exceptions. Not Sou. He was wary of white women, often driven by carnal desire, who donned dark makeup to sneak into Black clubs.

Sou took pride in running a clean club: no knives, no guns, no brass knuckles, no fighting, no profanity, no drugs, and no light-skinned women. He had one ironclad rule: "Act out and you're put out!"

If anyone got aggressive with a woman, used profanity, carried a weapon, started a fight, or disguised themselves as colored, they were on the street before God got the word. Of all these concerns, what kept him awake nights was the one Ida B. Wells called that "old threadbare lie"—that a Black man found in a consensual sexual relationship with a white woman would be branded a rapist and lynched.[1] Sou maintained a watchful eye over his musicians and cautioned them not to get involved with white women, as it would not only endanger their lives but could destroy his business, as it had his mentor's.

In 1934, after his grandmother Mary died, the family farm was sold and Sou inherited $420. With this inheritance, Sou purchased a new suit and pair of shoes for $150 and with the remaining $270 opened a three-table pool hall.[2] Two years later, despite being warned that a former Alabama plowboy couldn't make it in Nashville, he opened his first New Era Club. Determined to succeed, he sought advice from the city's most successful Black businessman, Bill James. In addition to running numbers, James owned the Grace Hotel, the swanky Blackhawk restaurant, a gas station, and a cab company. Rumors circulated that James had started the numbers racket with Stahlman, whose sports edition published the winning numbers. Whether Stahlman and James had ever been in cahoots, Sou never discovered.[3] He had his suspicions, because two of James's runners had been *Banner* pressmen who openly sold tickets to the staff. When James tried to organize a Negro political base in 1940, Stahlman went after him with the malice of a scorned lover. Word spread that James had become too cocky, and his blatant disregard for the tradition of Negro subservience led to his downfall.

Stahlman had himself appointed chairman of a grand jury investigating the numbers racket and ordered James's hotel raided by state police. The *Banner* published scandalous front-page headlines and lurid articles about interracial sex at his hotel. And the coup de grâce: the white woman at the center of this interracial carnal exposé wasn't just any random teenager, but Mary Davenport, the daughter of Albert Davenport, who was serving a ninety-nine-year sentence for the torture, mutilation, and murder of four teenagers—a tragedy of biblical proportions known as the Marrowbone Ridge Cabin Fire murders.[4] The only headlines that sold more newspapers than Marrowbone Ridge were those about crimes of interracial sex.

Stahlman hit the jackpot with this story, and Bill James was promptly

1. Ida B. Wells, "The Truth About Lynching," *New York Age*, June 25, 1892, 1.
2. William Bridgeforth, personal story pamphlet, July 2001.
3. Benjamin Houston, *The Nashville Way: Racial Etiquette and the Struggle for Social Justice in a Southern City* (Athens: University of Georgia Press, 2012), 31.
4. James G. Stahlman, "From the Shoulder," *Nashville Banner*, January 8, 9, and 15, 1940.

run out of town. Forced to flee to save his life, James turned over his numbers operation to Sou, who vowed to learn from his mentor's mistakes. Sou avoided association with whites and never flaunted his wealth, drove fancy cars, or flashed wads of cash. He gave away more money than he kept. He lived well but under the radar to avoid the wrath of any Bedford Forrest disciples.

When Malcolm told Sou that the white female owner of the Clarksville Highway nightclub had hired Jarrett, Sou intervened. He knew this woman seduced colored musicians who played for her. He gave Ted the file of *Banner* stories James had left behind when he fled. The *Banner*'s photograph of the raid of the Grace Hotel made the Black business district look like a crime-infested neighborhood in a Hollywood gangster film. Stahlman's editorial left little doubt how the newsman felt about interracial sex in Nashville:

Where Negro men go to bring in white women
for immoral purposes with Negro ex-convicts.
And that's in the City of Nashville. The Athens of the South.
The seat of Southern Culture. I thought things were pretty low-down here.
But I had no idea it had come to open consorting of the races.
That's lower down than I expected . . .
That sort of thing isn't going to go on in this community.
In the first place, it isn't moral. In the second, it isn't legal.
In the third place, it is downright low-down
and that doesn't even begin to describe it.
It is too low-down for decent people to contemplate.
And Nashville isn't going to put up with
Negro automobile scouts for white women as prey.
I'm saying it for the God-fearing people of Nashville.
For the law-abiding people of Nashville.
For those who believe in public decency.
For those who won't stand for any breaking down of racial barriers.[5]

5. James G. Stahlman, "From the Shoulder," *Nashville Banner*, January 9, 1940.

Sou was certain that after Ted read the file, he wouldn't fall victim to a trap that left many a man suspended from a poplar tree. Even James Stephenson, of the confiscated radio fame, escaped that fate only after he fled Tennessee immediately upon his acquittal.

The next week, Jarrett confided to Sou that the woman had propositioned him for sex.

"After what you showed me," Ted told Sou, "I hightailed it outta there so fast, I didn't even collect my pay."

Sou handed Ted the wages he would have made. "Never go back."

Wynonie Harris took the night train from New York to Nashville. He arrived in the afternoon without his normal pianist and checked into the Hotel Carver (formerly the Grace). After a shower, he went to the New Era to meet with Sou. Harris had been in Nashville many times before. He'd performed at Club Zanzibar and at the Ryman Auditorium with his friend Cecil Gant. Wynonie's Nashville trips had been his most profitable, as in addition to the concerts, Jim Bulliet had paid him to record four less-than-memorable songs for his label, Bullet Records. Wynonie learned from Gant that Sou hired musicians who performed at the Ryman or War Memorial for intimate, by-invitation-only shows for his bourgeoise patrons who didn't want to mix with the lower classes or be relegated to the colored balcony section of the big venues.

"Fast money makes fast friends," Sou said. He handed Wynonie a generous cash deposit for a private after-hours show.

"You must got lots of friends," Wynonie joked.

"More than most plowboys, I reckon," Sou replied. "Since WLAC started broadcastin' our music, this corner's become the musicians' first stop. They get off the night trains, then come here. They stay 'cross the street at the YMCA."

Wynonie was impressed with Sou's expanded club. Instead of the dirt floor honky-tonk of the first New Era, this was an upscale piano bar with wood-paneled walls and a real dance floor. He told Wynonie the patrons would arrive dressed to impress and that he'd hired an exotic dancer to perform before

Wynonie's set. For the women, Sou hired a few handsome gentlemen to ensure no wallflower went home without having been asked to dance. The gentlemen were virile young men from the roster of Sou's New Era Giants baseball team.

"Sou thinks of everything. No wonder he's so successful," Wynonie told Helen just before he went on stage.

Helen glanced around the room and recognized nearly everyone in attendance. They'd all dressed up for the occasion. Sou's table was crowded with women decked out in expensive suits, hats, and furs. Because he knew his guests would be eager to brag about this special by-invitation-only evening, Sou had hired a professional photographer and ordered custom mats to frame the photos. When the camera was aimed at Sou's table, Helen was the only woman who didn't pose as if she was the main attraction. She already had Sou's attention. Most of the other women craved it. Helen wondered how many she'd see at Westwood Baptist in the morning. Now that a photographer had memorialized the evening, the hypocritical church women who flirted with Sou on Saturday night and acted as if they didn't know Helen or had ever been to her husband's establishment couldn't deny it come Sunday morning.

Helen turned to watch Wynonie. He began his set with a song about a sinner who needed to repent for having thrown whiskey down a well. *How apropos*, she thought.

As with most cities in the Bible Belt, Nashville was never more segregated than on Sunday morning. Blue laws kept the retailers closed, and following a tradition older than the city, Nashvillians filled the first half of the Lord's Day with music, storytelling, and religion. Helen attended the uplifting Westwood Baptist service with her beloved stepfather, William Brown. The worship was full of good news and vibrant gospel music. She'd given up long ago on Sou attending with them. He told anyone who asked that he didn't attend Westwood because he was a member of St. Luke's Methodist. Technically, that was true. Sou provided generous financial support to St. Luke's, although he hadn't entered the sanctuary since he and Helen married—for the second time. Helen's family had belonged to Westwood

Baptist for three generations. She loved the festive services: the jubilance of voices united in song, the clink and jangle of the Pentecostal tambourine, the fervor of the sinner who begs forgiveness, and the triumphant drama of a sermon that began with despair and concluded with hope. At the conclusion of the service, Rev. Ambrose Bennett announced, "I hope you will all join Brother Crutcher and me Tuesday night at city hall to protest the opening of a liquor store in the vicinity of Meharry Medical College and Fisk. This places the devil's temptation directly in the path of our fine students. Our mission is to lead our youngsters toward a life of Christian values, not assist them into temptation."

Helen wondered how many of the Saturday night sinners she'd seen slam whiskey at the club a few hours before would participate exuberantly in Tuesday's liquor store protest. She kissed her stepfather's cheek, then snuck out the side entrance to rush home to her beloved husband. She couldn't wait to share the happy news that, after years of trying, she was finally pregnant with their first child.

On the other side of Union Station, Gab and Christine, along with Christine's extended family, attended church service at First Lutheran. Christine loved the solemn holiness of the ritual and the sacred hymns sung by her older sister, Bertha, the church soloist. Her family had been members of First Lutheran since her parents married here in 1895. As a result, there were few leadership posts that someone in Christine's family hadn't held. Christine was a member of the Ladies Auxiliary and the Mother Kuhn Missionary Society. Gab served as an usher.

Christine sat between Gab and Eddie, with their daughter, Gayle, beside Barbara, Christine's mother. By the time the sermon began, Eddie had become fidgety. Christine slipped him a piece of gum and told him to listen to Reverend Gernert. She turned her attention back to the pulpit and noticed the pastor seemed to stare directly at Gab when he spoke:

The church today has a larger field of service
in that it has so many avenues of approach
to the individual, not through the printed page
and pulpit alone. It has the radio, recordings

and documentary films. Later developments
tend to add to this . . . [6]

By the end of the sermon, Christine suspected the pastor had intended the
message as a directive for Gab to stop the race music broadcasts. He hadn't used
Gab's name or identified the station he believed was corrupting the airwaves
with the devil's music. Her suspicion was confirmed when Pastor Gernert
approached her in the narthex.

"May I have a word, Christine?"

Christine requested her mother take Eddie and Gayle outside.

Pastor Gernert lowered his voice. "You know how much I respect you and
your family. And while I hesitate to bring it to your attention—"

"Have I done something to offend you?" Christine interrupted.

"Not you. However, it's been mentioned, *repeatedly*, that Gab is behind the
promotion of the devil's music on WLAC. I'm concerned for his soul, as well
as y'all's personal reputation. Have you heard what they play late at night?"

"No, Pastor. I'm rarely awake past ten."

"I suggest you do, then try to talk some sense into Gab."

"Look, I know some race music can be offensive, but I believe they're broadcasting mainly spirituals, like the Jubilee Singers. Not sharecropper blues."

"During the day, you're right. But at night, they cross over to the dark side.
Listen to it."

"I will, Pastor. Thank you." Christine was disturbed by the pastor's comments and anxious to speak to Gab, but she didn't want to bring it up in
front of her mother and children. Barbara wanted to take them to Cross Keys
restaurant. Since Eddie had a crush on the owner's daughter, Betty, Christine
suspected Eddie had talked his grandmother into it.

Eddie spied Betty seated at the soda counter as they entered.

"There's your girlfriend," Gayle teased Eddie.

"Go on, say hello. But don't order anything," Christine said.

Eddie slid onto a stool next to Betty's. "Hey, girl," he said. "Feelin' better?"

Betty slurped her soda and smiled with her eyes. "I wasn't sick."

6. "On 25th Year of Pastorate," *Tennessean*, November 10, 1947.

"I saw you crying when you left Friday."

"Oh, that. Some dumb kid said my nanny couldn't go to heaven 'cause she's colored. When I asked him, 'Who says?' he said, 'The church!'"[7]

"I never heard that at church," Eddie said.

"Me neither, so I asked my Sunday school teacher. She said some churches say coloreds are cursed. And some say they ain't the same human as us. But Methodists don't believe that."

"I don't think us Lutherans do either," Eddie said.

"Well, it's just plain wrong to say stuff like that, and I intend to tell him."

Gayle tapped Eddie on his shoulder. "Table's ready. Mother says you gotta come."

"See ya later, Betty," Gayle said sweetly.

Betty waved to Eddie and he waved back. As he followed Gayle through the crowded dining room, Eddie watched colored men in white jackets as they cleaned tables and carried heavy trays. He wondered if these men knew some churches taught heaven was like restaurants and restrooms, where whites were allowed but coloreds weren't.

Later, Christine said bedtime prayers with the children: "Now I lay me down to sleep. I pray the Lord my soul to keep. If I should die before I wake, I pray the Lord my soul to take."

"Where does the Lord take coloreds' souls?" Eddie asked.

"That's a silly question," Gayle said. "It depends on if they were good or bad."

"But if they're good? Is there two heavens or just one?"

"Why are you—" Christine said.

Eddie interrupted. "Is heaven like here? Is there one heaven for us and a different one for coloreds? Betty said some churches say coloreds don't even go to heaven, no matter what. If that's true, why would they even try to be good?"

"Listen, just 'cause one nutty church says somethin' doesn't make it true," Christine said. "Don't you worry 'bout the coloreds. Love God, say your prayers, follow the Golden Rule, and leave the rest to God."

Eddie thought his mother's answer seemed incomplete, but he wanted to

---

7. Oral history interview with Betty Chiles Nixon, June 19, 2007, accessed in Nashville Public Library Civil Rights Collection.

get back to his book, *Thirty Seconds over Tokyo*. It was an adult book with no pictures, and Eddie was determined to finish it. He wanted to be just like his dad, always the most well-read guy in the room.

Christine had intended to tune in to WLAC, until she remembered that Gene didn't broadcast on Sunday nights. She'd listen to him the next time she couldn't sleep. Anyway, she was too tired to think about the devil's music or where coloreds went to heaven.

6

CALL IT STORMY MONDAY

Nashville is as much a mood as it is a place. It comingled remnants of a self-professed genteel Old South, and reminders of a Confederate past with the bustle of New South commercial town, the bawdiness of a river city and the fundamental roots of a religious city.

—BENJAMIN HOUSTON, *THE NASHVILLE WAY*

Like all of Gallatin, Bill Allen had been impressed by Agnes Jones's and Randy Wood's mail-order businesses. Bill and Agnes's son, Ellis, were cousins who had been buddies since elementary school. They still called each other by their childhood nicknames, Hoss and Big Foot. In the summer of 1947, Ellis and Hoss were home from college. One Sunday, over a fried chicken meal, Agnes speculated about how much revenue WLAC must be generating from the sale of scrub roosters. This led the two college guys to contemplate what they might sell on WLAC. It didn't take long for Hoss to find the perfect product. A friend who sold novelty items to drug-stores had an excess supply of round, wire-rimmed sunglasses like those worn by

Dizzy Gillespie. Hoss decided to brand them "Bop Sunglasses" and sell them on WLAC.

Gab welcomed two tall, handsome young men into his office. Without removing their sunglasses, they introduced themselves as Bill Allen and Ellis Jones from Gallatin. Gab listened to their pitch for "Bop Sunglasses." Impressed with the young men and their idea, he suggested a per-inquiry sales promotion and retail price. Gab scribbled out a commercial and Gene recorded it. The men approved the thirty-second spot, signed a contract, and gave several pairs of the sunglasses to Gab and Gene. By the time Bill and Ellis returned to college, they had sold tens of thousands of pairs and become Gallatin's third most profitable mail-order business. The joint venture between Gab and Hoss was a harbinger of greater things to come.

Despite Cecil and Mamie's disapproval of his theatrical ambitions, Bill held several lead roles in Vanderbilt theater productions. He played the deranged judge in *Winterset*, the former boyfriend in *The Male Animal*, and, foreshadowing the iconic role he'd one day play on air at WLAC, the title character in the Shakespearean tragedy *Othello*. Bill's portrayal of the dark-skinned general, mocked as a "Barbary Horse," who endured racism after he married a white woman, was so stellar it earned him a scholarship to the most prestigious theater company in New England. Nevertheless, Mamie and Cecil put the kibosh on Bill's dream of an acting career. They demanded he withdraw from the Priscilla Beach Theatre on Boston's South Shore, which left the handsome heartthrob role to a tuition-paying understudy: Paul Newman.

When she learned that a local car dealer planned to launch a radio station in Gallatin, Mamie insisted that Bill come home and follow Mrs. Bingham's advice. Bill was able to do at WHIN what he'd wanted to do at WKDA—turn on the microphone and gab.

On September 1, 1948, Bill "Hoss" Allen debuted his afternoon radio program, *The Harlem Hop*. He featured big band music until phone calls and letters informed him that WHIN's audience didn't like big band music. They wanted to hear what Gene Nobles aired the night before: Wynonie Harris, Bull Moose Jackson, T. Bone Walker. Hoss got Randy to share Gene's playlist with him so Hoss could play the same music. And what they played, Randy sold.

Six months later, on Monday, March 26, 1949, during a meeting, Gab told

Mary Elizabeth Hicks, WLAC's effervescent staff keyboardist, "Meet me at the Hermitage Hotel."

Everyone laughed. No one interpreted it as inappropriate, because the phrase was a common punchline for jokes about the Bourbon Aristocracy, whose home turf was the hotel's Grille Room. Gab had been born into this clan of patriarchs who played the cityscape as if it were a Monopoly game. At the *Banner* he'd been considered an outlier due to his lack of wealth, education, and power. Since having joined WLAC, he was branded an antagonist—a disrupter to the delusion that their "Confederate lost cause" was never lost, just temporarily misplaced.

On his walk to the Hermitage, Gab ruminated over a conversation he'd had after church with one of the elites who objected to Gene's broadcast. The complaints had become so prevalent Gab was forced to pen a canned response for switchboard operators to read. He had anticipated race music might rile up a few racists; however, he had underestimated how vile the calls would be. After Gab listened to one of the initial rants, it triggered his first migraine since he'd left the *Banner*. He instructed the operators that if they heard the words *nigger music*, or any similar statement, they were to respond, "If you don't like our broadcast, change stations. They'll be happy you tuned in. Just as our listeners are happy with us." Then hang the hell up!

Gab felt as if he were fighting a war on three fronts: against Jimmy's crowd, the Bourbon Aristocracy, who used wealth and influence to control the city; the Dixie Gestapo, who called themselves "White Citizens' Councils" and hid under white hoods to use intimidation as a weapon; and finally, the Morality Police, religious leaders of *both* races, who protested the music as the devil's handiwork and deejays as his soldiers.

Each Monday, Gab was forced to defend Gene for something. The first call this day had come from the Morality Police. Rev. Ambrose Bennett of the Westwood Baptist Church insisted Gab remove Gene from the air because he drank Sterling Beer on the job. Bennett wasn't the only pastor who complained—he was just the most recent. Gab had assured them all that Gene didn't drink beer on air. He acted as if he did only because Sterling Beer sponsored the broadcast. Gab didn't disclose that what Gene actually drank while on air was whiskey with cola.

Gab explained to Bennett, like he had to others who complained, that just because a kid sees a beer billboard doesn't mean the sign should be chopped down. It's advertising. And unless listeners want to pay to listen, it's the only way radio can work. Since prohibition ended, alcohol manufacturers had the same right to advertise as churches. If Bennett wanted to sponsor a gospel show, Gab would be happy to sell him airtime. And if he preached on air that the music they broadcast was the devil's handiwork, Gab would defend his right to say it. This is, he was fond of saying, a country of free speech, and that includes, within certain limits, the airwaves.

The more Gab was lobbied to end the broadcast, the more he realized how influential WLAC had become. Gene's program was beloved by nearly every colored person east of the Missouri River—and all of whom, the mailman complained, Gene had heard from personally. Willie had been correct when he'd claimed everyone 'cept the preacher would listen. Gene had become the most popular announcer in the country. There was no way Gab would turn off his microphone. Especially now that the FCC had granted WSM's television license. WLAC stood to lose many of their prime day-time advertisers the moment WSM-TV went live. If anything, Gab needed to extend the station's race music broadcast hours in preparation for that downturn.

Gab arrived at 221 Sixth Avenue, the city's most prestigious address, home to the bejeweled queen of Nashville, the Hermitage Hotel. He had come early to greet the representatives of Knoxville's JFG Coffee Company. Today was the inaugural broadcast of his new show, *Coffee Quiz*. The JFG executives were enthusiastic about having their brand associated with Tennessee's most exclusive hotel. They wanted a live show, but Gab convinced them to do a two-hour taped delay so the participants could listen to themselves on air later. JFG sponsored the show, hopeful they could replicate the success the Cheek family fashioned after claiming President Teddy Roosevelt had declared of their Maxwell House brand: "Good to the last drop!"

The Hermitage Hotel owners were equally keen to have the show recorded at their Grille Room. Mary Elizabeth Hicks was a popular draw, who would liven up a room normally filled with stoic businessmen. Mary would play a melody, then the WLAC host announcer would ask diners to name the tune.[1] Whoever named the most songs would win JFG-sponsored prizes.

Gab crossed the hotel's soaring lobby, descended several steps to the Grille Room, and conversed with the hotel manager and the JFG executives. Mary Elizabeth Hicks arrived minutes later. She socialized with diners and answered their questions about the contest, a job intended for the host, who had not yet arrived. Gab glanced at his watch. It was fifteen minutes to showtime and his announcer was already thirty minutes late. When he finally breezed into the room, Gab asked, "Where've you been? We're ten minutes to show."

"I'm not doing the broadcast unless you pay me what she's getting!"

Gab glanced at Mary. "Oh, hell no! She's the star, *and* she's been here doing your job."

"I'm not working for less than a woman. If you don't pay me equal, I'll quit."

"Then quit. You'll be easily replaced."

The announcer stormed out. Mary rushed over to Gab. "What just happened?" she asked.

"He quit. Stall while I call another announcer." Gab called the station. Herman Grizzard jogged around the crowd of lunchtime shoppers on the sidewalks. He arrived out of breath, but the show went on as planned.

After *Coffee Quiz* had been broadcast, Gab and Truman tuned in to listen to "this fresh kid with a magnificent voice on air in Gallatin."[2] Four days later, Gab put a familiar and handsome face to the voice and hired the former "Bop Sunglasses" salesman—Bill "Hoss" Allen. Bill took over some of John Richbourg's news announcements, which allowed Gab to shift John to the more lucrative nighttime broadcast. Gene's show had already been extended to three hours. The hour before Randy's was now sponsored by Ernie Young, who owned a record store in downtown Nashville. The hour after Randy's was sponsored by Sterling Beer.

The three straight hours had started to wear on Gene. Gab had been concerned that a reduction in Gene's hours would cost them listeners, after college students voted Gene the most popular deejay in the country. The students were hooked on Gene's quirky double entendres: "If your gal is mad at you, why

---

1. Egerton, *Nashville*, 173.
2. Gab's index cards for the speech at Hoss's retirement party, April 27, 1992.

don't you give her a good Gruen [wristwatch]?" (rhymes with "screwin'")[3] and his provocative advice to buy petroleum jelly and "keep workin' and jerkin'."

After Ernie Young complained to Gab that he felt Gene did a better job selling records for Randy than for him, Gab gave Gene's first hour to John. Gene continued to host the next two. Gab had initially arranged for Gene and John to be paid a 10 percent per-inquiry commission. They turned out to be too good at it. In one of his first weeks as a pitchman, John earned $700, which adjusted for inflation is more than $10,000 today. A lot of money for selling records and baby chicks. The bookkeeper told Truman that deejays should not make more money than a bank president downstairs. Truman delivered the bad news to Gab, who broke it to Gene and John. Gab had to cap their commission so they couldn't make more than $300 or $400 per week."[4] And soon the record producers arrived with stacks of cash to make up the difference on record sales.

On Monday, April 25, 1949, Pie Hardison, Mayor Cummings's porter, told Sou that things were about to get stormy for numbers runners.

"Law's coming down on y'all," he said. "Memphis is about to arrest all the runners. You're in need of more protection than just the mayor and police chief or you're next."

For years, Sou had paid Pie to keep him abreast of what went on in the mayor's office. Pie proved invaluable and had never provided inaccurate information. Pie had been instrumental in convincing the mayor and police chief to hire several colored policemen. The colored officers were permitted to work only within the boundaries of colored neighborhoods and prohibited from arresting a white person regardless of where the crime occurred. Initially, Sou celebrated this victory. He had hired several of the officers to work for him as bouncers and it had proven effective. He now realized those colored badges had come at an enormous price.

"Are you saying I'm gonna get raided?" Sou asked.

3. Smith, *Pied Pipers*, 87.
4. John R. Franklin, "The Hit Maker," *Take One*, March 1978, 15.

"I'm sayin' gots to be honor among thieves. Colored police cain't make what white officers ain't. You gots to pay 'em all," Pie explained.

"All who?" Sou asked.

"All cops. If one colored's paid, every white's gotta be paid same."

"How many we talkin'?" Shorty asked.

"Hundred. Give or take."

Sou was dumbfounded. "Let me get this straight. You're sayin' I gotta pay *one hundred* white policemen to look the other way because two coloreds do legit work here off duty?"

"I'm sayin' onliest way you ain't gettin' arrested for numbers and liquor is if you pay every white police what you pay them two. You got a new baby, Sou. You want her growed up while you's in the county workhouse?"

"This is a shakedown!" Sou exclaimed.

"Not just of you," Pie said. "All y'all's competition gotta pay too. Fair's fair."

"Maybe we wait," Shorty suggested, "see what happens in Memphis."

Sou shook his head. "Nah. Pie says gonna happen, it will. Let's get Good Jelly on it. I don't like it, but Pie's right. I'm not going to the workhouse!"

Henry "Good Jelly" Jones was a charismatic former minstrel performer and petty criminal who had started his illicit career hawking numbers for Bill James. Good Jelly was considered Nashville's greatest-of-all-time street hustler. Jelly had refined the gift of blarney to such a degree that despite his fifty-plus arrests—operating a disorderly house, vagrancy, impersonating an officer, operating a taxi without a license, drunk and disorderly conduct, carrying an illegal weapon, grand larceny, driving while intoxicated, pawning stolen goods—he'd spent nary a day behind bars. Jelly could charm anyone. From streetsweeper to county judge, he collected friends and favors like librarians collect books. Only someone with Jelly's charisma and connections could negotiate a deal between the colored nightclub owners, numbers runners, and one hundred white police officers. Jelly recruited a professional gambler to serve as mediator. Three days later, an agreement was reached. The odds payout for winning numbers would be reduced from 500-to-1 to 400-to-1. The runners' margin of ten cents per dollar would double, with half given to white police officers and high-ranking officials for "protection."

Sou arrived home in the wee hours of April 28, relieved to tell Helen they'd reached a settlement. He found her asleep in their bed with Harriet nestled beside her. He kissed Helen lightly on the forehead. She woke instantly.

"It's settled, Funny. Odds is being lowered to pay them. You can sleep soundly now."

"Thank goodness," she sighed.

He lifted Harriett and carried her into the nursery. "Until the next administration," he whispered to his baby daughter. "But that's our secret. Don't worry your mother about it."

When Sou slid into bed, Helen snuggled next to him.

"How're you gonna get word out that payouts is being clipped?" she asked.

"Stahlman'll announce it in the *Banner.* Jelly's giving him the scoop. Come Sunday, May 1, odds is lowered to four hundred to one."

On April 29, 1949, the *Banner*'s front-page headline read: "The 'Payoff'— Lower Number Odds for 'Protection.'"

Nashville's "numbers" racket had declared a new deal, it was learned today, and beginning at midnight Sunday the current 500 to 1 "payoff" odds will be reduced to 400 to 1 with a large percentage of the racketeer's "saving" to go to "protection."[5]

Adjacent to the odds story was this AP article:

Memphis, April 28—Twenty-two Memphis Negroes were arrested last night in what police termed "the smashing of the biggest policy racket in Memphis in many years."

Two days later, on a busy Saturday night, the city's clubs were raided in what the *Banner* described as a "citywide 'vice' clean-up."[6] Slot machines were confiscated or destroyed. Sou's was one of the only clubs to escape the raid unscathed. The white officers who carried out the raid left his slot machines untouched. They thanked Sou for his generosity, then left.

5. Richard S. Battle, "Lower Numbers Odds for 'Protection,'" *Nashville Banner*, April 28, 1949.
6. Robert Battle, "Vice 'Clean Up' Forces Withdrawal Of Games," *Nashville Banner*, April 30, 1949.

The following week, Nashvillians went to the polls to vote on the city auditorium referendum. Gab paid little notice to the announced results because he was too distracted by another citywide vote that had taken place that day. Christine had been elected president of the Nashville Council of Church Women, a prestigious position normally held by Bourbon Aristocracy wives. With a mixture of pride and trepidation, Gab read the announcement in the *Banner*. His wife was now the leader of the most influential Christian women's organization in town—an association aligned with the Morality Police, who regularly protested the scandalous, immoral, low-life portrayal of sexual braggadocio and innuendo of the devil's music.

Gab wondered if Christine's election might be a sneak attack on his broadcast. Then he dismissed the thought as irrational. Christine was a superb choice to lead an organization that promoted Christian family values. She was an excellent wife and mother, and people were drawn to her—John Richbourg, the most recent. He'd turned to Christine for advice with his marital problems and asked her to speak to his wife, Lilli. When Christine spoke to Lilli, she was dismayed to hear Lilli confess she hated life in the South and regretted having married John and having children. Christine tried to counsel Lilli, to no avail. Eventually, Christine told John that when a woman doesn't want to be a wife or mother, there's little anyone can do, except pray. Gab was impressed with how faithfully Christine prayed for John and Lilli, though her prayers went unanswered.

John turned out to be the perfect replacement for Gene's first hour. Not only did John bring in more listeners, but the show's sponsor, Ernie's Records, experienced tremendous sales growth. The late hour enabled John to be home with his children after school and for dinner. With his Broadway experience, baritone voice, and low-country, rural drawl, he developed an on-air personality perfectly suited to a race music show. When Gab heard John's commercials for Ernie's, he couldn't believe the voice that pitched the Blue Ribbon Record package came from the same mouth that read the news with impeccable elocution. Gab thought John's Black idiomatic dialect was so pitch-perfect that listeners might believe the musicians had pitched Ernie's record packages themselves.

Ernie called Gab to express his delight with John's broadcast. Gab predicted John would make Ernie rich. After Ernie raised concerns that John's barely literate audience couldn't spell Richbourg, John changed his on-air name to "John R," pronounced "Arrr," as a pirate might.

After John became John R, he decided the music also needed a better name. The terms used to denote Negro music—race music, sepia records, and the devil's music—needed a more accurate and respectable appellation. John invented a new name and christened this music "rhythm and blues."

NASHVILLE JUMPS

I was a baseball fanatic. And I loved funky music.

—WILLIAM SOU BRIDGEFORTH

MAY 27, 1949

Helen hadn't been able to spend much time at the New Era since Harriett was born. When she did, she came to support the musicians who were also her friends, like Cecil Gant. Helen had missed several of Cecil's previous shows; however, this year she promised him she'd do better. Following his performance earlier in the week, Cecil invited Helen to see his new home. She had agreed to drop by after shopping on Saturday. Sou promised to meet her at Cecil's after golf.

Helen had waited for over thirty minutes while the uppity clerk in Cain-Sloan's credit department proceeded to help every white person first, irrespective of how long Helen and the other colored women waited. Fearing she'd miss Sou at Cecil's, Helen felt her patience vanish.

"I've been waiting for over half an hour and I'm in a hurry," she said. "If you can't help me promptly, I'll just return these newfangled charge-a-plates and go to Castner's."

Knowing she was one of Sloan's best customers, Helen demanded immediate attention. The snobby white lady surely knew how much money they spent, as she'd processed Sou's statement for years. And that was before they'd gone all fancy and mailed these two dogtaggy-looking metal charge-a-plates—unsolicited.

Helen hated having to flaunt Sou's wealth to get attention. She knew he wouldn't approve. Yet if she didn't protest, who would?

"Helen, I'll get to you next," the clerk insisted. A few minutes later, she yelled, "Helen!"

It annoyed Helen that the white women had been called Mrs., yet they insisted on calling her Helen, like they were friends. *As if!* Helen took a Mr. Charge-it charge-a-plate from her pocketbook and slid it across the counter.

"You mailed two charge-a-plates. They both say W. S. Bridgeforth. There's only one W. S. Bridgeforth. Please reissue mine to *Mrs.* W. S. Bridgeforth."

The clerk slid the plate back. "You're Sou's wife, you can use it."

"I don't want to use it, because I'm not Mr. Bridgeforth. I'm *Mrs.* Bridgeforth."

The clerk sighed. "We don't put *Mrs.* on coloreds' charge-a-plates."

"But you put them on whites'?"

"We do. Same as we call you Helen and not *Mrs.* Bridgeforth."

"Ha! Ya just done did and thanks for nuthin'. Lemme speak to your manager."

"Thought you was in a hurry, *Helen.*"

"I am. Don't get snippy."

"I ain't snippy. *Mister* Sloan hisself said we cain't issue charge plates to *nigras* with *Mister or Mrs.* on it."

Helen pulled the second charge-a-plate from her pocketbook, plunked it on the counter, and snapped her purse closed. "Then you go tell *Mister Sloan hisself* he can keep Mr. *and* Mrs. Bridgeforth's charge-a-plates."

"Ladies," she said to the two colored women who had waited with the patience of Job, "I'm headin' to Castner's. Wanna join me? Mrs. Bridgeforth is feelin' mighty generous today."

The women followed Helen to the elevator. When the operator closed the door, Helen announced, "I'll pay off y'all's Cain-Sloan's bills if you turn in your charge-a-plates in protest over them refusing to call us Mrs."

Forty minutes later, Helen left Castner-Knott with two heavy shopping bags while her two new friends left with cash to pay off their Cain-Sloan accounts and two pairs of fine Sunday silk stockings, courtesy of W. S. Bridgeforth.

Helen checked her wristwatch. "I've got to hurry, ladies, but do me a favor." She handed the receipts for her purchases to one of the women. "Show these to that ol' biddy!"

Helen hailed a cab. "Twenty-Sixth and Booker," she told the driver. When they passed the new Cain-Sloan store, still under construction, Helen thought she'd miss shopping in that soon-to-be-opened showplace. "Sometimes you gotta stand up for yourself and your tribe," she said, thinking out loud. "Ain't that right?"

"Sho-nuff," the old Black cabbie replied. "Trick's not to get lynched doing it."

Cecil toured Helen through his new bungalow in the city's first planned, deed-restricted, colored subdivision. It had been advertised as "the only high-class Negro subdivision in Nashville. Free water tap with each lot." Cecil showed her his gas stove, electric icebox, and hot and cold running water taps. He pulled lemonade from the icebox that his wife, Alma, had prepared specifically for Helen. As he poured the drinks, Cecil confided that with such a fine home, he wasn't much interested in leaving.

"If not for them boys at Fort Campbell, I wouldn't even go that far," Cecil said. "Gots no wish to sweat through another hot Southern tour, sleeping in cars and eatin' standin' up. Onliest time I enjoy travelin' South is when them leaves change. I loves them fall colors. Maybe, head west later. Right now, I's happy to play for Sou. Pays my bills."

Helen thought that since Louis Armstrong had covered Cecil's hit, "I Wonder," and "Another Day Another Dollar" hit the Billboard chart, he probably didn't even need Sou.

Sou arrived and Alma greeted him at the front door. Helen carried two glasses of lemonade to the porch, handed her husband one, and sat beside him. She watched her husband run his fingers along the grout between the stones of the front wall.

When they'd first met, Sou had been a popular bricklayer. His uncle Nick had taught him that good workmanship was the best advertising and would always guarantee him work. She'd heard Sou frequently repeat Nick's advice:

"If you can't be tops in a field, find another where you can be tops."[1] She wondered what he thought of the workmanship on Cecil's home.

Cecil turned on the radio. "I sit here most nights listenin' at myself and my buddies on Randy's," he said. "Wynonie, Jordan, Hooker, Milburn. We all revel in knowin' millions of colored folks is listenin'. It's like Randy's done made us a jukebox in the sky. I hear myself come outta this box and think I's dreamin'."

"Heard 'I'm a Good Man but a Poor Man' just charted," Sou said. "Congratulations."

"From the looks of it, don't seem the song's true no more, Cecil," Helen teased.

Sou raised his glass. "Well done, my friend."

"Nobles said Randy's and Ernie's sold a million records last year—*each*. And fifty thousand was mine! Couldn't've dreamed that when I recorded 'I Wonder.'"

"I Wonder" had topped the 1945 Harlem Hit Parade chart. Cecil had recorded it the year before while in the army in Los Angeles. This was before any significant radio station broadcast race music, and there had been no organized distribution system for race records. "I Wonder" had become a hit after Pullman railroad porters bought hundreds of copies in Los Angeles and resold them at stops along the way. Four years later, when Cecil returned home to Nashville, he discovered a new industry had been created, literally, out of thin air. After WSM and WLAC used a skip propagation signal to bounce programming into the ionosphere and back to Earth here, there, and everywhere, a multitude of wise men—musicians, producers, and advertisers—followed the station's beacon like the holy star of Bethlehem.

Randy Wood was even inspired to turn the station's multidirectional signal into an infectious jingle: "Randy's Records is on the air—here, there, and everywhere."

WSM's signal brought thousands of country music devotees to the Ryman Auditorium and honky-tonks, while WLAC's wooed a similar crowd to the colored nightclubs. On the weekends, Nashville's streets were crowded with

---

1. William Bridgeforth, personal story pamphlet, July 2001.

aspiring musicians. It became easy for natives to spot these budding music makers by the instruments on their backs and hopeful expressions on their faces.

Of all the Chitlin Circuit nightclubs, Sou's was Cecil's favorite. He was the most generous benefactor of musicians and ran the tightest club. Artists never had to worry they'd be stiffed, shortchanged, overcharged for liquor and food, docked for damages to the venue, or wind up stuck in jail if the place was raided. Sou even arranged a driver for his guest artists. Sou was a class act who treated his musicians as class acts. For this reason, Cecil wanted Sou and Helen to be the first guests he welcomed into his new home.

"Look, Teddy Acklen's place is fine too," he told Sou, "but nuthin' nowhere beats the Era."

"Speaking of Teddy, we're playin' ball at the Dell tomorrow. Why don't you come?"

"You and him, or just y'all's teams?"

"I'm playing," Sou said. "Can't say for sure about Teddy."

"You was good in the day, but ain't you a bit old for the mound?"

"Satchel's a year older."

"Yeah, 'cept he's Satchel. And you ain't," Cecil teased. "But sure, I'll come."

Summer Sundays found Nashvillians segregated by more than just race and religion. The residents were divided by baseball, as the game reached a level of veneration normally reserved for the sacraments. For Sou, baseball was more of a religion than a game—one that had informed his character, honed his determination, and ignited his passions. It was on the mound that he first felt invincible. He'd learned to sharpen his senses, focus his mind, and harness his physical prowess to propel a hardball sixty feet six inches with such velocity that it would arrive within a seventeen-inch window in the time it takes to blink.

After Sou had pitched his first high school no-hitter, he realized if he applied this same focus to everything he did, he couldn't help but be successful. He'd applied the strategy to bricklaying, his businesses, golf game, and, most importantly, his pursuit of Helen.

On Sunday, May 28, 1949, at age forty-two, Sou walked onto the historic pitcher's mound at Sulphur Dell Stadium and wondered if Cecil had been correct. Was he too damn old to pitch? He'd surely pay for it later. The aches and pains would be worth it.

"Grand old dame, you're even older than me," Sou said as he kicked the dirt and settled his spiked metal cleats into the soil. He caught a whiff of the ground's telltale rotten-egg smell. The ancient ballpark, built atop an underground sulfur spring, was at the precise location where Union Army soldiers first introduced the game to Nashvillians.

Sou could always tell when a game was in progress, as the Era was within earshot of the Dell. Occasionally, when the wind blew in the right direction, and there were no trains on the track or barges on the river, he could even hear the crack of a bat and call of a strike. These echoed resonances were as intoxicating to Sou as Gene's broadcasts were to musicians.

Sou told Funny to bring the baby so she could watch him pitch. His wife thought Harriett was too young for baseball, but Sou insisted. He reminded her that she knew when they married—both times—he was a man of many passions. Sou loved to work, but he wasn't a workaholic, because he was equally passionate about his hobbies: gambling, golf, the blues, and baseball. Helen knew it was true. She never doubted his love for her and the baby; however, she believed that of all Sou's loves, baseball was his first and truest. Sou didn't have the heart to tell her she was right. Nothing made him feel like this did—to stand on a mound, face a batter, an umpire, and a stadium crowded with noisy fans.

Sou had come by his love of baseball honorably. His father, Isaac, told him that he loved baseball so much he had walked fifty miles to play a baseball game and thirty miles to watch one. When Isaac first sent Sou to live with his grandparents, Isaac visited frequently. After Isaac remarried, his visits became far fewer. After Isaac had additional children, the visits dwindled to twice a year. Sou surmised the only way to regain his father's attention would be through baseball. If Sou became a ballplayer, his father would drop everything and walk miles to watch.

Thus motivated, Sou quickly progressed from an Athens, Alabama, sandlot (where he earned the nickname Steel Arm Red) to lead his high school team to an undefeated championship season. Sou had hoped to become a professional ballplayer, and he'd been good enough. But Sou's uncle Nick insisted games were for boys, and with Mary recently widowed, Sou needed to become a man and provide for his grandmother as she had done for him.

Helen had tagged along to ball game after ball game when they first married. She'd watched his sandlot games and professional exhibition games. She enjoyed watching stars like Satchel Paige, Jackie Robinson, and Roy Campanella. However, Funny drew the line at high school games. Sou tried to never miss a Pearl High game, as he was ever on the lookout for talent he could nurture. He loved nothing better than to identify a future Negro League player and help him hone his skills through his New Era Elite Giants team.

Before Sou threw his first pitch, he scanned the seats for Funny and the baby. He spotted them in the front row, just to the left of home plate. Helen sat between her aunt and stepfather in seats normally reserved for whites. On this day, the sections were reversed so coloreds got the best seats, while whites were relegated to the seats usually intended for coloreds. Sou saw fewer than a dozen white spectators, mostly boys who looked like ragamuffins compared to the colored fans. Those men wore their Sunday suits, ties, and fedoras. The women—his wife, her aunt, and even baby Harriett—sported fine spring dresses, straw hats, and, in Funny's case, pearls.

Sou usually served as the New Era Elite Giants relief pitcher; today he decided to pitch first—for Harriett. Helen thought Harriett would be unable to sit still and watch the game, yet Sou knew better. His earliest memories were of crawling around in the hot, dusty dirt of a North Alabama ballpark. Plus, he was concerned this could be his last season. After one inning, he'd have to ice his shoulder for a week. He wasn't the stallion he once was, but he still felt the same thrill. He glanced at Helen and the baby, wound up, and let his first pitch fly. A strike. It felt just as good as the first strike he'd ever thrown.

When the inning ended, Helen asked her aunt to take Harriett home for a nap. She knew they'd both grown bored. Helen watched her husband roll his shoulder a few times and hoped he'd send one of the young men to the mound soon. Taking Harriett home would help. Sou could now tell his daughter she'd once watched her father pitch at Sulphur Dell.

A few hours later, Helen's aunt returned with Harriett.

"That was a quick nap," Helen said as she pulled her daughter into her lap.

"While I was at your house, Henryene Green called from Baltimore. Said Vern passed away and wanted Sou to know."

Helen allowed the news to sink in. She watched Sou signal the first base runner to advance. Moments later, she burst into tears.

"Now, sugar," her stepdaddy said, "you know Vern's been sick a spell. Didn't realize you's so fond of him."

Helen wiped her tears. "I'm not. Wasn't."

"I see. Is you worryin' Sou'll buy Vern's team?"

"Uh-huh. Likely before his obit hits the papers."

Helen feared that if Sou owned a real professional team, she'd lose her husband forever—to his first and truest love.

JINGLE BELLS

Why should the devil have all the good tunes? Music-making ought to have loftier purposes than just sensual entertainment.

–JOHN WESLEY, FOUNDER OF THE METHODIST CHURCH

Shortly after Christine became president of the Nashville Council of Church Women, she met with Pastor Gernert. He advised her to redirect the council's focus from Europe and look instead to her own backyard.

"Our agenda was set before my term. The national organization pledged a million pieces of fabric, thread, and needles to European refugee camps. 'Pieces for Peace' is the slogan."

"That's admirable, but shouldn't charity begin at home? How can you send our limited resources overseas when the most basic human need—fresh water—is going unmet right here? Just blocks away, children live without running water, heat, or electricity. They get water from fire hydrants and use outdoor privies, which contaminate the underground reservoirs. Knowing this, how can you justify sending money overseas?"

"But, Pastor—"

"Nor is there anywhere here coloreds can send their physically or mentally handicapped children. Humanity survives collectively. Shouldn't fresh water be accessible to every resident of this city, irrespective of race?"

"Of course. But I can't do anything until next year."

"Well, let's just hope that's not too late!"

Christine placed her notepad in her purse. Pastor Gernert followed her to the narthex.

"Did you listen to Gab's nighttime broadcast, as I asked? It's full of the devil's music. Gene promotes premarital sex with his double entendre and endorsements for products like petroleum jelly. More out-of-wedlock births will only make an already bad situation worse."

"Pastor, you really should speak to Gab directly."

"Gab is not president of the Council of Church Women, an organization that promotes Christian values. One of our members' sons was caught listening to Gene's program. It's your responsibility as the leader of a high-profile Christian group to take a stand against this immorality. Listen and decide if you'd want Eddie tuning in to Gene's show."

Christine thought he had likely overreacted, but when she listened to Gene's broadcast, she realized the pastor wasn't wrong. Gene began his broadcast with a Tarzan-like, chest-thumping yell from his "cohort." He promoted petroleum jelly and advised his listeners "to keep a jar in their glove compartments for whatever might come up."

Pastor was right. Gene's sexual innuendo was directed to people having sex in cars—meaning students. And she definitely didn't want her children influenced by that. She had to confront Gab. What the hell was he thinking?

One month later, on July 16, 1949, Christine read the *Banner* and wept. Her goal to address the freshwater issue had come too late for the nine dead babies and 150 children hospitalized in the city's diarrhea epidemic. The health department identified the seasonal heat combined with unsanitary living conditions and lack of clean water as the cause of the outbreak.

Many years before, when Christine was a student at Peabody, her class had volunteered at Bethlehem Settlement House. It was the first shelter of its kind for Negroes in the South, a place where they could go for a meal and a bath. Christine could still recall the smell of the multitude of unwashed bodies, heads full of lice, and bellies full of parasites. People would come in after five or six long, hard days over hot irons or presses, from the fields or the railyards, and despite having worked from "kin to cain't"—a reference to the early morning when you can just discern the difference between a brown and black mule and the time in the evening when you can't—they were paid such a pittance that even water was beyond their means. The only place they could enjoy a hot bath was the shelter. Christine cared for the children while the mothers bathed. The expectant mothers and those who had recently given birth tugged at her heart. She volunteered there until she became pregnant herself.

"It's just tragic." She wiped her tears on her napkin. "I feel sick. Pastor warned me."

"Honey, you're in a position to do something," Gab said. "Concentrate your efforts on helping them." He added under his breath, "And quit worrying me about my broadcast."

To Christine's way of thinking, just because her organization's focus was on issues of substandard housing and water didn't mean they couldn't also work to get immoral programming banned from public broadcast.

"Gab, it's my job. Not just as a leader of a Christian organization, but as a mother!"

"We've given voice to people who didn't have one before, and their lives are better for it, Christine. Some have even made enough money to buy nice homes. Cecil Gant just bought a new home nicer than ours. I know you don't approve, but I've got news for you: we have a target audience, and you and your church lady friends are not it."

"I'll say." She had half a mind to show up unannounced sometime. Something told her Cecil Gant hadn't just strung a few words together when he composed "Nashville Jumps." She suspected the rollicking misbehavior he sang about extended past Jefferson Street to follow the musicians wherever they went. And that included the radio station.

Christine sipped her ice water and savored the taste. Of all life's simple pleasures, ice-cold water was one of the best. How inconceivable it was that in Nashville, for thousands of people, ice water wasn't a simple pleasure but a rare luxury.

As summer turned to fall, Christine shifted her attention to the promotion of World Peace Day. On a Saturday afternoon in October as she and Gayle shopped along Church Street, Christine paused to watch a blind man and a boy of nine—about Gayle's age—play the spoons. When the song ended, Christine spoke to the man.

"How's Ovalla and the family, William?"

His face lit up. "We be just fine. Hal's in Okinawa with the army. Who that askin?"

"Christine Blackman. I knew Ovalla at Bethlehem. Y'all played for us each Christmas."

"This here's Bobby, our youngest," the man said. "He good, ain't he?"

"Very. Hello, Bobby," Christine said. "And this is Gayle. Y'all have a blessed day and tell Ovalla hello from me." She dropped a dollar in the basket.

When they crossed the street, Gayle asked, "Why haven't you spoken to him before, Mother? We've seen him here before."

"I didn't think much about the Hebb family until Pastor reminded me. William and his wife are blind. Years ago, he made brooms and sold them on the street corner. My family always bought them. His were the best brooms ever. The Hebbs got lots of children. I've no idea how they manage. Last I heard they were a family of eleven in a one-bedroom home near Hadley Park."

Gayle stopped in front of Tinsley's display window. Lettering on the glass proclaimed: *Fall in the Smokys.* Behind the glass, a mannequin sat amid piles of colorful leaves on a haybale beside a fiddle. She was outfitted in a green evening gown with a fox stole draped over one shoulder. White-gloved fingers held a lacy pink fan in front of her face.

"It's like a scene from Hollywood," Gayle exclaimed. "What's her story, I wonder?"

"You're asking the wrong parent," Christine said. They both laughed.

Later, Gayle described the window display to her father.

"It's social commentary on the Opry crowd at the Ryman," Gab surmised. "It's about country-fried musicians getting rich singing about how great it is to be poor. They still wanna live the country life, but they want everyone to know they ain't po' no mo'!"

"Or it could just be a colorful display with no point whatsoever," Christine said.

"Every display tells a story," Gab said. "I worked at Castner's, remember?"

"Well, if that's so, maybe I could get a few stores to tell the Pieces for Peace story."

Gab thought it was an excellent idea and offered to give her a list of store managers.

"Soliciting merchants isn't easy," he said as he handed her the names. "They'll want to talk about themselves and their wares. Let them. But look for an opportunity to connect what they want with something you want. It should be a win-win."

Christine studied the list and ranked the stores in order: Cain-Sloan, the premier store with the wealthiest customers; next, Harvey's, as its carnival atmosphere drew the biggest crowds; and finally, Castner-Knott, with the most loyal customer base. All others were second tier. Christine felt if even one major retailer would agree to showcase her event, it would be successful.

John Sloan welcomed Christine into his office. Blueprints and sketches for their new forty-thousand-square-foot store cluttered his desk. He showed her renderings of the escalators, the tearoom, a five-hundred-seat auditorium, and the multilevel parking garage.

"Have you considered using the windows to promote local charities?"

"Now, why wouldn't I have thought of that?" Sloan replied.

Christine told him about Pieces for Peace.

"That's great, but I've got my own campaign, Community Chest. Our goal is to raise half a million, and I'm looking to bring in half myself. If I promote a charity, it'll be mine. But thanks for the window display suggestion."

"If y'all raise that much money, maybe you'd consider getting the slums fresh water."

"Why? That's why we're proposing a new auditorium. Now, show yourself out and have a great day, Mrs. Blackman."

By the time she left Cain-Sloan, "Have a great day, Mrs. Blackman" was a comment worn as thin as their dollar-a-pair stockings.

She went to Harvey's and rode the escalator past the carousel horses and zany funhouse mirrors. She'd hoped to have better luck with Fred Harvey.

Shortly after Gab joined WLAC, they'd collaborated on a Christmas jingle. Gab claimed Fred bought airtime for the jingle to be heard every four minutes during the holidays. Harvey's "Jingle Bells" lyrics were now as familiar as the original:

> *Harvey's has it! Harvey's has it! Christmas gifts galore.*
> *Oh, what fun it is to shop in Nashville's largest store!*
> *Escalators up and down, Gifts on every floor . . .*
> *Oh, what fun it is to shop in Nashville's largest store![1]*

Fred told Christine to meet him in the shoe salon. He probably thought she'd buy something. After Christine told Gab how much she and her sisters adored Harvey's shoe salon, Gab sold Fred on the shoe salon having their own jingle. Another advertising first. The salon sponsored "A Song for You" weekday mornings. It opened with the jingle "One, two, buckle my shoe. Make sure it's a Harvey's shoe. Three, four, open the door, make sure it's a Harvey's door . . ."

Fred nixed Christine's request for a Pieces for Peace window almost immediately after she pitched the idea.

"Who've you asked so far?" Fred inquired.

"Only John Sloan. He turned me down because he's got his own charity campaign. I would be surprised if he's not creating a Community Chest window now as we speak."

"You should have come to me first. Harvey's leads. We were first to install escalators, give six days' pay for five days' work, open on Monday nights, offer cycle billing, and use a radio jingle. Our innovation has grown Harvey's from a half million in sales in 1946 to a projected nine million by year-end.[2] It's been said that if Harvey's picked itself up and walked down the middle of Church Street and jumped into the Cumberland River, there would be those stores that would follow.[3] I'm not gonna give you a charity display. How 'bout I treat you to one of our famous Hatfield club sandwiches?"

---

1. *Tennessean*, November 2, 1947, 7.
2. Don Doyle, *Nashville since the 1920s*, University of Tennessee Press, Knoxville, 1985, 138.
3. *Tennessean*, April 9, 1947, 7.

"Thanks," Christine said, "but I'm not hungry." She was famished but found Fred's Monkey Bar with its live, caged monkeys off-putting.

Christine achieved success at Castner-Knott. The elevator ride to the top floor had taken longer than it took the advertising manager to agree to her window display.

"We'll package a Pieces for Peace special on fabric, thread, and needles and advertise it in the paper and in our windows," he said. "And thanks for bringing us this opportunity."

Christine's last stop was Tinsley's, a "white gloves and pearls" kind of place—white gloves required, white-glove service, white women only in the dressing rooms. If a colored woman made a purchase, it was final sale only. While she waited for the manager, Christine studied the colorful ballgowns. A clerk pulled one from the rack for a young lady, who smiled at Christine.

"This should capture the eye of a certain beau at Belle Meade's bachelor ball," the clerk said as she handed a gown to the woman. "Mr. Allen's bound to notice you in this. Model it for us."

While the girl changed, Christine asked the salesclerk if she meant Bill Allen of WLAC.

"Who else? I've no idea how many men attend that ball, but for the ladies in this town, he might as well be the only man there."

Christine left Tinsley's with a dress for Gayle, a promise of a window display for Pieces for Peace, and some gossip to tell Gab.

Gab chuckled when he heard what the clerk said about Bill. "Maybe I oughta have him record a commercial for some sexy product," he said, thinking out loud. One look at Christine's face and Gab realized he'd put his foot in his mouth. "Just joking," he added.

They both knew he wasn't.

On the evening of November 22, Gab, Christine, Eddie, and Gayle, along with other employees' families, watched the annual Christmas parade from the warmth of the station. The corridor was set up like a grandstand. Rows of wooden stepstools had been positioned in front of the windows along Church Street. Giant balloon characters floated past: Alice in Wonderland, Bugs Bunny, Humpty-Dumpty. Gayle wanted to be on the street with the massive crowd that was crammed onto every inch of sidewalk. "Even the fire escapes, rooftops, and platforms that supported theater marquees had been turned into viewing platforms."[4]

Gayle aspired to be a dancer. And no one in town could dance like the majorettes from Tennessee A&I. Gab had read the parade lineup in the *Banner* and knew that when Superman floated by, they needed to take their seats on the street. He'd paid a colored couple to sit in folding chairs he'd positioned on the sidewalk earlier. Of the fourteen bands in the parade, A&I's was always the top draw. Nothing compared to their over-the-top, energetic performances. Gab lifted Gayle to his shoulders and muscled his way through the crowd until he reached the seats the couple held.

Each year, the crowd wondered how the A&I band would top their previous year's performance, and every year they did. This year proved no exception. Gayle stood on her chair, cheered, waved, and hollered as the majorettes danced and pranced. Outfitted like Christmas trees, the dancers sported electric lights on their uniforms, boots, and batons. The band members followed in similarly lit uniforms, their drums encircled in neon lights, as they played a frolicking, tambourine-heavy rendition of "Jingle Bells."

Many of the spectators sang along, replacing the original lyrics with Harvey's jingle. Hearing this, Gab felt inspired to promote more jingles. When an audience knew the jingle as well as iconic Christmas lyrics, it validated the station's influence. *Next up, John Sloan*, he thought. There was such a rivalry between Cain-Sloan and Harvey's, and keeping John and Fred trying to one-up each other was almost enough to keep a radio station in business.

The next day's *Banner* reported the A&I marching band gave the best performance parade viewers had ever seen. Among the spectators who watched in awe were Sou and Helen, with baby Harriett. After Sou watched the performance, he called A&I and offered to sponsor the college's band for a Christmas concert at Hadley Park. He hired William Hebb's Kitchen Cabinet Washboard Orchestra as the opening act. They watched the runners hand out candy canes and dollar bills.

"You're a good man, Bridgy," Helen said.

"The Nashville community has been good to me, I'm trying to be good to them."[5]

---

4. H.B. Teeter, "Midstaters Roar Welcome to Santa," *Nashville Banner*, November 22, 1949.
5. William Bridgeforth, personal story pamphlet, July 2001.

PART 2
THE 1950S

The influence that WLAC wielded in the R&B world, it just can hardly be overstated. It provided a shared cultural experience for millions of African Americans while also transforming the lives of millions of white teenagers.

—MICHAEL GRAY, COUNTRY MUSIC HALL OF FAME

GOOD ROCKIN' TONIGHT

Gene Nobles was the deejay pioneer in playing
Black music for both Black and white listeners.
Believe me, he was the first; he was so far ahead of
everyone else, not just in the South, but everywhere.

—RANDY WOOD

Roy Brown and his Mighty Men arrived in Nashville on January 18, 1950. They'd driven from Waterloo, Iowa, to Flint, Michigan, before visiting Cincinnati, Ohio, and Paducah and Madisonville in Kentucky, doing five concerts in five days. Roy's driver had a copy of *The Negro Motorist's Green Book*, yet it hadn't helped, as neither Paducah nor Madisonville listed any accommodations for coloreds. Roy's band had slept on the bus for three cold nights. Fortunately, Cecil Gant invited Roy to stay with him while the Mighty Men were booked at the colored YMCA, so they'd all finally get a hot shower and a bed.

Cecil greeted Roy with a highball. Before Roy finished his drink, Cecil asked if Roy would sit in for Cecil's gig at the New Era later that evening.

"I's slap wore out and still gotta see Gene, and that announcer they got for my concert."

"Rest up, then," Cecil said. "You got time. And Sou pays tops, in cash."

Roy drained his glass and headed to the guest room. He wanted to refuse Cecil's request, but he wouldn't. Years earlier, Roy had composed "Good Rockin' Tonight" for Wynonie. After Wynonie decided not to record it, Roy took it to Cecil, who had Roy sing it to a producer over the phone. The producer loved it. Roy's version went to number thirteen. Then Wynonie covered it and his version topped the chart. Roy would muster the energy to play the Era because he owed Cecil.

John Richbourg sent Bill Allen to Ernie's Record Mart to pick up flyers for Roy's concert. Roy was set to go live on John's show later, and they wanted posters up in the lobby when he arrived. Bill ran into Ted Jarrett at Ernie's.

"Roy's comin' in tonight," Bill told Ernie. "John wants you to swing by." He turned to Ted. "You're welcome too, Ted."

"You sure?" Ted asked.

"You do know Roy's colored, don't ya, Ted?" Ernie teased. The men laughed.

"So, tonight then," Ted said.

Bill smoothed the poster onto the glass at the Third National Bank. "It's just for today," he told the banker nearby.

"Be good rockin' upstairs tonight, I reckon," the banker said. "I'll pass the word."

"Sure," Bill replied. He should have let the banker know Gab felt the parties had gotten out of hand and they were trying to cut back on the guests, but Bill was distracted by the pretty, busty elevator operator who'd just entered.

Later that evening, Bill flirted with the elevator operator as he waited for Ted.

When Ted and Bill stepped into the elevator, Bill pronounced, "I've had this feeling for y'all's music all my life. It's like it transports you from your ordinary life to a better place."

"Yeah, kinda the point of slave spirituals," Ted deadpanned. The operator laughed.

Ted followed Bill into WLAC's lobby. The expansive skyline view was a twinkling cityscape unlike anything Ted had seen of his hometown, twelve stories high, suspended between the lampposts and the stars. Up here, one shared the perspective of the slate-and-ivory snowbirds that rested on the windowsill.

Soon, these juncos would spread their melodies from here to Canada, without awareness of borders, barriers, or the separate Jim Crow universes below. They flew above the city's tangible barriers, like the Cumberland River that separated downtown from East Nashville and the railroad tracks that divided the haves from the have-nots.

Prior to Gene's late-night program, what little race music was broadcast was carried on signals so weak they were confined within segregation's boundaries. That changed after Gene blasted his 50,000-watt megaphone into the segregated sky. If one could have seen WLAC's skywave transmission, it would have appeared to arch along with the curvature of the earth, until it bounced like a bad check and was returned. If visible, it would resemble a rainbow. And the mischievous creature with a pot of gold at the end—no fairytale—that was Gene Nobles.

Ted heard someone shout: "Bellhop's escortin' a gal from the strip joint!"

Someone else yelled: "Gene! Cue 'No Name Jive'!"

"It's *git-down* time," Bill announced. Ted followed Bill into a crowded hallway where men stood on stepstools with binoculars they aimed across the street to the Noel Hotel.

"Git-down time mean the same here as on Cedar?" Ted asked. "Time for pimps to put his ladies on the street?"

"Yep. Gene's calling the Bird Watchers to a meet."

"That's these guys?"

"Ah-huh. WLAC, home of the 50,000-watt Peeping Toms."[1]

Without binoculars, there wasn't much to see. Ted followed Bill until they arrived at a cavernous, opulently decorated room. Lit by a crystal chandelier and covered floor to ceiling in damask, the room was sparsely furnished with a French provincial desk (cluttered with liquor bottles), a grand piano (piled high with coats, hats, and binoculars), and a long velvet divan. It was eclectic— massive enough to house an orchestra yet occupied by a small gathering of men who seemed trespassers.

When "No Name Jive" blared from a speaker, Bill handed binoculars to Ted and kept another for himself. Ted glanced around, reluctant to join the

---

1. Smith, *Pied Pipers*, 85.

peepers. He recognized Louis Brooks and Cecil Gant and assumed the other colored guy was Roy Brown. Ted sent Cecil a look as if to ask, Dare I go? Cecil shrugged.

"I'm gonna say hey to Cecil," Ted told Bill.

"Not now! Come on."

Ted dutifully followed Bill to the corridor. With all the stepstools occupied, the five-feet-six Jarrett couldn't see what the six-feet-two Allen could, although he was well aware the men were watching a stripper perform oral sex on a john. Ted didn't need to see the action, as one could discern what transpired from blow-by-blow comments. This brought to mind how often Ted had overheard Woodmont members complain about WLAC's "vulgar" broadcasts. Ted wondered what those country club Jews would think if they knew what really happened here. This was misbehavior that would get you banned from the New Era—*for life*. No wonder Sou called the Bourbon Aristocracy the Bourbon *Hypocrisy*. The men spying on guests at the Noel Hotel were the same snobs who demanded Nashville's hub of vice, Harlem, be demolished because it "damaged the city's cultured reputation."

As more men arrived, Ted excused himself from the hallway. After all, it wasn't that long ago that a Black man caught spying on a white woman would turn up dead—with a few body parts rearranged. Ted wondered how many people knew of this activity and if that's why preachers were so riled up over Gene's broadcast. His provocative double-speak, sexual innuendo, and the music's suggestive lyrics had sent both Black and white clergy to the pulpits to condemn WLAC's sinful programming. The preachers called race music the devil's music and had branded Gene "Satan's collaborator" as the lyrics tended toward themes of sex, particularly infidelity; liquor; and death.

Ted followed a tall, thin man with dark-rimmed, Coke-bottle glasses into the strange room. The man held the door for Ted, then closed it behind them. He then placed a microphone near the piano.

"Aw-right. Hush up, everybody. I'm going live," the man announced. Ted recognized the voice. This was John Richbourg, who sounded like a young, hip colored man and not the skinny, professorial-looking, middle-aged white guy he really was.

Red lights flashed: *ON AIR*.

"Let's do this thing, shall we, Roy?" John said into the microphone. "Yeah man, I got Roy Brown hisself here tonight. Tell us where you're playin' next, Roy."

"We's at Nashville's War Memorial *tomorra*. Then we's travelin' all over the South through March," Roy announced. "Probably be near all y'all, soon."

"You sure get around," John said.

"Yeah, me and my Mighty Men been everywhere from Iowa to Cuba recent. Early March, we play Tuskegee. I'm real excited 'bout that."

"Yeah, you're big on college campuses, I hear," John said. "I'll bet those students would like to hear some 'Good Rockin' Tonight.' Let's kick it off with that."

As the song blasted from the speaker, Ted pondered whether John would sound the same in conversation or if his colored patois was an act for radio. When the song ended, the lights flashed and John returned to the microphone.

"You want that record of Roy's, or any others, then get yourself together and write to Ernie's Record Mart, Nashville, Tennessee, 'cause Ernie's is nowhere else."

The lights went off, doors opened, and men from the hallway entered, along with two busty girls in stripper costumes.

"Is it always like this?" Ted asked Bill.

"Is whenever talent's here."

"Who are these people?"

"Well, them two's from the alley strip joint. Men with 'em are record producers."

"Randy Wood here?" Ted asked.

"Nah. He's a family man and don't care for these. Mosta the younger guys are assistant engineers, and the older ones, salesmen." He pointed to the men near John. "You already know Roy and Ernie. The little guy's Gene Nobles. He gets over *three thousand* letters a month. Boss hired him ten secretaries, and now John gets nearly as many."

"Wow! Is the boss here?"

"Yeah," Bill pointed to Gab. "That chatty guy in the tweed jacket's Gab Blackman. We call him Blackie. He runs the sales departments and nighttime programming. Guy with him's Jordon Stokes. They just helped Randy launch a record label."

"So the bosses are okay with this?" Ted asked with a nod to the strippers.

"Not exactly. It started when Blackie told sponsors they were welcome here whenever a musician was live. But it snowballed. Now if someone sees a colored guy enter at night, word travels. Next thing you know, record producers, talent managers, even the attorneys, bankers, and insurance guys with offices downstairs show up. At least they bring stuff—liquor, binoculars, record producers with cash. It's been a windfall for Gene and John. They're making more that-a-way than's in the paychecks. Who you wanna meet?"

"Everyone. First, Jordon Stokes," Ted said.

"Blackie, Jordon," Bill said. "This here's Ted Jarrett. He was navy and now's studying music composition at Fisk."

Gab took a good look at Ted. "We've met somewhere before."

Ted nodded in agreement. When Ted considered how many white men's shoes he'd shined or golf clubs he'd carted over the years, he wouldn't be surprised if he had crossed paths with everyone here. What did surprise Ted was that this white man remembered. Few men of Gab's status noticed the colored men who shined their shoes, carried their clubs, washed their cars, or mowed their lawns. Whites tended to consider servants as a collective group, interchangeable, and unworthy of remembering.

Ted turned to Stokes and said, "Thank you for your work on behalf of colored railroad workers. You're from the Stokes family that defended the rights of free Negroes, right?"

"I am. That was my great-grandfather and founder of our firm."

"And you're still fighting for us and involved with the Highlander Folk School, right?"

"Yes. At Highland was the first time I ever sat down to eat with coloreds. Up there, everybody's equal. Gives us something to aspire to."

"Aspire to!" Bill said. "Hell! I been sittin' down eatin' with coloreds my whole life."

Stokes extended his hand to shake Ted's. Another first. This was the first time a white Nashvillian ever offered to shake Ted's hand. Ted shook hands with Jordon, then Gab.

"I remember you now," Gab told Ted as their hands touched. "Pin boy at Belle Meade!"

"And you paid me to attach strings to pegs so you could balk," Ted suddenly recalled.

"Balk!" Bill exclaimed. "A bowling ball?"

"Sure," Gab said as he mimed the action of hurling a bowling ball. He froze midway through the toss, then after Ted made a crashing sound, Gab completed his follow-through.

"Blackie's always coming up with ways to make us laugh," Jordon said. "Look, I gotta head out. Ted, if you ever need legal help for your music, call me. Musicians are my specialty."

"I'll do it," Ted said.

"Yo, Ted!" Cecil called. "We's headin over to the Era. Wanna go?"

"I do!" Bill said.

"They ain't let no whites in," Cecil said.

"Who said I's white?" Bill asked.

"You sayin' you ain't?"

"Well, Anna Day raised me, 'n she's dark as molasses. Ask any colored from Gallatin who's Day's boy. They'll say it be me, *Hoss* Allen."

Ted noted the change in Bill's voice. He certainly sounded colored. Either Bill and John were talented actors, or they had split personalities, one from each side of Jim Crow.

"You just playacting or's that true?" Ted asked.

"It's the gospel truth, and anybody at the Era from Sumner County'll verify it."

Ted took note of Bill's ability to speak a bilingualism—Vanderbilt English and Soul. The former pretentiously flat, the latter poetically street savvy. With Bill's full lips, ruddy complexion, and dark wavy hair, he was ever so slightly African enough to pass as a light-skinned colored. Sou wasn't much darker himself, and some folks called him mulatto. If Allen was colored—he was what old Southerners called an octoroon or one-eighth Black—eighty-seven years ago, that would have been enough to enslave him.

Gene's voice blasted from the speaker: "Well, jerks and fillies, I'm gonna have to hurry as I'm getting a little behind. Here's your favorite, 'No Name Jive.'"

"He just played that," Ted said.

"He's signifying," Cecil said. "Let's skedaddle, 'fore we's pulled into that peepster nastiness!"

"I'm comin' with ya," Bill insisted. "But remember, I'm Hoss, not Bill."

Sou noticed the tall, light-skinned man with Jarrett, Cecil, and Roy Brown. "Who's he?" Sou asked Pie Hardison, the part-time bouncer.

"He a drummer from the army," Pie said. "Met him with the mayor once."

"Get him over here."

Ted went with Hoss. "Sou, this here's Hoss Allen," he said. "Works over to Randy's settin' in for Gene some."

"You white?" Sou asked without preamble.

"Birth certificate says so, but Miss Anna Day done raised me, and she ain't."

"I'm lettin' you stay on account of who brung ya, but stay away from the women."

"I'm here for the music, not women. See, I'm a bit of a jazz drummer myself."

"Um-hum. Cause trouble, someone hereabouts might up and cancel that white birth certificate you got. So be careful."

"He's lettin' me stay," Bill told Cecil as he straddled a chair at Cecil's table.

"You's first white I seen sit here," Cecil said.

"I told him I's raised colored."

Cecil laughed. "Oh yeah? What church?"

"First Baptist Gallatin. Doctor Rucker was the preacher. He was the principal of the high school and the doctor and dentist too, and I looked up to him."[2]

"Then know this'n?" Brooks sang: "I'm going home . . ."

Hoss completed the gospel line: "Ol' arks a-moving an I'm a-going home."

"Can ya sing it full verse?"

Hoss sang the slave spiritual exactly as Anna had taught him. His enunciation and tremolo conveyed a bona fide familiarity with Black preachers and pray-ers. Cecil nodded approvingly. Hoss leaned back in his chair and absorbed

2. "Rock and Roll; Renegades; Interview with Hoss Allen (Part 1 of 2)," Open Vault.

everything—the chatter, the music, the flavor of the food, the fragrance of the women's hairdressing, the shine of the men's oxford swings—and felt an aching homesickness. He could return to his family's manor house, but he couldn't go home. Anna's shack in the back had been torn down.

The ache Hoss felt was familiar and primal. He'd felt it first when his father left, then when his mother abandoned him to travel the world. He recalled how at eleven years old, his mother finally let him accompany her to Europe. He'd stayed in London only a few days before she sent him back home alone. The entire journey Hoss had feared the boat would sink, and he wouldn't be missed. When he'd shared this with Gab, the boss said something memorable. "Well, someone must have loved you, because nobody survives childhood unless they're loved." Yes, Hoss had been loved—by Anna Day. He felt more at home at the Era than he did at the family house because the Era felt like Anna, sounded like Anna, and smelled like Anna. He breathed in her essence and turned his attention to the stage. Decades later, Hoss would fondly reminisce:

> I remember it so well, Roy strolls into the spotlight so casually that he might have been just passing though. He moans . . . the band answers, he moans again, again the band answers. So easily he pulls the audience all the way into himself as the number begins. . . . It builds . . . some urge him on. . . . Yeah, Roy. . . . Come on, Roy . . . and then seeming to sense that they are truly with him, he leans back, closes his eyes and moves into "Trouble at Midnight" and he is instantly transformed from a performer on stage into a downhearted pouring out his pain into a woman who has walked all over his heart.[3]

Hoss didn't simply *hear* Roy's music; he *felt* it. As Gregory Clark details in *Civic Jazz,* the experience of listening to jazz is immersive, emotional as much as intellectual, even spiritual when it lets two or more people feel themselves transcending the differences that divide them for a moment or two."[4]

---

3. John Broven, *Walking to New Orleans: The Story of New Orleans Rhythm & Blues* (Gretna, LA: Pelican Publishing Company, 2016), 22. This footnote shows Hoss's faulty memory as the date (1948) and song don't correlate. The song was likely "Boogie at Midnight" and the date January 18 or 19, 1950.
4. Gregory Clark, *Civic Jazz* (Chicago: University of Chicago Press, 2012), 10.

Sharing this experience with Ted provided solace and meaning for Hoss. Obviously, meaning doesn't reside solely in a song's lyrics. Because meaning is context dependent, Hoss recognized Roy's call-and-response as reminiscent of a preacher and congregation. In the Black church it is believed that the congregation's response empowers the preacher, anointing him with the Holy Spirit. Thus anointed, the preacher delivers divine guidance. And the wisdom is transmitted not only through sermon but also through music. This symbiosis between heaven and earth, preacher and congregant, melody and lyric creates a vibrant dynamism unrivaled in any other Christian church.

When this gospel music, conceived in jubilance in the church, was emancipated from the sanctuary and unshackled from the confines of segregated ghettos, it soared throughout the ionosphere, spreading a message of liberation. This message would inspire a little Black woman in Alabama to refuse to give up her seat; empower an elementary student with courage enough to take her seat at an all-white school, despite the bomb intended to dissuade her; give college students the endurance to suffer beatings for having the audacity to sit at the same lunch counter as Gab—and to open Gab's eyes to the harsh struggles Southern Blacks faced daily.

Hoss said of Gab, "He was the first person to see the commercial potential in this Black music and this Black audience that no one had ever tapped."[5]

When Gab first targeted a Black audience, his motive was strictly financial. It wasn't until long *after* he'd proven the commercial viability of race music that he realized his innovative programming had a value far greater than anything quantified in dollars.

Only after reflecting on his experiences, especially when sharing them with his teenage granddaughter, did Gab fully grasp that WLAC's revolutionary race music program had inadvertently proven Beethoven's premise true: "Music could change the world."

5. Broven, *Record Makers and Breakers*, 99.

10

TROUBLE AT MIDNIGHT

As far as he [James Stahlman] was concerned, his
purpose was not so much to inform as it was to work
for his own cause, which was the cause of the South.

—DAVID HALBERSTAM

"Honey, you're *not* gonna believe this!" Gab said. "Jimmy hired a colored reporter."

Christine pulled the skillet off the heat. "Seriously? After givin' reporters pistols with instructions on how to kill one, he's now gonna sit one at the next desk?"

Gab lowered the *Banner*. "So says the *Banner*. I'm telling ya, he read the article in *Sponsor Magazine*. Remember? 'The Forgotten 15,000,000'? They reported how Negro-targeted radio advertising was the best way to reach that billion-dollar-a-year market. Whether Jimmy will admit it or not, Gene and I created that Negro market and made it a national force."

"Eat these and lemme read that myself." Christine put a plate of fried chicken hearts on the table. While Gab enjoyed the snack, she read about Robert Churchwell, an army veteran and graduate of Fisk, who was now a *Banner* reporter.

"Why in tarnation would a smart nigra like that work for Jimmy?"

"Money," Gab said. He took a sip of ice water, then finished his thought. "Same reason we all did. Gotta admit, I feel vindicated after hearing Jimmy yak for years 'bout how television was gonna kill radio. Told me I was committing professional suicide leaving the paper."

"I remember. Somebody said Jimmy was considered 'the most violent anti-radio newsman in the world.'"[1]

Gab mimicked Jimmy's voice: "'Coloreds' business ain't worth a bushel of black-eyed peas. Why advertise to folks who can't read?' he'd say." Gab reverted to natural voice. "Hiring Churchwell proves he knows I was right and he was wrong. Just like he was wrong when he said department stores would never spend money on radio."

It was well known that after Gab joined WLAC, the station had become unusually profitable. The 1948 National Broadcasters Convention featured industry experts who detailed how WLAC had created the country's first national minority-targeted programming. This strategy had every New York agency able to quote the numbers of baby chicks and records WLAC sold.

"*Banner*'s circulation in colored neighborhoods is almost nonexistent," Gab explained. "Only page ever crosses Charlotte Avenue's the sports edition with the winning numbers. They call it the *Damn Banner* for a reason. Coloreds feel Jimmy's refusal to capitalize Negro and still print 'nigger' in editorials is an attack on their dignity. Jimmy finally figured out insulting a quarter of the population affects his bottom line."

"So Churchwell's hiring is about money, not giving the paper perspective?"

"Darn right! No colored reporter, no colored readers, no advertisers selling to coloreds. Jimmy's the dumbest smart guy I know. Then again, that's Vanderbilt's specialty."

"Hell, no! I'm not working for the *Damn Banner!*"[2] Robert Churchwell said when he was offered the job. Eventually, Churchwell acquiesced and took

1. Craig Havighurst, *Air Castle of the South: WSM and the Making of Music City* (Urbana: University of Illinois Press, 2007), 76.
2. Halberstam, *The Children*, 183.

the $35 per week offer—what garbagemen were paid—because he'd gotten engaged and couldn't find any other white-collar work. This was typical in Nashville, as the four Black colleges graduated more students than needed for white-collar jobs open to Negroes. Thus, white Nashvillians prided themselves on having college-educated maids, nannies, porters, and sanitation workers. In return for a wage barely above minimum, Jimmy insisted Churchwell work from home, pay his own expenses, and limit his reporting to noncontroversial social, church, and school events.

The collegiate camaraderie that Gab, Fritz, Jack, and Ben had enjoyed at the *Banner* was never extended to Robert. Throughout his thirty-year career at the *Banner* Robert worked in a perpetual "state of loneliness."[3] When Robert became affiliated with the paper, the friendly reception he had previously enjoyed at the Elks Lodge deteriorated. Most members snubbed him as an Uncle Tom. Fortunately, the lodge had an astute member who actually read the *Banner* daily—Sou. He challenged the move to ban Churchwell, arguing that having someone aware of what the town's most powerful man was doing and thinking was a good thing.

"Know your enemy," Sou insisted. "Getting someone near Stahlman's better than not knowing anything." Because having Hardison keep tabs on the mayor had worked out so well for Sou, he had no doubt it would work equally well with a man far more influential than the mayor.

"Churchwell's more Jackie Robinson than Uncle Tom," Sou argued. "He'll prove to those peckerwoods he's every bit as capable as them. How's that gonna happen if we interfere?"

Sou believed that every colored man who achieved success in arenas previously restricted to whites was a victory for all Negroes. He was disappointed to learn Churchwell wouldn't get a desk in the newsroom (supposedly due to a lack of space), but Sou wasn't surprised. An integrated newsroom was still a bridge too far.

Churchwell told Sou that the executive editor, Charles Moss, seemed like a nice enough guy. However, Robert couldn't shake the feeling that Stahlman himself was secretly hoping Churchwell would fail.[4]

---

3. Halberstam, 699.
4. Halberstam, 185.

Moss suggested Churchwell begin his reporting with the Council of Church Women's upcoming event, as it included the entire church community. Moss handed Robert the name and phone number of the chairwoman, Mrs. Galbreath Blackman.

Christine was surprised to receive a call from Churchwell. "I know who you are," she said. "I read 'bout you in the *Banner*. Congratulations. I can't imagine what it must be like for you there. Anyway, Gab's not home."

"I called to speak with you, Mrs. Blackman."

"Me? Whatever for?"

"World Day of Prayer. I was wondering if you could advise me about—"

"Of all the colossal gall! Gab proved Jimmy wrong about y'all's business, and he just couldn't leave well enough alone, could he?"

"Ma'am, I have no idea. Charles Moss gave me your number and—"

"And Charlie just conveniently forgot I was forced to resign because of my husband promotin' devil's music!"

"What? I, I—"

"Jimmy musta told Charlie to tell you, *a colored*, to call me so's they could rub it in Gab's face! Well, listen to me, Robert—you'd best watch your back, 'cause Jimmy'll feed you to the lions first chance he gets."

Christine's blood pressure soared. She said a curt goodbye, clicked the handset hook, then dialed Gab. "Galbreath! I just got off the phone with that colored reporter Jimmy hired."

"Come again?"

"He called to humiliate me. Whyever else would Charlie give my number to a colored?"

"Honey, our number's in the directory. What'd he want?"

"To talk about my being ousted from Council of Church Women. Which was *your* fault—you and your damned devil's music, forcing my friends to have to demand my resignation." She changed her voice to mimic the up-North-educated-speak-like-a-dictionary dialect of the Methodist pastor's wife. "How is it, Christine, that our mission is to promote family values, yet our leader's husband is the devil's music promoter-in-chief?"

"Now, calm down, Christine. It was unintentional, I'm sure. What'd you say?"

"That I was no longer president and he should watch his back."

"You didn't tell him about the pistols, I hope."

"Land sakes, Galbreath! What kinda fool you take me for?"

"What can I do? And don't say stop the music, 'cause that train's left the station."

"Then I have nothing more to say to you!" She hung up, poured herself another cup of coffee, and recalled the second most humiliating moment of her life. Initially, she wasn't sure she'd heard the pastor's wife correctly. The devil's music, yes. But Peeping Toms? Christine had no idea what the woman was talking about when she'd said, "It's been brought to several pastors' attention that Gab's employees are spying on guests of the Noel Hotel. A bellhop confessed that the bellboys and the desk clerks were paid by men inside WLAC to place ladies of the night in the rooms visible from the station—and Gab knew and let it happen!"

Christine had recalled the hallway cluttered with stepstools, the multitude of binoculars, complaints about ribald stories Gene broadcast, or calls urging Gab to go to the station because things had gotten out of hand. Christine was angry with herself for her naivete and furious with Gab for not telling her. And to add insult to injury, when confronted, Gab had defended the announcers! "That's who they are, honey. They drink, carouse, push the envelope. It's all part of the package."[5]

Christine was hurt by Gab and ashamed to have let down the women she'd been so proud to lead. "Please accept my resignation and my deepest apologies," she'd told her board.

"You've steered us in the right direction," the pastor's wife replied. "It's just public perception, you understand." The pastor's wife served the remainder of Christine's term. By the time the meeting concluded, Christine's anxiety had turned her bowels to water. Rather than go home, she went to her doctor's office. The quickest route to Buchanan was through the poorest Negro neighborhoods. Seeing the conditions in which they lived made Christine feel worse. She'd just read the mayor's report, which stated this area was home to 70 percent of the city's colored population. They lived in wooden shacks

5. Smith, *Pied Pipers*, 103.

without water or power, which created unsanitary conditions that led to chronic health problems. The below-poverty wages and redlined segregation left nowhere else for them to go. The analysis showed how in 1929—the same year Christine volunteered at Bethlehem Settlement House—of the 1,800 Negro children who had started first grade, only 52 were still enrolled in their senior year.[6] Poverty forced these children into the workforce. Christine had wanted her organization to help remedy this dreadful situation.

"Is there anything you can prescribe that'll prevent me from smacking Gab with my skillet?" she'd asked Dr. Price Duff, her friend since elementary school. The doctor prescribed paregoric, a mild opiate. Shaken by the call from the reporter, Christine was relieved to find she still had a bit of that delightful tincture.

Gab hung up from the call with Christine and turned to Hoss. "Sorry, where were we?"

"Maybe now's not the best time," Hoss said.

"Never is. What happened last night?"

"Well, ah, I, I, must've been . . ."

A warning light flashed in Gab's head. Hoss could normally carry on a conversation with a fencepost. That he stammered meant it was bad. "Out with it!" Gab demanded.

"You know the elevator gal with the stuffed-tighter'n-a-ballot-box sweater?"

"Uh-huh."

"Round about midnight, me, Gene, and his cohort got to wondering if her bra was Christmas-goose stuffed with flesh . . . or . . . anyway, I volunteered to . . . you know, find out. For the fellas. After I honeyed her up like a biscuit, I gave her a tour. Gene's buddy manned the elevator so's we could test out the casting couch. Well, unfortunately the divan was already occupied, so we wound up in Binns's office 'cause he's got that nice—"

"Couch. Yeah, get to the bloody parts!"

"'Spose I'd downed a few too many and her sexy wiggle musta misled me so, I, ah, she slipped as I chased her. Hit her head on the corner of Binns's desk. I, I, never seen so much blood. And, ah, you know, I served."

---

6. Doyle, *Nashville since the 1920s*, 49.

"As a drummer! Cut the crap—"

"She went down, stone cold out. For a bit there, we thought she's dead. Gene's buddy suggested we drop her down the elevator shaft, you know, to make it look like an accident. But then, ah, we'd have to use the stairs—"[7]

"WHAT THE HELL'S THE MATTER WITH YOU!" Gab pounded his fists like a drummer's fermata. "You got every debutant in town chasing your sorry ass and you're hound-dogging common country trash at work!"

"I wouldn't say she's trash. Country yeah, but—"

"Just stop! Where's she now?"

"I, I, I, was getting there. So, Gene, figurin' best not to have an ambulance draw attention, got Binns's apprentice to call a cab. We sprang for the taxi fare, hush money for the cab driver and medical expenses. She got ten stitches and's gonna say it was a car accident."[8]

Gab sighed. "Who else knows about this?"

"Well, other than us, the emergency room doc and, I guess, Binns. We cleaned up, but the papers on his desk got bloodstained."

Gab had half a mind to fire Hoss. He was already concerned about Hoss's drinking. Gene, weighing half Hoss's weight, could drink a full bottle of whiskey and stay sober. After three drinks Hoss was tanked stupid. These nightly bacchanalia could likely jeopardize their television application. "This debauchery's gotta stop! What's in her sweater? What are you? Fourteen? Get your ass to Belle Meade and find you a wife."

"But Blackie, them belles don't know Wynonie from Wyoming. They think pot-likker's a drink and I'm the prince's gonna crown 'em Queen of Bal d'Hiver. They're just looking to wear pearls while they play bridge all day. Only thing they care about's my last name and the money I'm set to inherit. How's a guy to live like that?"

"You'll figure it out. Go tell Binns I wanna see him."

"So? I still got a job?"

"For now, but since you're such a schmoozer, I'm movin' you over to sales. If you're not on air, you'll sell it. And if I find you chasin' tail here again, I'll

7. Smith, *Pied Pipers*, 105.
8. Smith, *Pied Pipers*, 105.

throw your ass in the Cedar Street gutter myself, 'cause that's where you're heading."

"But Gene—"

"You're not Gene and never will be! He's got fans from Cuba to the North Pole, and all you got's a damn fine voice. Time you use it to make me some money 'steada smearing biscuits with honey."

F. David Binns, the station's chief engineer, and Gab discussed Truman's concerns that the nightly antics put the station at reputational risk. The race music program, while profitable, had already marred their standing in the community.

"What can we do?" Gab asked Dave.

"I can remove the switches so the lights in that corridor don't shut off. Least that way, the Noel's guests'll see the peepers. And I'll rewire the speaker above the divan. They rigged it so it receives *and* sends. Probably why Hoss took Miss Busty to my office. Problem is, whatever I fix, my apprentice engineers can unfix."

"Reckon it's better'n us having bad engineers," Gab said.

"Speaking of apprentices, one of my former ones, Sam Phillips, called. He's opened a recording studio in Memphis. Told him if Gene promotes him, the little carnie'll make him rich."

"For sure. He's like King Midas, spinning vinyl to gold."

"And getting roosters to lay golden eggs. How many chicks he sold lately?"

"One-point-two million past four months," Gab said. "Listen, do what you can and I'll let Truman know it's fixed—for now."

11

ROCKET 88

David Binns was a wonderful man who taught
me an awful lot about electronics. Gene Nobles
in his own particular way was a damn genius.

—SAM PHILLIPS

Sam Phillips had worked at WLAC, filling in for John Richbourg while he
served in the navy. Phillips came highly recommended by an employee who
believed in Sam despite his having lost his previous job after having a nervous
breakdown. Binns and Nobles had taken the likable young Phillips under their
wings. Binns taught him to adjust soundboards prior to the invention of the
standardized equalization curve, while Gene taught on-air delivery.

Sam had been hired as a temporary until John returned, so when Sam
heard of a permanent opening in Memphis, where he'd long dreamed of living,
he decided to apply.

"Sam had never flown before and was so nervous," Binns told Gab. "I
sent Ira Trotter, one of my board guys along with him.[1] We all worried Sam's
anxiety would become a panic attack and ruin his chances, and we wanted
him to succeed."

---

1. Guralnick, *Sam Phillips*, 47.

"You helping Sam get set up like you did Randy?"

"He don't need help. Sam's got this uncanny knack for sound. Think his overly sensitive moods are the result of a hypersensitivity to vibration. Anyway, said he plans to record the great Negro musicians there, since no one else will."

"He's not gonna have trouble findin' talent," Gab said. "Even the sidewalk bums on Beale all play a mean harmonica. Next time I'm in Memphis, I'll go see him."

"He's still on WREC, so you might wanna wait till he sends Gene something to promote. Speakin' of, see he's not influencing Hoss to any more carnal crimes. Hopefully, the kid's found a nice gal and's not trolling the colored clubs."

"From your lips to God's ears," Gab said, although he suspected both were true. Hoss, the light-skinned Black, was regularly at the Era, while William T. Allen III, bachelor beau of Belle Meade, had met his match. Hoss had told Gab about Nancy Hoffman, a Knoxville deb, when they'd driven to Gallatin to see Randy. Gab had asked if Nancy was the gal for him.

"She might be," Hoss said. "She's down-to-earth and open-minded, not haughty. Of all the debs I dated, Nancy's the only one that approves of my love of race music, my colored friends, and me going to the Era with Ted."

Hoss shared that Nancy's opinions on racial issues were unusually progressive for a University of North Carolina graduate, likely because she'd attended a preparatory boarding school in New Hampshire, then Bradford Junior College in Massachusetts, before Chapel Hill. She now worked in advertising at a Knoxville department store.

"She's sassy, stylish, outspoken, and, most importantly, head-over-heels in love with the real me, Hoss. Not Belle Meade Bill."

"Then you'd better marry her quick before she comes to her senses," Gab teased. "Adjust the radio. Let's see if WDIA's got any new advertisers we can poach."

WDIA Memphis was one of a multitude of regional stations that replicated WLAC's late-night format to attract WLAC's listeners during the day. Gab had met Bert Ferguson of WDIA at a broadcaster convention, where the success of WLAC's nighttime program had been featured. Gab wasn't surprised when, months later, Ferguson launched a race music broadcast and hired a few colored announcers, as Memphis's population was 40 percent Black. Shortly thereafter, Ferguson called Gab to ask how they'd handled death threats. Gab said the operators told callers they were free to change stations, but no one had ever threatened to kill anyone at WLAC.

"Hey, that's Riley King!" Hoss said, referring to the WDIA announcer. "He's my friend from the Era. He's got a roadhouse band plays there."

"That's the colored deejay you talked about?"

"Yeah, and he's a pitchman, truck driver, and gambler. Likes Sou's place because Sou advances him his take so he can gamble *before* the gig. Riley sells some kind of tonic."

"Pep-ti-kon?"

"Yeah. You know it?"

"Of course. We gotta know who's advertising elsewhere so you can poach clients. We'd go broke if we only sold to virgins." As if on cue, King gave his Pep-ti-kon pitch.

"Want me to pitch Pep-ti-kon?" Hoss asked.

"No. That's Ferguson's own brand. This busy bee King's a born salesman, though. Keep in touch with him in case Truman ever lets me hire a colored."

"Well, for all practical purposes, I'm colored."

"You don a pale blackface to get into their clubs. That's a huckster."

"Which is my job, right?"

"Touché." Gab pulled an *Ebony* magazine from a stack of periodicals on the seat between them and handed it to Hoss. "Check it out."

"Whoa! Notre Dame's admitted Negroes," Hoss exclaimed. "Good on them."

"Not the articles, knucklehead. The ads! Look who's advertising. See anything we can sell and ship, anything COD?"

"Shoes?"

"Nope. Boomerang. They'll be returned."

"Hats?"

"Don't ship well."

"Liquor?"

"That's a sponsor. Not a COD product."

"Headache powder, hair pomade, scalp cream?"

"Bingo! Sell me some scalp cream."

Hoss slid his hand through his hair. "If you want good-looking, shiny hair so you can be sexy, sexy, sexy like me, then you need Hoss's sexy supreme hair cream."

Gab laughed. "It's radio, they don't know what you look like."

"Still, men wanna look like me. 'Cause women wanna look *at* me."

"Your cockiness is as sexy as socks on a rooster. Why else would you buy scalp cream?"

"They got an itchy head?"

"Convince me Hoss's sexy supreme hair cream'll stop the itch."

"Hoss's sexy supreme hair cream makes your hair look fine and stops the itch too."

"Make it stronger . . . personal."

"Now friend, if you got a itchy head, then you got a diseased scalp. Hoss's sexy supreme hair cream'll clear up that scalp in no time so you won't have no itchy head."

"You might have a future in this business after all. Make a list of who's advertising hairdressing in *Ebony*. You can record that as a prospective ad and call on 'em. Well done."

When Nancy Hoffman's engagement to William T. Allen III was announced, Tennessee's debutants, their mothers, and their grandmothers cried into their cheese grits. Southern belle wisdom held that handsome Vanderbilt grads from founding families with old money fortunes came along only once a generation. Christine told Gab that Bill's engagement was all her friends at bridge could talk about. "They all asked, 'Why her?'"

"What'd you say?" Gab said.

"He loves her, I guess. I don't know. Of all the debs, why Nancy?"

Gab smeared sweet sorghum on a biscuit. "She's everything Cecil and Mamie wanted: beautiful, well-mannered, well-dressed, with a wealthy father, a monogrammed silver service, real pearls, and, of course, the requisite family deviled egg recipe—"

"You're makin' fun of me and my friends."

"Now, honey, let me finish. And Nancy cares about all that as much as he does, which is not a bit. He made a great choice. God bless her."

Gab served as an usher at Bill and Nancy's wedding on December 9, 1950. Christine cried throughout the ceremony. Afterward, as they drove to Knoxville's Cherokee Country Club, Gayle asked Christine, "Mother, why do you always cry at weddings?"

"Because we have no idea what future heartbreak awaits," Christine said. "I cry for the unknown inevitable. Everyone eventually pays a price for having loved. Think of my mother. She buried my father, brother, and three of my sisters. Sometimes I wonder just how much heartache one woman can endure."

Gab had heard this from Christine before, but on this day, her words felt eerily prophetic.

In mid-March 1951, Gab was on the phone with Ben West when Gene entered Gab's office. Ben had informed Gab he planned to challenge Mayor Cummings in the upcoming election and asked for help with publicity. Because Ben had recently spearheaded the campaign to change city council elections from at-large to single-member districts, he believed his newfound support from colored voters could carry him to victory. Gab promised to help, then hung up and gave Gene his undivided attention.

"How's Midas?"

"You wanted to know if Phillips produced somethin' I could spin to gold," Gene said as he handed Gab a record and a letter. "Sam thinks this'll make him a millionaire. Don't know if it's that good, but I'm laying on it and John is too."

"'Rocket 88'? Like the car?"

"Yeah. Come listen to it." Gab followed Gene to the studio. John was seated at the boards. A minute into the song, Gab wondered if the settings were off. "Why's it so fuzzy?"

"That's the hook," Gene said. "Tied to the hottest thing on four wheels and sounds like an airplane. It's gonna be huge."

"Melody's not new," John added. "Liggins recorded a similar tune, but this's magic."

Gab didn't hear the magic, just jump blues on a blown speaker. "You think a million folks'll buy that?"

"We ride it hard enough, they will," John said.

"What's Hoss think?" Gab asked.

"Thought you'd made him a salesman," Gene said.

"I'm trying him out as a pitchman case you don't come back from the track. Sales's best place to learn it."

"Carnival midway's better," Gene said.

"Cain't y'all picture that?" Gab said. "Huckster Hoss at the fairgrounds?"

"Wearin' that white sport coat he loves," Gene added.

"I gotta see 'Rocket 88' top the charts before I believe that noise is gold," Gab said.

"Boss, it's more than a race record," Gene said. "Just wait."

Two weeks later, Gene dropped a newspaper on Gab's desk. The headline read, "Rocket Becomes Flying Disc, Spins toward Record Glory."[2]

"Guess this proves how little I know," Gab said.

"Here's Phillips's letter. He thanked me for playing the record and believing in it."[3]

"Hey, I never said you weren't a genius," Gab replied. "Now, see if you can teach our pedigreed pup whatever it is that makes you so irreplaceable around here."

Gab read the article and letter from Sam. Two things stood out: B.B. King, the ambitious disc jockey, musician, pitchman, and truck driver had sent Ike Turner, a teenager, to Sam to make a record. Sam echoed what Gene said, that "Rocket 88" would jump from race to pop. Gab believed Gene was a strange kind of genius. He'd recently told Christine that Gene reminded him of the little engine that could. When all the other engines were too proud, too powerful, or too prejudiced to haul race music, Gene took it to heights no one could have imagined.

On May 10, 1951, Sou turned up the radio so his patrons could listen to WLAC's election coverage. Everyone there had voted for West in gratitude for

2. Lydel Sims, "Rocket Becomes Flying Disc, Spins toward Record Glory," *The Commercial Appeal*, March 28, 1951.

3. Guralnick, *Sam Phillips*, 107.

working to get a colored city councilman elected. Sou voted for West, despite knowing this change in the mayor's office could jeopardize his numbers business. Sou couldn't afford to lose revenue now that he'd offered Henryene Green $10,000 for the Baltimore Elite Giants of the Negro League.[4]

Now that the major leagues had integrated, Negro baseball teams were terrible investments. He'd told Funny if he broke even, he'd consider it a victory on par with a World Series championship. Only by running numbers could he keep a team financially afloat. With Pie reporting on Mayor Cummings, and the police on his payroll, Sou's racket was safe. Without that protection, however, Sou's house of cards could collapse. Plus, it was no secret that West owed his allegiance to Stahlman.

John Richbourg announced, "Ben West has defeated the four-term incumbent, Mayor Cummings, 13,189 votes to 13,162."[5] The New Era's crowd erupted.

Sou joined Shorty Banks in the office. "When's West takeover?" he asked.

"Four weeks."

On Sunday afternoon, June 3, Helen stepped onto the back porch and read the thermometer. It was ninety-three and not yet summer. She heard the front door and knew Sou had returned. He seemed worn out but happy. "How's Atlanta, Bridgy? How'd the game go?"

"Good. Don't get too close," he cautioned. "I'm needin' a shower and a nap."

When Sou lay down for a rest, Helen joined him. "Did ya get by your family place?"

"Nearby."

"We prayed for rain in church," she said as she rubbed his arm. "Farmers are sufferin'."

"Yeah, drought's terrible," Sou said. "I seen livestock bad off. Passed dry ponds and streams, tobacco plants dead in their beds, and whole cotton fields plowed under. My stepbrother come by. Said his sweet potato crop's worst anyone remembers."

"Folks over to Shantytown's worried city hydrants are gonna run dry. Said pressure's a trickle. Supposedly, superintendent of waterworks told Pastor there's

---

4. Bob Luke, *The Baltimore Elite Giants* (Baltimore: Johns Hopkins University Press, 2009), 131.
5. Dick Battle, "Ten Council Runoffs Set," *Nashville Banner*, May 11, 1951.

adequate supply, but some folks is stockpiling water, fearing Cummings'll retaliate for coloreds givin' West the win."

Sou was sympathetic to the beleaguered farmers' plight; however, he hoped the dry spell would hold another day. Come Tuesday, the Dell could flood until the Krispy Kreme donut sign's hole became a waterfall, but on Monday night, he expected to watch the season opener from the dugout. A full stadium was necessary to fill the coffers, and no one packed the stands with Black *and* white fans like Satchel did.

The next morning, Sou read the *Tennessean* aloud as Funny put coffee in the percolator:

Satchel Paige, the rubber armed pitcher who helped the Cleveland Indians win the American league pennant three years ago, will be the headline attraction in Sulphur Dell tonight when the Baltimore Elite Giants meet the Chicago American Giants.[6]

"Big game tonight and you're coming," he said to Harriett as he tickled her tummy.

Later that afternoon, as Sou and Shorty sorted dimes, nickels, and quarters into galvanized buckets, a car honked repeatedly.

"Who's the fool—" Shorty moved to the window. "Sou, come look."

Sou glanced down to the street. A gray Cadillac blocked the intersection of Fourth and Cedar. It was Paige's car surrounded by a small crowd. Sou stuck his head out the window and yelled. "Yo, Satchel! Save the autographs for the game."

"Got's me a strategy, Bridgy!" Satchel shouted back. "Best bring your A game!"

A light rain started to fall and Satchel climbed back into his car, headed to the stinky, rightfield-sloping stadium he called Suffer Hell. "The greatest pitcher in baseball history considered this trip a homecoming of sorts. He had returned to where in 1926 his professional career had begun."[7]

Satchel went to the broadcast booth to say a quick hello to WLAC's

6. "Paige Pitches in Dell Tonight," *Tennessean*, June 4, 1951, 14.
7. George Leonard, "Satchel Paige Scotches Some Of Legends Built Around Him," *Nashville Banner*, June 5, 1951.

Herman Grizzard, who had been the voice of Nashville baseball for as long as Satchel could remember.

The light drizzle that started that afternoon continued steadily and was still falling when the lanky one took the mound at the bottom of the first inning. Chicago had scored one run, and while the crowd (estimated at 1,500) hadn't cheered for Chicago's batters, they welcomed Satchel like a returning war hero. Local baseball aficionados of every race stood in the rain to applaud the legend. Satchel crouched, read the catcher's signal, cranked his arm twice, paused at the top of his windup, then uncoiled to send a crossfire rocket over the plate. Sou's second baseman, Chilson, watched it fly past.[8] Chilson walked. Right fielder Brice singled. Then the team's best batter, Henry Kimbro, approached the plate. Satchel passed Kimbro with an intentional walk. The bases were loaded with no outs. Sou had three strong, young hitters on deck. In quick order, Satchel Paige struck them all out. The maestro of the mound had given the crowd what they braved the rain to see.

In the third inning, Satchel demonstrated how at age forty-four, wisdom trumps brawn. Knowing it would take more than fast pitches to beat Kimbro, Early in the game, Satchel had intentionally walked him, fooling Kimbro into believing Satchel was afraid to pitch to him. The strategy worked, and it provided Kimbro and Sou a story with which they could entertain baseball enthusiasts for the next fifty years.

In 1996, Sou told journalist Randy Horick, "Satchel looked around and saw Kimbro was coming up and loaded the bases just to get to him. Then he *struck* him out."[9]

Satchel struck out the batters behind Kimbro, then left the stinky, soggy field and headed to the locker room for a hot, rotten-egg-smelling shower. Satchel had allowed four hits and no runs. Sou's southpaw rookie, Searcy Kelly, pitched all nine innings to claim the 5–4 win. The opening game did not produce enough revenue to cover the cost of renting the stadium, but for Sou to see Satchel cheered on by a diverse crowd, including Sou's wife and baby—everyone braving the rain for the love of the game—was the experience of a lifetime.

After the game Satchel said, "If the way had been open for my race, I could

8. Leonard, *Nashville Banner*, June 5, 1951.
9. Randy Horick, "They Might Have Been Heroes," *Nashville Scene*, May 2, 1996.

have started pitching major-league ball when I was eighteen. There's no telling how long I might have stayed up. I might have won twenty-five games in the majors ten years ago. I was two or three times faster then."[10]

When Satchel entered the Era, the house band struck up "Rocket 88."

"It's like your fastball," Sou said. "A rocket hurtling at ya 88 miles an hour!"

"Eighty-eight's my slow fastball," Satchel said. "I gots four fastballs faster'n that!"

Later, in the wee hours, Sou slipped into Harriett's room. "Baby girl," he whispered softly, "someday you tell folks you once seen your daddy and old Satch play a Negro League game at stinky old Sulphur Dell, where back in the day, Yankees brung us two of the best things God ever created—freedom and baseball."

10. Leonard, *Nashville Banner*, June 5, 1951.

12

DON'T DO IT

Sou ran a clean club, no vulgarity, no fighting.
He did not tolerate it. . . . The greatest night
of my life occurred at the New Era.

—CHRISTINE KITTRELL

Sou spent the summer traveling with his team. By late July, with his funds nearly depleted, he sold Sidney Bunch's contract to an MLB minor-league team. He hated to let Sid go, yet he was happy the kid had a shot at the majors. When Mayor West organized a send-off parade for Sidney, Sou discovered Sid's mother was West's maid. The fortuitous coincidence allowed Sou to have eyes and ears on city hall again. Pie had warned West would come under pressure to shut down numbers. After Sid's mother confirmed this, Sou worried a grand jury was forthcoming. Before going back on the road, Sou told Shorty to save any news articles related to numbers. Shorty despised the *Banner* and delegated the task to their flirty new single-mom waitress, Katherine "Kat" Nuble. Whenever Sou returned, he'd spend a day reviewing the articles. So far, nothing indicated an investigation was imminent.

"While's you gone," Shorty said, "Looby filed an injunction so's we can play city golf courses. Guess the Supreme Court ruled on links in Florida. So West's promised us a course."

"But," Kat interrupted, "Mrs. Otey's got a petition going 'round saying that thirty-five thousand's better spent improving colored neighborhoods. That'll buy sewage, lights, streets, and better school facilities."[1] Kat handed Sou a folder of news clippings and sat beside him. Kat's interest in Sou was obvious to everyone.

Sou wasn't interested in Kat, as Funny had divorced him for infidelity once before. Sou shooed Kat away. His disinterest only seemed to further motivate Kat, as she returned with his mail and resumed her bid for attention.

"Go purr somewhere else," Sou insisted. "Woman's a damn nuisance, Shorty."

"Tap that pussy and put us all outta her misery," Shorty replied.

"And when she tells Funny?"

Shorty shrugged.

Later that evening, Sou saw Ted come in with his white-acting-colored friend, Hoss, who'd proven surprisingly helpful. Knowing in advance which records WLAC planned to promote had given Sou a booking advantage. Before "Rocket 88" even topped the charts, he'd scheduled Jackie Berenson.

Sou noticed Kat sidle next to Hoss, lean into him and rest her ample breast on his shoulder. If Hoss responded to Kat's flirtation, it could wreak havoc. Sou tried to signal to his policeman/bouncer, Bobby Baker, but his focus seemed locked on a voluptuous woman making her way to the stage from the audience. The woman whispered something to Jimmy Lewis.

Lewis announced, "This's for whoever requested 'Danny Boy' earlier. Sorry I didn't know the words. She do."

The woman sang: "Oh, Danny Boy, the pipes, the pipes are calling. From glen to glen and dooowwwwnnnnn the mountainside . . ."

Kitty stretched the notes like a candymaker pulls taffy. Hoss and Ted stood up, in awe of her melismatic delivery. She sang the folk tune with the fervor

1. "Local NAACP Holds Discussion About Golf Links," *Nashville Banner*, July 31, 1951, 15.

of a gospel singer and the sensuality of a nightclub songstress. Following her performance, Bobby brought the woman to Sou's table.

"This here's Christine Kittrell, my girlfriend," Bobby told Sou.

"My friends call me Kitty."

Sou laughed. "Another black cat, just what I don't need. Miss Kitty, you made me love a song I've never liked. You want a job here?"

"I sure do."

"You know how I know you're tops?" Sou asked. He pointed to Hoss and Ted. "You impressed them."

"I know Jarrett, but who's with him?"

"WLAC's Hoss Allen."

Kitty smiled. "My lucky night!"

Within hours of her impromptu performance, Sou gave Christine "Kitty" Kittrell a regular gig, and Ted negotiated a recording contract for her with Bill Beasley's Tennessee Recording Studio.

The following weekend, Helen came to hear the new singer. By the time Kitty concluded her first set, Helen had lost patience with the club's flirtatious waitress. Between her first and second set, Kitty joined Helen at Sou's table.

"That Kat's like a bitch in heat," Helen complained.

"Ain't she?" Kittrell said. "Whole club's noticed. I'll sing something about it next set."

When Kitty saw Hoss enter, she elbowed Helen. "That cocky peckerwood could charm the skin off a snake. He oughta be in movies, not on the radio."

When Kitty took the stage, she opened with "Don't Do It." Her breathy, sexy vocals, enhanced by Louis Brooks's sax and Jarrett's masterful keyboard, was torchy nightclub blues at its best. A month later, Beasley released the song as Kitty's first single.

Sou was relieved when the Elite Giants wrapped their season at the Dell with a pair of doubleheaders over Labor Day weekend. It was midnight when the final slugfest ended and the exhausted players limped out of the stadium. With his wallet as depleted as his players, Sou put his baseball dreams aside and redirected his energy toward his business and family. And none too soon, as two weeks later, once again his name graced the *Banner's* front page:

> While several of the community's better known professional gamblers are reported looking for greener and safer fields beyond Davidson County's boundaries, the perennially popular "numbers" racket moves on merrily and unmolested. Rumors have it that a new "banker" is now attempting to get into the business that has heretofore been dominated by Marcus Hackeman, "Soo" Bridgeforth, Theodore Acklen and a number of others. The banker has been getting an assist in this aim from a couple of men whose uniforms should normally identify them as being on the side of law and order.[2]

"The *Banner's* soliciting a grand jury," Sou told Helen.

"What'll you do?"

"You know what separates a professional poker player from the amateur? Amateur plays the cards he's dealt, while a pro plays what he makes you *think* he's dealt. Grand jury convenes, my best bet's a bluff."

"Least it ain't nuthin'," Helen replied. "Seein' as how you're so good at it."

Sou was stunned when Community Chest, Stahlman and Sloan's favored charity, asked Sou to head a "Negro Sports Division," with a goal of raising $10,000 from and *for* the colored community. Sou accepted the challenge because the charity did good works, and he feared if he refused, Stahlman would have another reason to harass him. Shorty speculated the *Banner* wouldn't simultaneously promote and attack Sou. Shorty was wrong.

A few days after having highlighted Sou's work for the Community Chest, Dick Battle's column appeared in bold type on the front page of the *Banner*:

> There's something wrong somewhere when the biggest and most flourishing numbers racket "kingfish" in Nashville can carry on his business openly and without any molestation by city or county law enforcement officials and brag about it. To be specific, I'm talking

2. Dick Battle, "City Hall," *Nashville Banner*, September 21, 1951, 2.

about the Negro night club operator, "Soo" Bridgeforth, who is now admittedly the biggest of the five or six numbers racket bankers in town and does a daily business ranging from $3,000 on up. The money comes in daily at a place adjacent to the New Era Club on Fourth Avenue, North. It comes in in bags and buckets beginning at seven o'clock in the morning and continuing until shortly after two o'clock in the afternoon. The tickets and the money are sorted and counted almost in full view of the street and it's been going on for a long time just like that. I don't know what sort of "Indian sign" Bridgeforth has, but so far it's worked with remarkable success.[3]

Sou wanted to know where Battle got his information. "Who blabbed?" he asked Shorty.

"Probably Bellamy. Started his own game, then learnt numbers ain't easy as its looks."

Kat pounced in, uninvited. "Y'all hear about the KKK burning a cross at Shelby? *Banner* reported teenagers seen white-robed men set it afire on the golf course."

"Klan don't want coloreds playing, but carrying they's clubs's fine," Shorty said.

"And the city makes us pay the same taxes for it," Sou added.

On November 5, the *Banner* reported that Nathan Bellamy was out of business, and the "top man in numbers was 'Soo' Bridgeforth of the New Era Club on Fourth Avenue."[4] Never one to hold a grudge, Sou instructed Shorty to rehire Nathan.

"After he stole your customers and ratted you to the *Banner*?"

"Yep. And get me a federal gambling tax stamp while you're at it."

"Say what? You're wavin' a Roll Tide flag at a bull! Federal stamp don't make gambling legal here; just proves you guilty. Swear, Sou, sometimes you ain't got the sense God gave a mule. That stamp'll put us in the county workhouse!"

"You gotta trust me, Shorty."

---

3. Dick Battle, "City Hall," *Nashville Banner*, October 11, 1951, 2.
4. Dick Battle, "City Hall," *Nashville Banner*, November 5, 1951.

"I'll do it, but ain't puttin' my name on it." He looked at the runners and chose one of Sou's Alabama kinfolk. "Be yours and your lousy nephew Woodson."

Sou had discussed the tax stamp issue with his attorney, who claimed the district attorney had privately insinuated the statute wouldn't withstand a constitutional challenge. It was a gamble, but that's who Sou was—a professional gambler.

Days later, Kat announced, "*Banner*'s here. You're on page one again!"

Sou scanned the front page. "Y'all ever notice how Battle spells Sou ever-which-way but right?" He read aloud for the benefit of the illiterate runners: "The professional gamblers of Nashville and Davidson County, their 'baby blues' gleaming with hope, are eagerly waiting for the holiday season of Christmas and New Year's . . . and are nervously apprehensive about the rumored renewal of Grand Jury activities after November 26."[5]

"Ain't a damn week since I filed for that stamp!" Shorty complained.

Sou continued: "Sou and his competitors are more afraid of a grand jury than publicity. Battle says he's got a hunch members of the jury'll continue their investigation into gambling."[6]

He lowered the paper. "Christmas parade before or after the twenty-sixth?"

"Couple days before," Kat answered.

"Why? You worried you'll miss seein' the marchin' bands from the workhouse windas?"

"Nobody's going to jail. Night *before* the parade'll be our last numbers night."

"Now, I knows you took a flyball to the noggin," Shorty said. "Parade night's numbers's best. Runners buys they's Christmas hams and chillun's presents off those tickets."

"Kat, count how many hams I'll need for my runners, club's employees, and house musicians. I'll tell the police they're off my payroll and my last lottery's November 19."

Two weeks later, Sou told Funny, "I gotta miss dinner so's I can play poker with Loser."

5. Dick Battle, "Gamblers Agleam for Yuletide," *Nashville Banner*, November 9, 1951, 1.
6. Battle, 8.

"Which loser? Thought you quit."

"Carlton Loser, attorney general." Sou kissed her cheek. "How do I win, again?"

"You bluff."

"In bluffing, timing's everything." He climbed into the cab and directed his driver to take him to the police station.

"You turnin' you own self in?"

"Could say that, I reckon, but to the *Banner*, not the police."

Dick Battle waited for Sou on the steps of the police station. The men walked around the public square and chatted like they were old friends.

"I did buy the stamp," Sou admitted. "Then surrendered it. Told the government men I don't even want the stamp. I just want to let you boys know that from now on I'm running the New Era Club on the up-and-up and that there'll not even be any numbers tickets around."[7]

"Your filing said you accept wagers on numbers, horse races, and other things."

"*Did*. We informed Loser I'm out for good."

"You'll just walk away from the $68,000 monthly profit you reported?"

"Better than jail."

Kat read Battle's column the following day. "*Banner*'s calling you the fast-buck gentry. Nicest thing they ever printed about ya, Sou."[8]

Sou's gambling enterprise stayed closed for months. His friendly competitor, Teddy Acklen, didn't close and was arrested. When Acklen failed to show for his arraignment, the *Banner* attacked. On February 1, Robert Battle wrote:

It's about time this town came of age, faced the facts of life, and realized that the professional gamblers, the bootleggers, the honky-tonk operators and the numbers bosses have in the past and are attempting to now cut themselves in politically anyway that will buy them a "break." There couldn't be a better time, today, tomorrow and seven days a week from now on for law enforcement officials to

7. Robert Battle, "City's Gambler's Appear To 'Be at a New Low,'" *Nashville Banner*, December 3, 1951.
8. Battle.

start putting the screws to these people and giving them a taste of workhouse food . . . that is if they are really in earnest about enforcing the law.[9]

"Stahlman's baiting West," Sou told Shorty. "Raid's coming. Keep us buttoned up tight." Sou had yet to tell Funny he'd decided to purchase the Birmingham Black Barons. Shorty's anger was already more than enough for him to deal with. He'd tried explaining that he couldn't *not* buy the Barons. They were the team his father had walked thirty miles to watch, that he'd dreamed of pitching for, and one that wouldn't likely exist if he didn't buy them. This was a circumstance where because he *could*—he *must*. The Barons' former owner and Sou agreed they'd make the announcement at the owners meeting in Chicago. Knowing Funny would be as angry as Shorty, Sou had waited until just before he left to tell her.

While he was away, he had Kat order flowers and chocolates delivered to Funny each day. They seemed to have worked, as Funny seemed genuinely happy to see him when he returned. However, Kat was snippy and Shorty was a nervous wreck, convinced they were workhouse-bound.

"Wear them Barons stripes now, ain't long we's be in county stripes," Shorty said. Shorty had developed a habit of pacing by the window, on the lookout for government cars.

On February 12, the cars Shorty expected arrived. "They's here and that's Loser hisself!" Shorty yelled. Sou went to the window. Sure enough, the attorney general was on the sidewalk.

Sou called Funny. "Call my attorney. Loser's here," he said calmly. "Don't fret, I'll be out within an hour." He hung up and turned to Shorty. "Is Battle with Loser?"

"Nope. Different reporter, but *Banner*'s top photographer." Shorty's father had been a professional photographer in Memphis. By happenstance, Shorty and his dad were in Oklahoma at the time of Tulsa's Wall Street massacre. Shorty had been thirteen when his father photographed the aftermath of that bloody event. Ever since, the popping sound and acrid smell of exploding flash bulbs triggered Shorty's anxiety. He stuffed the last bite of pulled pork into his mouth. "Better eat, Sou," Shorty mumbled. "Workhouse food ain't fit for dogs, you know."

"Finish mine then," Sou said. He went downstairs and outside. "Good afternoon, gents."

Carlton Loser spun around. "Oh, Bridgeforth. I hear congratulations are in order. Business must be good if you can keep the Black Barons afloat."

Sou was caught off guard by the attorney general's polite greeting when he'd expected to be cuffed. Then again, white Nashvillians could be mercilessly polite right up to the point they strung you like Christmas tinsel on a tree.

"Gang's all here. Let's go in," Loser commanded. Sou stepped aside. "Oh, ya thought I was coming for you, did ya? Not today, Bridgeforth," Loser said. He led his men farther north.

John Malone, the *Banner*'s top photographer, followed. "He's raiding Dr. Jackson's," Malone told Sou. "Doc strangled a seven-month baby born healthy. *And* they say he's got slot machines to entertain the men while he kills their babies!"

Sou watched Malone photograph the sign: *R. B. Jackson, M.D. Physician + Surgeon.*

Shorty and Kat joined Sou on the sidewalk. "What's happenin'?" Shorty asked.

"Abortionist strangled a newborn *and*'s got slots," Sou explained.

"Which's they raidin' for?" Shorty asked.

"Probably depends on the strangled baby's color," Kat said.

Sou wondered if the grand jury's investigation of gambling had uncovered the newborn's murder. Sou wouldn't have believed any good could come of Loser's investigation, but if what Malone said was true, it had. A long-suppressed memory surfaced of his grandmother Mary clutching his hand as they knelt together in the loamy Alabama soil to bury Sou's mother and baby sister.

"All God's chillun's got-a-wings," he whispered, repeating Mary's words. "Now fly on home to heab'n."

13

THREE O'CLOCK BLUES

Black performers would come around with these
records; they were good records. They couldn't
get them exposed anywhere. Nobody would
touch them. But we decided to play them.

—JOHN RICHBOURG

Gab had agreed with the *Saturday Evening Post* article that claimed Nashville's
residents were overly attached to tradition. "Therein lies Nashville's greatest
weakness and its greatest charm," the *Post* reported. "The true Nashvillian is
more interested in living as his grandfather did than in having his city a model
of civic progress. In many homes, life moves along with an old fashioned ease."[1]
Thus, Gab was surprised when Hoss handed him a blue ribbon–wrapped cigar
on February 16 and announced his son would not carry the name onto the IV
generation.

"He'll be Charles Rogan, after my mother's father. We'll call him Rogan."

Gab passed the cigar under his nose. "Congratulations. Let's celebrate.
Cocktails at five."

"So just another ordinary day at the office," Hoss joked.

---

1. *Saturday Evening Post*, October 27, 1951.

The men of WLAC had plenty of reasons to celebrate during the spring of '52. On April 1, Truman, F. C. Sowell, Paul Oliphant, Dave Binns, and Gab flew to Chicago for the National Association of Radio and Television Broadcasters convention, where FCC chairman Paul Walker announced the freeze on new television licenses was being lifted. There were fourteen million televisions in US households, yet few received a signal. WLAC was eager to jump on the television bandwidth wagon. Truman informed his management team he'd quietly negotiated with Guilford Dudley Jr., president of Life and Casualty Insurance, to sell them the station.

"They can build out a state-of-the-art studio. We're butting heads with Tom Baker and WKDA for the license. L & C would give us the advantage."

Gab had long hoped for a career in television. Now that the association had implemented new censorship rules—which Gene's broadcast and Gab's advertising clearly violated—timing was ideal. Gene's sexual innuendo and consumption of alcohol on air, coupled with Gab's misleading product descriptions, were bound to rile up the FCC. Yet if everyone adhered to this new truth-in-advertising guideline, Gab suspected the entire economy would collapse. In anticipation of WLAC-TV getting the green light, Gab carefully studied *The Television Code*, the FCC's latest publication.

Upon their return, Truman signed the sales agreement with Life and Casualty. To prepare for the transition, duties formerly Sowell's or Truman's became Gab's. He now ran the sales department, managed the deejays and nighttime programming, represented the station at the state's broadcaster conventions, served on the board of the Nashville Advertising Federation, and chaired the Heart Drive's publicity campaign. In addition, he helped Christine with her drive to provide playground equipment for Negro children at the school for the blind. He'd been so busy, he almost forgot to buy baby chicks for Easter.

The Saturday before Easter Sunday, Eddie followed Gab to the driveway. "Dad, if you're going to Gallatin, I'd rather have records from Randy's than baby chicks from Mrs. Jones."

"*Buy* records? Son, producers give 'em to me."

"Cool. I'll make a list," Eddie said.

"That's not how it works. If you want records, you'll do chores to earn 'em."

"You just said they're free!"

"No. I said I don't *buy* them. There's no such thing as a free record, son."

"You just trying to get me to do more without paying me for it."

Gab lost his temper. "Dang it, Eddie! You idolize Buddy. Why can't you be more like him?" Gab had considered taking Eddie along, but with the boy's entitled attitude, neither of them would enjoy it. Gab didn't understand why Eddie couldn't emulate his cousin, Buddy. When Eddie was four years old, Buddy and his family had moved in with them. Christine's sister Clara; her husband, Sam Rogers; and their three children intended to stay briefly until Sam found a job. Gab had leased the expansive riverfront estate of his late uncle, former Nashville mayor Hillary Howse. There was plenty of room, and with Christine pregnant with Gayle, Clara was helpful.

They enjoyed being together so much that after Sam recovered financially and Gayle was thriving, they stayed. During this time, Gab grew fond of Clara's oldest, Buddy. An adventurous teenager who loved to fish, Buddy made friends with the river rats who fished for a living. They taught Buddy their secrets, and before long, Buddy was reeling in enough fish to host Friday night fish fries. Despite this hobby, Buddy never shirked his responsibilities. He did his homework and chores promptly, perfectly, and without complaint. When he was named his high school's valedictorian, Gab introduced him to Stahlman, who got Buddy a scholarship to Vanderbilt. Buddy completed his sophomore year and then took a leave to join the Naval Air Corps. He now served as one of the navy's most elite fighter pilots.

Conversely, Gab thought if slacking was a sport, Eddie'd qualify for the Olympics. Giving his spoiled son records just because he asked wouldn't turn him into Buddy. It wouldn't even make him like Billy, Buddy's younger brother, who'd just been accepted into the navy's pilot training program. Besides, if Gab wanted records, he'd call Ernie, who owed him a favor. Gab had helped Ernie's nephew Cal launch WSOX. Gab tuned in to 1470 to hear what WSOX broadcast on Saturday afternoons. As he listened to *The Ted Jarrett Show*, he thought about how far Jarrett had come since his days as a pin boy, which further fueled Gab's frustration with Eddie's lack of ambition. His son needed to learn how hard life could be for men with limited options. The best way to learn that was by doing hard, hot, manual labor.

WSOX was a 1,000-watt daytime station that copycatted Gene's broadcast. Gab helped Cal set up the advertising department. Ted set up the music library, hosted two shows, and recruited additional hosts. Ted worked as a pianist, composer, producer, talent scout, manager, and event emcee, leaving little time to hang at the Era with Hoss.

At WLAC, Hoss also juggled multiple positions. During the day, he was a reporter and salesman. At night, he was Gene's and John's backup, Nashville's favorite event emcee, and occasional actor in community theater. As busy as they were, Ted and Hoss made it a point to meet at the Era whenever B.B. King was in town.

By the time "Three O'Clock Blues" topped the charts, King was already beloved at the Era and WLAC. He'd wrap his early radio show in Memphis, drive to Nashville, swing by WLAC, then check in at the colored YMCA and walk to the Era to play craps, blackjack, or poker until showtime. Like most Chitlin' Circuit clubs, the Era had music in the front for the ladies and gambling in the back for the men. King was popular with both. Ladies loved his looks, his molasses-dripping voice, spry fingers, and sincere down-home humility. The men loved how he was a bad gambler but a good loser. Sou loved how, whenever B.B. was in the house, the cashbox would swell. The revenue B.B. brought into the Era stayed at the Era.

In early March, two of Sou's biggest numbers competitors, Teddy Acklen and Marcus Hackerman, were arrested along with twenty-seven of their runners. Sou immediately ceased his gambling operation. Once Teddy and Marcus were bailed out, a meeting of all the city's professional gamblers—white and Black—was called for the purpose of electing a "gambler friendly" sheriff. They selected Oscar Capps, a twentysomething war hero turned policeman. They tapped Pie Hardison and Good Jelly Jones to steer his campaign.

B.B. arrived in town on April 22, disappointed to learn he couldn't gamble. Shorty explained that with Teddy facing eleven months and twenty-nine days in the workhouse, gambling couldn't commence until after the election. B.B. had hoped to discuss business with Sou. B.B.'s new booking agency had contracted him for sixty gigs in sixty days, and although he was only halfway in, he was exhausted and felt they'd taken advantage of him. Unable to gamble, or to see Sou, who was out with his baseball team, B.B. walked three blocks downhill to WLAC. The conversation he'd intended for Sou happened with Gab instead.

Gab listened patiently, touched that B.B. would confide in him. Gab learned details of B.B.'s Steinbeck-novel-worthy life. He hadn't expected to hear a contemporary life story as inspirational as Ted Jarrett's, yet even Ted's hardships couldn't compare with King's. Gab never considered himself particularly privileged. As a boy, he'd been distraught over having to support his mother and disappointed to have lost his dream of Vanderbilt. The tragedies in B.B.'s life punctuated just how much being born white—especially in a city where your last name's a commodity that bestows mentors willing to impart knowledge—afforded true privilege.

When B.B. asked for advice, Gab considered the lessons his mentors shared that he'd found most beneficial.

"I'll share with you the sage advice my mentors gave me. First, be very careful who you get involved with. It takes years to build a good reputation, but an unscrupulous associate can destroy it in an instant. Secondly, my wise uncles advised, 'If you do business with the rich, you'll dine with the poor. But if you do business with the poor, you'll dine with the rich.'"

"How's that?"

"Believe that's what's happening to you. In part, means be wary of doing business with guys in big cars, who smoke big cigars, wear gaudy cuff links, and flash big wads of cash. Too often that's greed, and they'll beat you outta every last penny they can. You're better off with someone you trusted *before* you became successful."

"Mens drivin' big cars, smokin' big cigars—describes every record producer I know."

"Which says somethin' about the industry, don't it?"

"This puts in my mind Mr. Sou over't the Era. Never seen him in a fancy car, flashing cash or jewelry. He takes cabs everywhere and lives on the down-low."

"I've never met Sou, only spoke on the phone, but it's well known around town he gives away more money'n he keeps. Hoss says anybody with talent—music, sports, whatever—he'll bankroll 'em. He didn't just take an interest in you *after* you topped the charts. He promoted you from the get-go."

"Before I made enough to gamble," B.B. said. "So'd y'all. Thank you. Oh, and the index cards and thesaurus helped too."

When B.B. had last visited, he'd mentioned the three books that lived on Gab's desk: a Bible, a dictionary, and a thesaurus. When B.B. said he'd never used a thesaurus, Gab explained how invaluable he found it while writing commercials. B.B. decided to try one for lyrics.

"Try this, too," Gab had advised. He'd shown B.B. his index cards, explaining how he wrote on the cards snippets of information, new words, quotes—anything he wanted to remember. He'd riffled through them until he found the Christmas card he'd received from Ferguson at WDIA with B.B.'s picture. He mentioned how he and Hoss had speculated B.B. would be a star. That's why he'd kept the Christmas card.

"I was intimidated at first," B.B. confessed. "This place, so fancy, so high in the sky, I stuttered, and you said to call you Blackie. Told me you weren't no Vandy brat, just an undereducated overachiever. Said you started tap-dancin' in minstrels and never imagined them dancin' shoes'd lead you to peddlin' baby chicks and records a-penny-per."

Gab smiled. "I remember. You'd said you'd been pickin' cotton a penny-a-pound, which is why I'd said it that-a-way."

"And now I'm pickin' strings a-nickel-a-record. Ain't it somethin'? Born Black on a Mississippi plantation? Plowboy's all anybody expected I'd be."

"Reminds me, Eddy Arnold came by with his dogcatcher of a manager who calls himself a colonel. They were looking to sell a show. Anyhoo, Eddy said the New York promoters call his music *cowboy*." Mimicking Arnold's voice, Gab parroted: "Them city folk don't know South's got no cowboys—only *plowboys!*"

B.B. laughed, and Gab continued. "Those highfalutin New Yorkers, like our Belle Meade snobs, look down their toffee noses at country and R & B musicians, but they got no problem getting rich off 'em. And then they come hat in hand asking us for donations to keep their symphonies afloat cause they can't sell enough tickets. Then who underwrites their pretentiousness? Us!"

"And ain't that always the way?"

After B.B. left, Gab thought about how he'd worked with the Madison Avenue agencies long enough to know they failed to understand segregation

Gab Blackman, Faye Emerson,
Christine Blackman, and
Bill "Hoss" Allen on July 28th,
1953 at Hermitage Hotel.

Gab with Black caddies at the
Woodmont Country Club.

John R.
WLAC Personality

Don Whitehead
WLAC News

James Brown

TO: Paula and Michael
A significant historical event
Nashville, Tennessee
1969
from
Don Whitehead
WLAC Radio

John Richbourg, Don Whitehead,
and James Brown on April 27th, 1970
at the Nashville Civic Auditorium.

Christine and Gab
Blackman at the 1968
Grammy Awards.

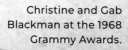

Sou Bridgeforth and Ted Acklen circa 1947 at the New Era Club.

Helen and Sou Bridgeforth circa 1946.

WLAC Nauta Line, the Gab Blackman family in July 1969 at Old Hickory Lake.

Gab and Christine Blackman with grandchildren Paula, Brett, and Cris circa 1968 in Nashville.

Gab at a retirement party with Bill "Hoss" Allen, Gene Nobles, Don Whitehead, and Spider Harrison in September 1973.

1953 telegram.

Gab Blackman with Baby Chicks supplier Mrs. J. Carter, circa 1947.

Perplexed little boy stands before wreckage of Hattie Cotton School in Nashville on September 10th, 1957.

Students March to Tennessee State Capital on April 19th, 1960.

Mayor Ben West, Reverend C.T. Vivian, and Diane Nash on the Nashville courthouse steps on April 19th, 1960.

Injured student Ewingella Bigham at segregation student protest on May 10th, 1963 at 6th Avenue, Nashville.

Hell's Half Acre circa 1950 at Capitol Hill, Nashville.

Photo courtesy of the Metro Archives, Nashville Public Library.

Hell's Half Acre circa 1950 at Capitol Hill, Nashville.

Photo courtesy of the Metro Archives, Nashville Public Library.

Colored YMCA Circa 1961 @ 4th Avenue North, Nashville.

Photo courtesy of the Tennessee State Library.

Harriett Bridgeforth Jordan circa 1955.

Gab Blackman at WLAC microphone on September 20th, 1960, Nashville.

Sou Bridgeforth golfing circa 1950.

NEW ERA CLUB
ENTERTAINMENT NIGHTLY
NO COVER CHARGE

Nashville's Finest

WM. SOU BRIDGEFORTH, *Proprietor*
E. J. BANKS, *Manager*

415½ Fourth Avenue, North
Nashville, Tenn.

New Era Club—Nashville's Finest—with Sou Bridgeforth circa 1940.

Photo courtesy of Harriett Bridgeforth Jordan.

Anne Duff Blackman, Eddie Blackman, Christine and Gab Blackman, Dr. and Mrs. Price Duff in August 1956 in Nashville.

L&C Tower in downtown Nashville on November 2nd, 1962.

Bill "Hoss" Allen and Mrs. Robert Worth Bingham in May 1946 at the Bell Meade Country Club, Nashville.

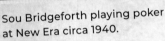

Sou Bridgeforth playing poker at New Era circa 1940.

Sou's house guitarist George Yates playing at The New Era in 1962.

and how that would make B.B.'s back-to-back engagements untenable. Gab tried to explain segregation to his reps at the Katz Agency, who'd responded, "So the South's gotta have two of everything."

Not everything, Gab tried to explain. They'd rattled off a list and when they mentioned golf courses and swimming pools, Gab admitted the city was divided, but not equally. This led the admen to see Nashville as two cities, each with its own ad market. One of the Madison Avenue geniuses then suggested that if Nashville wanted to be considered a business city and compete with Atlanta, they needed to get the time zone border moved west so at least the white side of town was in the Eastern Time Zone. This was all too reminiscent of Jimmy Stahlman's long-running battle with daylight saving time. Gab recalled how, when he worked at the *Banner*, Jimmy refused to change the clocks seasonally. When he stepped across the line in the lobby that separated the *Banner* offices from the *Tennessean* offices, the time shifted. It drove him crazy scheduling meetings and ad deadlines.

Jimmy and his Bourbon Aristocrat friends would probably embrace the idea of moving the time zone border and shifting the city's redlines so coloreds were on a different time zone than whites. They were moving forward with their scheme to build a swanky new auditorium so they could kill two birds—move the plowboy whites away from the central business district near the Ryman and bulldoze the Black plowboys away from the city square, thus evicting colored residents from land too precious to house a Negro ghetto.

Ted left his home near the city square's ghetto to meet Kitty at Bill Beasley's studio. They needed one more song to make an album. Kitty had grown tired of Ted's nitpicky criticism. She carried a bottle of whiskey to Bill's office and poured herself a drink.

"Whatcha doing?" Bill asked.

"Just sittin' here drinkin'."

"Great line for a lyric. Let's write it."

Ted came in later with more complaints that Kitty ignored. She and Bill kept drinking—and writing—until they had a song. A few nights later, Kitty debuted "Sittin' Here Drinkin'" at the Era. The record was released in July. *Billboard* magazine reported:

> Kittrell does "Sittin' Here Drinkin'" for the label and it sounds like it will go. Miss K had penned a moody opus here. It's a torchy blues which she delivers with good effect. Fine after-hours wax.[2]

When Sou heard Kitty's song on WLAC, he knew his songstress would soon be touring. He asked her who she suggested might replace her while she toured.

"Got a guy camped on Momma's couch now who'd be perfect," Kitty said.

"Bring him by."

Days later, Kitty came in with a young man dressed in Royal Canadian Dragoon uniform with heavy eye makeup, fake lashes, and a six-inch pompadour. Sou looked at the distinctive man. "This's who's camped out at your Momma's?"

"Yeah. He's a great entertainer."

"Oh, I remember," Sou said.

Several years before, Good Jelly Jones had seen the performer's act at a homosexual "circus" club on Gay Street. Jelly had brought him to the Era. Sou'd thought Jelly had brought a date and that the boy was a woman. Jelly explained the boy's dress and makeup were part of his act. Sou gave the boy the stage and then watched the most manic, rollicking, wild-ass show he'd ever seen.

"Little Richard Penniman," Sou pronounced. "How the hell you been?"

"I's seen better times. Daddy got murdered. I'm havin' to support my whole family."

"I'm sorry to hear that," Sou said. "Take my stage. I'll work something out."

Little Richard had been fending for himself for years. He'd traveled across Georgia and Tennessee with carnivals, gospel and minstrel shows, and blues and variety revues. In 1951, he'd recorded "Every Hour" in Nashville. Afterward, he'd told his family he'd made a record. Not everyone believed him,

---

2. *Billboard*, August 2, 1952, 104.

until one night Gene broadcast "Every Hour." Richard ran through the house screaming, "That's my record! My record! That's my record!"[3]

Richard stayed close to Gene forever after.

From May to August, Sou traveled the ballpark circuit. Business stayed healthy at the Era, and the shows were as good as anything in Harlem or Atlanta. On any given night, one might see Little Richard, Kitty Kittrell, John Lee Hooker, Little Esther, Ruth Brown, or Ray Charles. When Clarence "Gatemouth" Brown played the club, his pianist, Edward "Skippy" Brooks, stayed and took over the Era's house band. Skippy's combo featured Freddy Young on alto sax, Clifford McCray on bass, and Kid King on drums. Ernie Young renamed the Era band Kid King Combo. He recorded them in WLAC's studios to launch his new label, Nashboro.

Hoss's visits to the Era became infrequent because his friend Paul Mountcastle Jr. had gotten into the car business, and they became stock car racing fans. Hoss announced the races at Nashville's Speedway track. He even did a weekly segment on his sports show about the races, featuring "up-to-the-minute information on drivers, mechanics, and heaps."[4] Considering Hoss's many responsibilities, Gab frequently accused him of being as busy and nutty as a nutcracker at the GooGoo candy factory.

After the sale of WLAC to Life and Casualty was approved, L & C's chairman, Paul Mountcastle Sr., and their president, Guilford Dudley Jr., invited WLAC's management to a dinner party at Mountcastle's home, Hunters Hill. Dudley Sr. had built the home to resemble an English castle. Constructed of gray stone, it was ornamented with turrets, towers, and stained-glass windows and furnished with European antiques, including a pair of five-hundred-year-old chairs that were replicated to accommodate sixteen dinner guests.[5]

3. Smith, *Pied Pipers*, 67.
4. Eddie Jones, "TV Planned at NES Opening," *Nashville Banner*, May 8, 1952, 48.
5. Louise Davis, "Hunters Hill," *Tennessean*, June 8, 1952, 97.

Gab marveled at the foyer's gold-leafed ceiling and immense chandelier. "We've entered King Arthur's court," Gab whispered to Christine.

"Think we'll see a round table and those medieval chairs everyone talks about?"

"Round? Not in this 'Who's your daddy?' town of lords, knights, and knaves."

"Why's everything such a story with you?"

"Because life *is* story. And we're here to find the moral in it."

"What's this'n's?"

"Tonight's story's about the Kingdom of Vandyville where a Vandy education *and* inherited wealth separate lords from knaves. The plot twist occurs when the protagonist, *moi*, our hardworking master of revels, ends up working for the court jester, Hoss. Moral is, be careful who you step on as you climb up the ladder, because they may step on you on your way down."

"You never fail to amuse me, Galbreath."

The table in the medieval muralled dining room was, as Gab predicted, an elongated rectangle. Gil sat in the five-century-old head chair, while Gil's much younger wife, Jane Anderson Dudley, sat five paces away in the other. After dinner, the guests retired to the terrace off the library. Paul Mountcastle Jr. and Hoss came out to join the executives. Hoss was so entranced by Jane he failed to notice when his wife arrived.

Nancy sat next to Gab. "She's my age, you know. I've always held women who marry for money in contempt."

"You think Jane married Gil for money?" Gab quipped sarcastically.

"Would she have married him if he was a lowly radio announcer?"

"Is this a trick question? Did Jane date Hoss before you?"

"Didn't he date every deb before me?"

Gab smiled and kept to himself that Hoss had dated more than just debutantes.

Nancy cuffed her hand to Gab's ear. "I'll let you in on a secret. Women think he's Prince Charming, but princes are like rummage sales. From a distance they're enticing. But up close you realize they're just full of shit you don't need."

Gab laughed. "I have to remember to tell Gayle that. What's he done?"

"Nothin' more than usual. Just leaves me and the baby at home. Now there's another on the way. Today our neighbors complained about our yard."

"Hire a yard boy."

"You know one?"

"Yeah, Eddie."

When Gab got home, he asked Eddie if he'd gotten a job yet.

"I'm still looking, Pop. Nobody wants to hire me till I'm sixteen."

"Well, you got one tomorrow. Hoss's lawn needs mowing."

When Eddie arrived, he discovered Hoss's yard was so overgrown the grass nearly reached his knee, and Hoss's mower was an ancient, manual push-blade. It took Eddie the entire day to groom the lawn. With the money he earned, Eddie put two gallons of gas in his Willis Jeepster and five into a gas can. He drove to the home of his best friend, John Malone Jr. They filled John's father's boat with gas and spent the following day waterskiing.

Gab was surprised to receive a call from Malone Sr.

"Blackie, I'd no idea they've been takin' my boat out every day till the men at the locks called to tell me the boys were safe."

"Safe?"

"They ran outta gas. Told them next time they're gonna do somethin' stupid, head upriver so the current brings 'em home."

Gab went home at lunchtime. He stormed into Eddie's room and woke him up.

"You're a spoiled slacker!" Gab yelled. He grabbed the phone beside Eddy's bed and called his friend Charlie. "Could you use some help? Eddie's available." Charlie inquired about Eddie's age and size. "He's fifteen, five-ten, and skinny but strong." Gab looked directly at Eddie. "Takes a lot of strength to waterski all day, every day." Gab listened to Charlie's instructions. He then told Eddie, "You think mowing grass's tough? Let's see how you handle crates of bottles. Report to Pepsi's loading dock at 6 a.m. sharp."

A few weeks later, Hoss told Ted how the jungle around his house became a lawn, thanks to Gab's son. And when the kid complained it was hard work, Gab got him an even tougher job. "Blackie's a taskmaster, man. One day he says I'm his problem child, and the next day, it's Eddie. Seems he's always picking at one of us. No doubt, he'll fire my ass someday."

"I hear ya," Ted said. "I like Cal Young, my boss, but the other day, he said 'Ted, where can we get a couple of niggers to cut the weeds and bushes that have grown up around the building?' I was horrified and never said another word. Had he forgotten I was Black?"[6]

"No. He perceives you differently. See, it's not so much skin color as it is economics," Hoss explained. "Think about it like this: we call violinists at the symphony musical artists, but fiddle players are hillbilly pickers. Now, if a hillbilly picker makes a record, and it charts, he's no longer a hillbilly *or* a picker. He's a *country musician*. You make Cal money, so you're a *colored* businessman. Guys who work the yards, well . . ."

"Yeah, like right now you're not my light-skinned colored friend; you're a peckerhead!"

6. Ted Jarrett, *You Can Make It If You Try: The Ted Jarrett Story of R&B in Nashville* (Franklin, TN: Hillsboro Press, 2005), 90.

14

LUCKY OLD SUN

Frank Clement was the greatest governor we ever had.
He was the most far-reaching and at the same time, both
incisive and reflective person that has ever run our state.

—SAM PHILLIPS

Baseball season ended mid-August. Sou's Barons won the league with a 51–6 record. While he was away, a new sheriff had been elected. John Cartwright wasn't the gamblers' first choice, though they felt they could work with him. Sou put a hundred policemen back on the payroll and rehired the runners. When a runner was picked up in late September, the grand jury called for an investigation, then an indictment.[1] On October 6, Sheriff Cartwright raided the Era but found no evidence of gambling.[2]

Kitty had sold enough records to tour with Big Joe Turner. Throughout the summer, Little Richard's fevered performances and ribald lyrics kept the house packed. He earned $20 per night, which made it possible to move into the colored YMCA and send money home to feed his family.[3]

---

1. "Pistol Halts Fugett and 'Non Fugit,'" *Nashville Banner*, September 25, 1952, 8.
2. John Seigenthaler, "Cartwright Can't Find Gambling in County," *Tennessean*, October 6, 1952, 1.
3. Martin Hawkins, *A Shot in the Dark: Making Records in Nashville, 1945–1955* (Nashville: Vanderbilt University Press, 2006), 146.

It had been a while since Hoss and Ted had been to the Era. Nancy had gone into labor prematurely and lost their baby. Hoss stayed home nights for the longest two weeks of his life. Finally, he met up with Ted to catch Richard's show.

"Baby, don't you wish your man looked like me?" Little Richard hollered.

"Yeah!" the ladies screamed.

"No!" yelled the men.

"Hell, no!" shouted Hoss.

Two of Sou's regular performers, Raymond and Mildred Taylor, then joined Richard on stage. As a trio, they called themselves the Tempo Toppers. Shortly after Hoss and Ted caught the act, the trio departed to join Kitty on tour. Sou replaced them with Gay Crosse and the Good Humor Six, featuring John Coltrane on alto sax.

When Kitty returned, Ted hired her, along with Gay Crosse's band, to record his original composition, "Gotta Stop Loving You." Coltrane's bluesy, screaming alto-sax riff kept the song from crossing over to the pop charts as Ted had intended.[4]

In January, Kitty worked on her next record, while her boyfriend, Bobby, worked the police beat. Fats Domino's eight-carat diamond ring was stolen on the same night that Melfi's restaurant's thirty-by-thirty-inch safe was taken, along with a middling ham and a pork shoulder from the smokehouse.[5] Bobby kept an eye out for unlikely gamblers betting large.

Pie Hardison died unexpectedly in March. Sou served as a pallbearer at the funeral, where he ran into Mayor West. West assured Sou he had no intention of shutting down numbers.

"Lottery's just too ingrained in the culture to wipe it out," West explained. "Way I see it, money gambled here stays here. You just keep it circulating. Right now, I'm working to get Frank Clement elected governor. He sees it same as me."

Ever the gambler, Sou'd put the odds of the thirty-two-year-old Clement defeating the incumbent Browning on par with a *yo-eleven* bet. Browning had the support of the state's kingmakers, Stahlman and Memphis's Crump, which

---

4. Hawkins, 144.
5. "Bandleader's Ring Missing; Singer Held," *Nashville Banner*, January 3, 1953, 2.

meant Clement would have to roll each vote the hard way. Sou wrote a check to the campaign anyway and sent a runner to deliver it to West.

The entire state was stunned when Clement defeated Browning.

After the election, Ben West shared with Gab how he and the *Banner*'s political reporter had tried, unsuccessfully, to get Stahlman to support Clement.

"We sent Clement's dad to see Jimmy. Afterward, when Jimmy was asked what he thought, Jimmy said, 'I don't know about trusting a son of a bitch who wears brown shoes with a blue suit. I thought about telling him how wrong it was, but I was just too upset to say anything.'"[6]

Gab laughed. "Tell ya what, next time Jimmy's speaking somewhere, let's get a bunch of guys to wear blue suits and brown shoes to sit right up front, see if we can't unnerve him."

"Great idea," West said. "I'm saving you a seat at the swearing in. Hurry over."

Gab arrived at War Memorial Auditorium just in time to hear Clement say a prayer:

> I pray not for Frank Clement's personal success or glory, I pray not for power and riches, I pray not for any of the material blessings of life, I pray instead as did Solomon of old, and humbly beseech God, in the words of Solomon: "Give therefore, thy servant, an understanding heart . . ."[7]

When Frank and Lucille Clement moved into the governor's mansion, they decided to make it a showcase for Tennessee's musicians and music lovers. Lucille was an accomplished pianist and vocalist, while Frank loved country music. Clement became the first politician to recognize Nashville's potential as a "Music City," though it would be years before the slogan was officially adopted. Clement was an evangelical-minded progressive who'd promised to bring Tennessee into the modern era. He set up his transitional office at the Hermitage Hotel and extended an invitation to his longtime friend James

6. Halberstam, *The Children*, 119.
7. Halberstam, 119.

Edwards to join him for lunch. Edwards was a former marine who'd fought in the Pacific before serving as a guard at the Fort Meade prisoner stockade.

"I'm planning a few reforms that some people are not gonna take kindly to, starting with mental health and prison reform," Clement told Edwards. "I'd like you to replace Swafford as warden of the Tennessee State Prison."[8]

Sensing Edwards's reluctance, Clement requested Edwards tour the prison with him to offer advice. They drove to the Gothic sandstone fortress on the banks of the Cumberland River (as depicted in *The Green Mile*). Built in 1898, the cells were bug-infested, six-by-eight-foot hovels with three walls and an iron trellis door. After the tour, Edwards told Clement, "You need Jesus Christ to do the job. Conditions are intolerable."[9]

Clement believed that Edwards's Christian faith and values made him the perfect crusader for the job. "Swafford's Graveyard," as the prison was known, had long been run by people who believed jails housed "only two types of prisoners, niggers and white trash, and both were treated with equal disdain when it came to physical punishment."[10]

By the time Gab returned to the station from the inauguration ceremony, Edwards had already settled into the warden's office and issued his first order: that the whipping post be taken down. He then cut to pieces the leather strap used to beat prisoners, sometimes to death. The compassionate warden thought rewarding well-behaved inmates would be more effective than trying to beat the misbehavior out of them. He scheduled entertainment and withheld it as punishment. The prison hosted talent shows, wrestling matches, and Grand Ole Opry stars. Eventually, Warden Edwards's philosophy was proven correct.

The prison chaplain, Pickens Johnson, had requested that Edwards attend a Sunday service. Edwards arrived at the prison chapel astounded by the magnificent a cappella harmony that drew him inside. The following day, Edwards requested the records of the singers he'd heard: inmates Ed Thurman, William Steward, Marcel Sanders, John Drue, and Johnny Bragg, all noted for good behavior. Edwards told Clement how uplifted he'd felt listening to gospel singers. He wanted the governor to hear it himself. When Clement "went to the

8. Jay Warner, *Just Walkin' in the Rain* (Los Angeles: Renaissance Books, 2001), 65.
9. Warner, 66.
10. Warner, 43.

prison and saw the group perform in the auditorium, he was overwhelmed by the beauty of their harmony and the sincerity in song."[11] The benevolent governor, ever mindful of budgetary concerns, viewed the "Prisonaires" as a way to promote prison reform *and* Tennessee music. Soon the inmate singers were performing at gubernatorial social events. Ted Jarrett met the Prisonaires when the warden brought them to WSOX. Local record producer Jim Bulliet sold Sam Phillips on the idea of recording them.

On June 1, Bulliet drove the group, along with an armed guard, to Memphis. The jailbirds had practiced by singing into metal buckets. At the studio they sang their hearts out, but not well enough to satisfy Sam's critical ear. He felt Johnny Bragg had an enunciation problem. Sam took a lunch break, and while he was out, providence walked in. A teenager stopped by to inquire about booking a recording session and overheard Bragg and Bulliet discussing the enunciation problem. The teen volunteered to help. For an hour, the boy worked with Johnny. When Sam returned, they resumed the session, this time with the boy mouthing the words as Johnny sang them. When they had two songs worthy of distribution, they thanked the kid and asked his name.

"Presley," the boy replied. It would be several more years before Sam recorded the young man and the world would come to know him by his first name: Elvis.

The session wrapped at 8:30. The men were returned to prison, weary but joyful.

Gab watched the Prisonaires perform "Just Walkin' in the Rain" at an Exchange Club luncheon in the Hermitage Hotel. He told Gene that Phillips was about to strike gold—again.

Meanwhile, Hoss was given an afternoon show, *Take Five*. The live broadcast aired afternoons from 3:00 to 5:00. At 5:30, he returned to the air with the news. On Fridays he did a sports show, and when stock car racing resumed, he returned to Speedways as the track announcer.

Nancy had grown tired of her friends' admiration of Hoss. Rarely a day would pass without someone expressing adoration for the charming Belle Meade prince who'd become, among his many other duties, a beauty pageant

---

11. Warner, 75.

judge. Frequently, he'd arrive home after midnight reeking of liquor, chitlins, and cheap perfume. Nancy had reached her boiling point.

"My friends think you're Prince Charming. If only they knew you're more like Cinderella; at midnight you turn into an asshole."

"Thanks for the swell idea," Hoss said, slurring his words. "I need a better word, though. Censors won't allow asshole. What else do you call me? Oh, yeah. Nincompoop."

The next morning, Hoss suggested to Gab they run a prince or nincompoop contest.

"Most of *Take Five*'s listeners are housewives," Hoss said. "What if I asked them to send in comments about why their husband is a prince or a nincompoop?"

"And then what?" Gab asked. "A contest needs a winner and a prize. And we need to sell something. See, selling's how we stay in business."

"Yeah. I get it." Hoss stood to leave.

"Hold up, Hoss. It's a good idea. You just haven't thought it through. What'd make Nancy feel like she'd married Prince Charming—instead of you?"

"I don't know. Nice vacation, second honeymoon maybe?"

"Let's work on that."

As a prize for the best essay, Gab arranged for a week's stay in Miami, sightseeing tour, night on the town, matched pair of luggage, and complete outfits for the winning couple. He suggested the contestants write not only why they considered their husband a prince or a nincompoop but why he needed a vacation. A few newspaper reporters served as judges.

In early July, Hoss announced the contest winner, then hurried to Speedways Racetrack to introduce the between-race entertainers, WLAC's country musicians, Big Jeff and his Radio Playboys, and the Prisonaires. Hoss was impressed by the Prisonaires' lead vocalist, Johnny Bragg.

"Who wrote 'Walkin' in the Rain'?" Hoss asked Johnny.

"Me and another inmate," Johnny replied. "We recorded it in Memphis."

"You're a talented songwriter. When the record's released, I'll play it. We don't normally play race records during the day, but I'll play yours," Hoss said.

"We's already on WSM and WSOX, but that ain't gonna get us to the top. Onliest Gene Nobles's at your station can. Ever'body listens at him."

"I know," Hoss said. "I'm hoping to take over Gene's time slot when he retires."

Time slots were how announcers went from section player to concertmaster.

On July 28, Gab and Hoss, along with their wives, attended a party for the movie star Faye Emerson. The men entertained Faye with funny stories from the prince or nincompoop contest.

"Letters from husbands were the best," Gab said. "Mostly, they attempted to defend themselves, but instead we came away thinking calling them 'nincompoop' was being too kind."

"For example?" Faye asked.

"Well, one wrote, 'I wouldn't interrupt so much if she'd ever shut the hell up.'"

Faye joined Hoss on air the next day to weigh in on the prince or nincompoop premise.

The month of July ended with one of the worst days in Gab's life. He'd always been positive, a guy who didn't see a half-full glass—he saw a refillable glass with room for whatever else he wanted. Truman summoned Gab to his office on the thirty-first. Gab assumed his boss wanted to wish him a nice vacation, as Gab was scheduled to leave for Florida the following day. He hoped he'd hear the good news he'd been anticipating—his move to WLAC-TV upon his return.

"Now, Blackie, you know how grateful I am for all you've done," Truman began. "Without you, I doubt I'd be a millionaire today."

Gab didn't like the sound of this.

"We agreed that if I got a television license, you'd run it. Unfortunately, since the sale to L & C, that decision's no longer mine."

"Wait. Did the FCC grant our application?"

"Sort of. To end the competition with WKDA, Tom Baker agreed to withdraw his application in exchange for he and Fred Beaman each buying 25 percent of WLAC-TV. They'll own half, L & C will own half, and Baker'll run it."

Gab believed Baker'd had it in for him ever since Truman agreed to Gab's race music idea. Gene had speculated Baker left the station and launched WKDA in protest.

"Look, I told Paul and Gil you'd been promised that job and that you were the brains behind our profits. I told them they needed to make you a generous offer to stay. I just felt you should know before the press release goes out next week. I didn't want it to catch you by surprise and have it ruin your vacation."

Gab wondered if this had anything to do with the partnership offer he'd received from a local ad agency. Maybe word of the deal was already on the streets. Gab was uncharacteristically at a loss for words. "Thanks for telling me," he said as he stood to leave.

Truman's son waited in the hallway. "I hope you stay," Jimmy Ward said sincerely. "Father says you're the only person who can train me to take over here."

Gab knew the boy meant well, yet Jimmy's comment added insult to injury. He couldn't help but wonder if Truman was keeping Gab at the radio station for Jimmy or if Baker had objected to Gab running the television sales department. He left the office immediately after the meeting. Not wanting to spoil their vacation, Gab didn't share this news with Christine. Normally she would notice when he wasn't his usual self, but she was preoccupied with vacation preparations. Gab forced himself to look on the bright side. He'd leave for Florida in the morning and get to see Buddy and his newborn son, Chris. Buddy had just returned from Korea. Gab couldn't wait to hear about Buddy's adventures. Following dinner, Gab settled into his recliner to watch *Cavalcade of Sports*. He had nodded off when a loud knock on the door jolted him awake. Gab opened the door to a man in a Western Union uniform, holding an envelope.

"You E. G. Blackman?" he asked.

"Yep." Gab signed for the telegram, stepped inside, opened the envelope and read: *DEEPLY REGRET TO ADVISE YOUR NEPHEW ENS SAMUEL I. ROGERS, JR. USN DIED THIS HOSP 1:58 PM 31 JULY RES OF INJURIES IN PLANE CRASH.*[12]

The news of Buddy's sudden death hit Gab like a falling oak tree. His knees buckled. He loved Buddy as dearly as his own children. He moved to the couch and let the tears flow. The phone rang. Gab ignored it.

"Daddy?" Gab looked up to see his precious daughter, Gayle, come down

---

12. US Navy to E. G. Blackman, telegram, July 31, 1953.

the steps. She was in a robe with a towel on her head. "Daddy? You gonna answer that?"

Gab glanced at the phone on the stand beside him but didn't touch it. "Where's your mother?" Finally, the annoying ringing stopped.

"Fixin' to take a bath. What's the matter?"

Christine came to the stairs. "Go get dressed, Gayle. We gotta go to Clara's."

"Now?" Gayle said, glancing between her mother and father. "Why?"

Gab wiped his tears on his sleeve. "Do it, sweetheart. We'll explain on the way."

Gab met Christine at the newel post and wrapped his arms around her. "You heard about Buddy?" she asked. "Clara called. She's devastated."

Gab showed her the telegram. "He'd listed me as next of kin."

The vacation was canceled. Christine helped her sister Clara with the funeral arrangements. Tuesday, while Clara and Christine met to go over the details at First Lutheran Church, Gab swung by the station to collect Buddy's letters. He wanted to quote Buddy directly during his comments at the funeral. At the station, he discovered Hoss and B.B. in his office.

"Replaced me already, have you, Hoss?" Gab teased.

"Sorry, Blackie. Didn't think you'd be in, what with the funeral."

"I just came by to get something. Give me a sec, then you can have my desk." Gab riffled through his index card drawer.

"Blackie's nephew was a navy fighter pilot who flew dangerous missions over Korea," Hoss told B.B. "He just made it home only to crash on the runway in Jacksonville."

"I'm so sorry, Blackie," B.B. said.

Gab pulled out the small rubber-banded collection of letters. "He lived with me for a while. I couldn't love him more if he's my own."

"I understand better'n you could imagine," B.B. said. "Them from him?"

"Uh-huh," Gab said as he unfolded a letter. "Between dropping bombs and dodging MIGs, he'd order records from Randy's. Lots of navy guys did."

"Any of mine?" B.B. asked.

"Probably, but not in this one. Here, he orders Frankie Laine."

"The blue-eyed soul singer," B.B. exclaimed. "He's awright."

Gab handed the letter to Hoss. "Do me a favor. Since it's about time for you to go on air, play something Buddy ordered here and dedicate it to his family."

"You got it, boss."

When Hoss left, B.B. asked Gab about Buddy. Gab shared tales of Buddy's experiences and read excerpts from a letter. He showed B.B. a photograph Buddy had taken of Gab holding a huge string of fish, most caught by Buddy.

"That was taken when we lived by the river. The river rats shared their tricks with him and afterward, he caught fish like there's no tomorrow." Gab felt the sting of his own words—all Buddy's tomorrows were now in the memories of those who loved him.

"You know what that picture puts into my mind?" B.B. asked.

"Fried catfish and hush puppies?"

"Well, that too. Was thinkin' how us bluesmen was swimmin' upstream, gettin' nowhere, till y'all opened the sluice gate."

Hoss's voice came over the hallway speaker: "All of us at WLAC want to express our condolences to the family of Korean War veteran and navy pilot, Sam Rogers Jr. Wheels up to heaven, Buddy. This one's for you."

Hoss had selected Frankie Laine's "That Lucky Old Sun." *An ideal choice*, Gab thought as he listened and couldn't hold back his tears. He reached for his handkerchief, then remembered he'd given it to Christine. B.B. handed Gab his. When the song ended, Gab dabbed his eyes, then reached across the desk to return it. Rather than take the handkerchief, B.B. wrapped his hands around Gab's to hold them. Gab felt a heartfelt empathy flow from B.B.'s hands to his own.

Gab wasn't prone to melancholia, yet Buddy's death hit him hard. He'd championed blues music, but until Gab experienced a bout of the blues himself, he hadn't fully comprehended what solace WLAC's revolutionary programming provided to the disenfranchised, lonely, ill, or brokenhearted souls who couldn't sleep. In their despair, Gene, John, and Hoss kept these listeners company while B.B.'s music gave voice to their sorrow and offered comfort.

After Buddy's funeral, Gab went back to work with renewed purpose. He looked to add a gospel preacher to the broadcast and eventually settled on C. L. "Frank" Franklin. It was on WLAC that Franklin introduced his daughter Aretha to the world.

"Tonight, I'm not gonna preach," Franklin said. "I'm gonna introduce my daughter, and she can sing." Aretha sang "Never Grow Old."

As Gab listened to the gospel song, he reached into his wallet and pulled out the telegram notifying him of Buddy's death. He held it in his hands as he gave thanks for having the good fortune to have known such a remarkable young man.

Gab carried the telegram in his wallet for the remaining thirty-six years of his life.

15

SIXTY-MINUTE MAN

I did cry. Cried, cried, oh, oh, cried. When you
move, well, it's just like startin' all over again.

—WILLIAM SOU BRIDGEFORTH

The Barons played their final games of the 1953 season at Chicago's Comiskey Park. The Kansas City Monarchs bested the Barons in the first two games to clinch the championship. Sou returned to Nashville weary. He'd grown tired of being banned from Southern stadiums' white-only box offices. Even at the Barons' home field, Sou had to wait outside while someone white tallied *his* money. If attendance was nine thousand, inevitably he'd be paid for seven thousand.[1] No wonder most Negro League owners turned to some illicit activity to support their team. Fortunately, Shorty had kept the numbers rolling so Sou could keep his ballplayers fed and—at least north of the Mason-Dixon Line—in a bed.

In early September, as Sou, Helen, and Shorty waited for Big Joe Turner to take the Era's stage, Shorty brought Sou up-to-date on current events, including indications that Tennessee's new governor would be soft on victimless crimes.

"Shoulda been here Sunday," Shorty said. "That new warden did a benefit

---

1. Randy Horcik, "They Might Have Been Heroes," *Nashville Scene*, May 2, 1996.

at the Dell. Inmates played baseball, followed by a variety show with the Prisonaires. Tickets was seventy-five cents and done near sold out."

Kat carried a tray of drinks to the table and weaseled her way into the conversation. "Wish we could book the Prisonaires. They play everywheres 'cept colored clubs, even the governor's mansion. Probably shocks the hell outta Clement's fancy-ass guests."

"Don't know why," Sou said. "Jail's called workhouse for a reason . . . free labor."

Kat leaned over and slid a drink toward Sou so her low-cut blouse would leave little to his imagination. "Y'all hear 'bout the inmate workin' in governor's kitchen who got sent to solitary for makin' moonshine and apple julep in the mansion's garage?"

Helen's patience ran out. "Kat, don't you have paying customers to wait on?"

Kat made a clawlike gesture with her fingers and left.

A few weeks later, the *Banner* resumed its harassment of Sou. "Battle misspelled my name again," Sou told Helen. He read aloud: "Theodore Acklen and W. S. (Sue) Bridgeforth. In the past, each of these men and several others have been tied in with the numbers racket and each of them has stated from time to time that he was 'out' of the numbers racket."[2]

"His facts is right. You told him you quit for good, now you're runnin' again. Maybe he thinks you played him."

"Kat says Stahlman's got it in for me and won't let up till I'm in the workhouse."

"*Kat says!*" Helen snarked. "Maybe she's the snitch. Ever think of that?"

"Don't do me that-a-way, Funny." It hadn't dawned on Sou that Kat could be Battle's source, but anything was possible. The women had him in a pickle—Funny guarding home, Kat going for the steal.

On October 4, the *Sporting News* announced their choice of James "Junior" Gilliam Jr. as the National League's "Rookie of the Year." Sou was honored when Gilliam called to deliver the news personally. Junior was one of the high school athletes Sou had sponsored. When Gilliam started as the Dodgers' second baseman, replacing Jackie Robinson in the '53 World Series, he became the most successful of Sou's protégés.

2. Dick Battle, *Nashville Banner*, September 29, 1953, 2.

A week after the World Series, Sou and his team traveled to Virginia for an exhibition game against Roy Campanella's all-stars, including Gilliam. Then Campanella's stars followed them home to play the Negro American League's All-Stars at the Dell. Nashville gave Gilliam a hometown hero's welcome. Sou had known the Gilliams since his days as a bricklayer. They'd delivered the first stack of bricks Sou laid. The family had lived in a house near the river bottoms since 1910, and it had been flooded every year since. The unsanitary living conditions, combined with the grueling manual labor, resulted in most Gilliam men dying young. Junior's father had died at seventeen. Hence, Junior's grandmother, Mattie, felt bittersweet pride when Mayor West proclaimed October 12 "James Gilliam Day."

Mattie Gilliam had birthed seven sons and two daughters, yet on the day her grandson was honored, just a single son and daughter survived. After James ran away from the boardinghouse where he'd lived with his mother, Mattie had reared him as her own. She was a washerwoman who worked six backbreaking days a week for sixty years.

Sou arrived at the Dell early on James Gilliam Day. He'd long enjoyed watching the players warm up, and for a team owner, the warmup served a purpose. He'd scout players to consider acquiring. He watched Memphis Red Sox pitcher Charley Pride until a loudmouth drunk stumbling down the steps attracted Sou's attention.

"Junior!" the drunk screamed. "Junior Gilliam! You're *my* son! Ain't you?"

Sou glanced from the drunk to Gilliam. The quiet, gracious Gilliam snapped.

"You!" Gilliam screamed as he hurled a baseball toward the man. "You're the devil stepfather that put that bad scar on my momma's face, put me on the street hungry, with holes in my shoes and pants. Get away from me!" Security quickly threw the man out.

Mayor West arrived during the fifth inning. He presented Gilliam with the key to the city and a scroll commemorating James Gilliam Day.

"Your grandmother must be so proud," Sou told Gilliam when Junior showed him the scroll.

"Yeah," Gilliam said. "If only she could read this."

Sou kept business top of mind and put Charley Pride atop the list of players to acquire. The next season, Pride followed Goose Curry, Memphis's manager, to the Louisville Clippers. Word got to Sou that the Clippers were desperately in need of a team bus. Capitalizing on this tidbit of information, Sou offered Curry a Chevrolet bus in exchange for Pride's contract.

On May 23, 1954, Charley pitched his first game for Sou, allowing only three hits, to beat the Monarchs 5–1. Baseball provided a good distraction for Sou, as he was furious over the Capitol Hill Redevelopment project. The city announced an auditorium would be built on the corner where the New Era stood. Despite a lawsuit filed by merchants and property owners in protest, Sou knew before the year ended, eminent domain would take the Era. A top-tier entertainment venue, financed by tax dollars, would go up in its place.

People around town often said Sou had an uncanny ability to turn pennies into hundred-dollar bills. There was a kernel of truth to that. But what they failed to grasp was, as soon as the powers that be realized what he'd done, they'd take it and make it their own. Sou wondered how long before the government started playing numbers so it could profit from the lottery racket rather than the Black entrepreneurs who originated the game.

In late June, the team took a two-week road trip. Not all the players were fans of Charley Pride's singing on the bus, but Sou enjoyed it. He thought it helped ease the boredom while they traveled thousands of miles on bumpy two-lane highways, without air-conditioning, eating their bologna-and-cheese sandwiches and sleeping in their seats. After a grueling season, the team returned to Birmingham for their final game. Sou had "bought six dozen baseballs at a cost of ninety dollars. He didn't make enough from the sale of tickets to pay for the balls."[3] At least they won the championship.

August 31 found Sou at home confiding in Funny that he would dissolve the team. Now that the city had built a golf course for coloreds, he'd decided to switch sports and buy golf balls instead of baseballs. His decision to retire from baseball was essential because his club was empty.

"Where is everybody?" he asked.

"Billy Graham's in town," Shorty answered.

"What's that white preacher got to do with us?"

---

3. Randy Horick, *Nashville Scene*, May 2, 1996.

"He integrated his crusade and's got colored preachers," Kat explained. "He preaches on WLAC right before Randy's show, so most colored folks listen at him."

"Well, when's he gone?" Sou asked. "We need to replenish the coffers 'cause them city bulldozers'll be gunnin' for me any day."

"Ain't leavin' for weeks," Shorty said.

Stahlman hosted a luncheon at Belle Meade on September 11 for Rev. Graham. Governor Clement, Warden Edwards, and Attorney General J. Carlton Loser all attended. Afterward, the men went to the state pen to hear Graham preach to the inmates. Two days later, after Graham's newly redeemed sinners felt compelled to confess, Clement ordered the state patrol to "investigate allegations that local nightclub operators had bribed county officers."[4] Shortly after midnight, Sheriff Cartwright raided the Era along with five other clubs. Cartwright asked each club operator if they'd bribed officers. Each owner assured Cartwright that "they 'do not and have not' contributed to patrolmen in exchange for favors." The *Banner* quoted Cartwright saying that "he was inclined to believe the operators."[5]

Sou assumed that when the meddlesome preacher left, life would return to normal. It didn't. Instead, Sou was ordered to appear at the federal courthouse. He was charged with two counts of criminal information, for failing to purchase a gambling stamp and failing to register as a professional gambler. Sou hired the former US district attorney who'd been in office when the violations occurred, Ward Hudgins, to represent him. Hudgins assured Sou the sixty minutes he'd spent in custody would be all the time he'd serve.

A week later, the government added eight additional counts of attempting to evade excise taxes. Sou was the first person indicted under the new federal gambling tax statutes. And for the first time, Sou's name was correctly published in the *Banner*.

Locally, Sou's numbers game was a minor infraction. Somewhere between

---

4. Bob Battle, "Night Spot Operators Deny Bribes," *Nashville Banner*, September 14, 1954.
5. Battle.

a U-turn and a drunk driving arrest, which carried a fifty dollar fine. But this charge was federal, hence serious. And Graham fueled the fire, saying folks were "selling their souls to the devil for sex, thrills, and alcohol."[6]

Since WLAC broadcast Graham's show *Hour of Decision*, Gab was given VIP tickets to all of Graham's events. Randy Wood sponsored Gene's broadcast, which immediately followed Graham's Sunday night show. As a result, he'd become a devoted follower. Gab peddled Bibles before, during, and after Graham's broadcast and was selling nearly as many Bibles as records and baby chicks. The highlight of the events Graham invited Gab to was a Sunday golf outing at Bluegrass Country Club in Hendersonville. Graham played with Governor Clement, Randy, and another preacher, while Gab played a few foursomes behind. After the game, Randy grumbled he'd "played terrible."[7] Gab had enjoyed the day so much he considered joining Bluegrass. When the course opened, Gab had been offered a founder's membership, but with so many great courses near his home, he hadn't been interested. However, now that the Tennessee Valley Authority had dammed the Cumberland to create Old Hickory Lake, waterfront homesites near Bluegrass intrigued him. He missed the riverfront lifestyle.

Several years before, Gab had purchased Christine's childhood home. She'd claimed at the time that she wouldn't leave till she was carried out on a stretcher. But that was before the Supreme Court's school desegregation ruling. She now feared Gayle would attend school with coloreds and contract polio or some other dreaded disease. Christine's experiences at Bethlehem Settlement House had left her unreasonably fearful of germs and viruses. Gab didn't share her paranoia, yet he wasn't above using it to convince her to move to the waterfront.

On Saturday, September 18, Gab, Christine, and Gayle attended the grand opening of Hillsboro High School. The original building had burned down during Eddie's sophomore year, forcing his class to finish their education at

6. James Carty, "Shun Temptation, Grahman Urges," *Tennessean*, September 17, 1954, 12.
7. Joan Link, "Crusade Wives Fill Many Jobs," *Tennessean*, September 14, 1954.

Belmont. Eddie was now away at Tennessee Tech and Gayle was due to start her freshman year at Hillsboro on Monday.

Hoss was the emcee for the grand opening festivities. He introduced Pat Boone, a local Christian singer, who'd recently signed a recording contract with Randy, along with Dottie Dillard and Minnie Pearl. As Gab watched Boone's performance, he recalled how Gene had told him Randy planned to have Boone record covers of top R & B hits. Randy seemed to think Boone could do what Elvis did when he covered Arthur Crudup's "That's All Right Mama." Sam had speculated for years that he'd make a billion dollars if he could "find a white man who had the Negro sound and the Negro feel."[8]

Gab understood why Sam saw Elvis as this mythical Black-sounding white singer, but why Randy thought milquetoast Boone could do it, Gab hadn't a clue. Sam had come by the station with Elvis's record but had been unable to get Gene or John to play it. Hoss had a different perspective. Like Sam, Hoss believed music would bring the races together. He promoted Elvis on his afternoon show. Gab hadn't fully grasped the connection Sam and Hoss made between race music and integration until after he read an article in *Time* about the emergence of the Negro advertising market and its influence on race relations. Gab freely admitted music was something he'd never understand, but he certainly understood advertising. Because the airwaves couldn't be segregated, the marketplace would one day merge. And the proof was in the number of records John targeted for sale to coloreds that white teens ordered. First, they'd listen to the same music on the radio. Then they'd order the same records; they'd go to the same concerts, then the same movies until eventually segregation disappeared. Ultimately, so would discrimination. Hoss and Sam believed this was the power of music. To Gab, this was the power of advertising.

Sam brought Elvis to WLAC a few days later. He confided that his recording studio was bleeding cash and a hit was needed to bail him out. Gene and John were sympathetic, but they still wouldn't play Elvis's record. They suggested he try WSM. Gab was close to his WSM counterpart, Bud Wendell, and knew that Elvis couldn't walk into the capital of hillbillydom dressed like the truck driver he was.

---

8. Guralnick, *Sam Phillips*, 207.

"Don't take him looking like that," Gab said. "He needs to look like he belongs at the Opry stage." Gab called his clothier friend, Ralph Levy, who lent Elvis some snazzier clothes.

Even though Gab couldn't see Boone do an Elvis, he concluded Sam and Randy were two black-eyed peas in a green pod. Sam swore by his Black-sounding white teenage truck driver and Randy by his second-place-talent-show crooner. Only time would tell, Gab told Gene, whether Sam and Randy were just plain crazy—or crazy geniuses, like Gene.

At WSM, Sam managed to persuade the Opry to give Elvis a shot. On October 2, Elvis performed "Blue Moon of Kentucky" at the Ryman. They didn't offer him a return engagement.

Meanwhile, late the following evening, a trumpet player named Renald Richard drove Ray Charles to Nashville. On Sunday nights, Herman Grizzard filled the final broadcast hour with gospel music. When he aired "It Must Be Jesus," Ray and Renald sang along, reworking the lyrics from spiritual poetry to bawdy ballad. The following morning, Renald and Ray got together to compose their altered version of the spiritual. They titled the song, "I Got a Woman." Ray performed it in Nashville and recorded it in Atlanta a few weeks later. The record was released in December and "hit like an atom bomb."[9]

Kitty spent most of 1954 on tour. She'd started on the West Coast with Earl Bostic and headed to New Orleans in the fall. She came home to the Era in November and reconnected with Little Richard. One night after Sou closed the club, Bill Beasley borrowed some equipment from WLAC to record Kitty, Little Richard, and the New Era's house band. The songs "Lord Have Mercy" and "Sittin' Here Drinking Again" were also released in December.

When the ball dropped on New Year's 1955, no one—not Sou, Gab, Gene, John, Hoss, Mayor West, Governor Clement, not even the musicians—realized how much change was going to come as this new era dawned, the era now called civil rights.

---

9. Peter Guralnick, *Looking to Get Lost* (New York: Little, Brown, 2020), 39.

16

TUTTI FRUTTI

I was in heaven 'cause I was gonna finally
see this black man [John Richbourg] I had
listened to since childhood. Then I saw he
was a white man—I almost fainted.

—JACKEY BEAVERS

Sou took note of the shimmering icicles suspended from the lampposts and street signs at Fourth and Charlotte. The city's firehouses had created these ice sculptures, as if to remind onlookers that this smoldering wreck of a ruin had once been the dazzling Duncan Hotel, where the Vanderbilt family stayed when they visited the university, and once was home to a young inventor named Thomas Edison. The building was well into its dotage when Sou opened his first New Era Club inside the Duncan's hallowed walls. Demolition had been underway when the building burned to the ground on February 3, 1955. Sou anticipated the same city wrecking ball that demolished the location of the first New Era would soon come for his current club.

With his trial postponed due to the judge's illness, Sou solicited his uncle Nick's help to secure a new location. The city's urban renewal project had left few properties available for sale. Sou worried if sellers knew he was the buyer, with the trial looming, they could be reluctant to sell. He settled on a building at Twelfth and Charlotte—not an ideal location, a bit far from the hub of downtown, close to the noise of the railroad, yet hopefully far enough to avoid the landgrabbers inside city hall. The purchase contract and deed were issued in Nick's name, as were the contracts for renovations. Sou hoped to be fully operational by May 1, but to play it safe, he scheduled the grand reopening celebration for the Fourth of July. At Kitty's suggestion, Ivory Joe Hunter was booked to appear.

Kitty had learned a lot about jazz from Earl Bostic. Modern jazz versus Dixieland jazz had been a frequent topic during long bus rides. Kitty had been schooled on the Southern, New Orleans–style jazz, where saxophones in a jazz band were considered sacrilegious. On the other hand, Bostic, considered the "King of the Alto Sax," believed one couldn't play jazz *without* a sax.[1] One night over drinks at the Era, Kitty asked Hoss his opinion. Hoss presented the question to WLAC's resident Dixieland jazz aficionado, Papa John Gordy. Gordy ran white Nashville's version of the New Era—the Celtic Room—where Eddie Blackman and John Malone Jr. spent nearly every night when they were home from college.

Gordy claimed, "No self-respecting musician south of the Mason-Dixon Line would have a saxophone in a jazz band."[2] With Hoss's help, Gordy bet Bostic $5,000 in Confederate currency that his Dixielanders could outplay Bostic's orchestra. *Confederate currency!* These were fighting words. When Hoss added that no Negro musician or patron had ever been allowed in the Celtic, war was declared! Advertised as the "Battle of Jazz," the event sold out in hours. A second night was added, then a third. Nashvillians would have filled the club for weeks, but Bostic had other commitments.

Bostic's jazz militia marched into town as prepared for battle as any Green Beret ever was. And they played with the same gallantry as Steedman's Thirteenth Colored regiment displayed in 1864 on Peach Orchard Hill during the Battle of Nashville. Before Bostic left town, he told Sou his win at the Celtic toppled one more domino in segregation's long line of demarcation.

Sou agreed. "You won the battle, but not the war. We'll know we're

---

1. Eddie Jones, "$5,000 (Confederate) Riding On Coming Battle of Jazz," *Tennessean*, February 11, 1955, 10.
2. Jones, 10.

victorious over the Confederacy when those final dominoes—the monuments to the enslavers—fall. Until that time, those slave masters still dance on the graves of our grandparents."

In mid-February, Gab visited International Electronic Industries (IEI), a local company owned by James Pugh, a ham radio enthusiast, and Alan Holiday, a Peabody College chemistry professor. Pugh and Holiday had invented an "electrolytic capacitor used to manufacture the TR-1, America's first all-transistor miniature radio."[3] Gab had pitched Regency, the company that made the radio, on sponsoring a WLAC program. Since Regency couldn't keep up with demand, they weren't interested in advertising. Yet they were impressed with WLAC's ratings and arranged for Gab to tour Pugh's operation. A few months later, Pugh invited Gab to IEI's anniversary celebration, where TR-1s were given as party favors.

Gene had recently told Gab that Randy was offered a million dollars for his recording business, and as a stockholder, Gene would receive a financial windfall when Randy sold. Gene advised Gab he planned to retire then. The TR-1 would make the perfect gift to commemorate all they'd accomplished together, Gab thought. He returned to the station to present the radio to Gene. Together, they marveled at the ingenuity contained in the little red plastic box.

"Sure you don't want it yourself?" Gene said.

"Way I see it, no one deserves this more than you. I've made up my mind. I'm gonna build me a house on the lake, get a boat, and join Bluegrass. None of it woulda been possible without you. Smartest career decision of my life was coming here, working with you."

"Thanks, but targeting a colored audience and sellin' to 'em COD was your idea. I just executed it."

"Exactly. Ideas are worthless until someone executes 'em. Lots of folks probably had the *idea* of making a miniature radio, but Pugh made this thing possible."

Gene scanned the radio's instruction booklet. "It's gonna change everything."

"How's Randy's negotiation coming?" Gab asked.

---

3. Albert Cason, "Nashville Firm Plays Vital Electronics Role," *Tennessean*, February 6, 1955.

"He wants to hit a million records sold a month before he sells. He's close. The big shots in New York and LA hate that this little nobody from Gallatin outsells them."

"Hope he doesn't hit the bull's-eye soon. Don't know how I'd manage without you."

"Get a new Lothario to mesmerize the housedress brigade and move Hoss to my slot."

"It's the Lothario that worries me. Can you imagine? We can't have some poor gal fall down the elevator shaft in the new building. With all the drunks we got here, I told Dudley he best put us on the first floor when we move," Gab said in reference to the thirty-one-story skyscraper L & C was building across the street.

"Dudley may not understand our audience and music, but liability, he gets."

A few weeks later, Gab finally made a trip to Memphis. Hillsboro High was playing in the state basketball championship and Gayle's class was going to cheer on the team. While Gayle and her classmates toured Memphis's Cotton Row to learn about the hardscrabble lives of cotton pickers, Gab visited George Long, the owner of the J. Strickland Company.

Strickland manufactured White Rose Petroleum Jelly as well as haircare items specifically formulated for Black hair: Royal Crown Hairdressing, Hoyt's Hair and Scalp Conditioner, Silky Straight. After seeing Strickland's ads in *Ebony*, Gab had pitched Long on Hoss's haircare shtick. George Long now joined Randy Wood, Ernie Young, and Mrs. Carter of the baby chicks fame as Gab's top-grossing advertisers. Gab and Long discussed how the new transistor radio would expand radio's ad reach. Long agreed to sponsor six nights of programs.

As Gab had predicted, WLAC's advertising revenue increased in direct correlation to the number of transistor radios sold. So did the complaints. Gab received calls from every faction of the Morality Police. For years the complaints had been a steady trickle. However, since the *Brown v. Board* ruling, complaints had skyrocketed. Most came from White Citizens' Councils, organized groups of segregationist parents who believed the music and commentary broadcast on WLAC late nights corrupted young listeners' morals. Several callers insinuated Gab or his jocks could be jailed, reminding him Mae West had been jailed for corrupting the youth with a provocative Broadway play.

"Which made her career," Gab responded. "Thanks for the idea, I might have one of my guys pull the same publicity stunt." Gab was pretty sure sooner or later one of his guys would end up in jail. He only hoped it was for something they could put a positive spin on.

The Nashville Council of Church Women also took issue with his broadcast. Even Christine complained after she heard Eddie sing "Work with Me Annie." Christine's bridge and garden club friends insisted songs with lyrics that promoted premarital or extramarital sex should be banned from public airwaves. When Christine realized her husband couldn't be persuaded to censor the jocks, she introduced her Christian Council friends to Gil Dudley, who agreed with the ladies. Shortly thereafter, WLAC became the first radio station in the country to create a self-censorship board. Christine and her friends declared victory when "Work with Me Annie," "Honey Love," and "Get out of the Car" were the first songs banned.

In early May, Randy recorded Boone's pop version of Fats Domino's "Ain't That a Shame." Hoss debuted the record on his afternoon broadcast. John continued his ban of white covers of R & B hits, insisting WLAC at night had become the "colored town square" and playing Black music hijacked by whites was disrespectful to his audience. Gene made an exception for Randy's covers, as he was part owner of the company and had a vested interest in the record's success.

Gab had immense respect for John, whose opinion on the white covers issue was indicative of his exceptional character. They'd worked together for years, and Gab had no idea how John kept it all together. John's wife, Lilli, was perennially unhappy. She complained about being stuck at home with children yet refused to learn to drive. When things got really bad at home, John's schedule was rearranged to allow him breaks to feed his kids and get them to and from school.

In mid-May, Dudley told Gab he wanted Hoss to emcee Steeplechase. Nine years had passed since Hoss had heckled patrons in the VIP boxes over the Monkey Simon Mule Race, and to Gab's knowledge, Hoss hadn't returned. With Dudley serving as this year's chairman, he insisted his popular afternoon announcer man the broadcast booth.

"I don't know, Gil. You got a mule in the race?"

"A mule? Hell no! I'm riding Fighter Jet in the Truxton."

When Gab told Hoss that Gil requested they run the Steeplechase broadcast booth, Hoss complained. "Guess this makes us official Bourbon Hypocrites."

"I wouldn't go that far," Gab said. "I'm no fan of Steeplechase either. Back when I tapdanced for nickels, the old timers'd sneer at me saying, 'Look how far the mighty Blackmans have fallen.' After they built a track and started racing horses, gambling became 'the downfall of the Blackman family.'"[4]

Hoss announced Andrew Pratt had won the best costume in the mule race. Referring to Andrew's red gingham dress and flower-embellished hat, Hoss's voice blared over the loudspeaker: "Andrew, your look's worthy of a *Vogue* cover." Responding to comments from the VIP section, he added, "I stand corrected. An *Ebony* cover."

Hoss switched off the microphone and turned back to Gab. "Can you imagine riding a mule in a dress? Chaps my cheeks that colored jocks have to race mules. Anna's oldest was a hell of a horseman. Taught me to ride. Here, they'd make him play the fool on a mule. Pass me that whiskey, Blackie!" Gab poured a single swallow into a jigger and passed it instead.

After Hoss announced that Gil Dudley and Fighter Jet had won the Truxton purse, Gil invited Gab and Hoss to his victory party. Later that afternoon they were served mint and apple juleps beside the pool in which Fighter Jet's horseshoe-shaped pink rose victory bouquet floated. Gab monitored Hoss's drinks. After the fourth, he called Nancy.

"Come get him and make him nap. He needs to be sober to emcee the Hunt Ball."

Hoss was normally immune to Belle Meade's Old South reenactments, yet the Hunt Ball gave him plenty of ammunition to mock the Bourbons. "You shoulda seen the strutting peacocks," Hoss told Gab. "The men wore pink coattails with boutonnieres the color of their horses' silks while the women could wear only black or white. The walls were covered in 'saucy foxes, glittering hunt crests, and silk flags.'[5] Only thing missing was Hattie McDaniel fannin' the ladies."

---

4. Maury County Historical Society, *Historic Maury County, Tennessee, in Pictures* (Columbia, Tennessee, 1966), 11.
5. Betty Banner, "Betty Banner Dances At Brilliant Hunt Ball," *Nashville Banner*, May 16, 1955, 14.

On May 26, Roy Hamilton, Erskine Hawkins, and LaVern Baker arrived to headline the "Biggest Rhythm and Blues Show of '55" at the Ryman. In addition to the stars, the show featured the Drifters, Willie Mabon, Jimmy Reed, Della Reese, and others. The previous evening they'd performed two sold-out shows in Memphis, one for a Black audience and another for a white audience.

Hoss was on air with *Today's Top Five* when Della Reese and Roy, LaVerne, Erskine, and Clyde McPhatter of the Drifters stopped by. Roy joined Hoss in the booth to plug his hits, "Unchained Melody" and "You'll Never Walk Alone." Hoss would have preferred to feature Clyde's "Sixty-Minute Man," one of Hoss's personal favorites, but that was strictly an after-hours tune. When *Top Five* wrapped, Hoss joined the impromptu party in the big studio.

When he entered, he caught sight of Della Reese. One look at her and the breath left his lungs. As he came closer, she beckoned him with her musky mix of perfume, hairdressing, and sweat. From the stylish crown of her sexy curls to the polished red tips of her sandaled toenails, everything about Della was utterly irresistible. And the way she looked at him, with one perfectly groomed brow arched, it was as if her gaze shot a dagger into his heart and left him wounded and aching.

"I apologize for staring, Della," he said by way of introduction. "You've no idea how many times I've held *A Date with Della* in my hands. I couldn't help but compare you in the flesh to your album cover."

Della took his hands in hers and guided them to her shoulders. "Feel the difference?" The energy that passed between them was kinetic. It seemed to reverberate throughout the studio, changing the chemistry.

Gab felt it and moved to put distance between them. "Della, John wants to speak with you about how you'd like to be introduced tonight," he said.

As Della walked away, Hoss said, "Now *that's* a woman to be reckoned with."

"But not by you!" Gab warned.

John had been hired to emcee the concert that night and the next night when the Blues Show of '55 moved onto Chattanooga. After the musicians left, Hoss volunteered to do the Chattanooga show.

"Keep the money. I'll travel so you don't have to leave your kids," Hoss offered.

"Thanks. But the family's going with me."

By the time John reached Chattanooga, he wished he'd taken Hoss up on the offer. He and Lilli fought all the way to Chattanooga and then again all the way back. When they neared home, Lilli had a meltdown. While their children cowered in the backseat, she screamed, "I'm sick of all you! I wish I'd never married or had kids!"

John had reached his limit. "If you're so damn miserable, leave!" Later, John asked Lilli what life she'd rather have.

"The life I had in New York before you."

John agreed to buy Lilli a new wardrobe at Cain-Sloan's and a bus ticket to New York.

Three days later, with the children in the back seat, John drove Lilli to the bus station.

Sixty-seven years later, when John and Lilli's daughter, Ellen, was asked what she remembered about that day, she recalled, "Her shoes. I remember her wearing these new slingbacks Daddy bought her for her new life. She walked away from us in fancy new shoes."

Sou was convicted on four counts of failure to pay excise taxes and one count of failure to buy a federal gambling tax stamp. Fortunately, his sentencing was postponed until after the July Fourth weekend. Helen tried to put on a brave face in the courthouse. The courtroom fell silent when Judge William E. Miller issued his ruling. Sou was "fined $5,000 and sentenced to four eighteen-month prison terms and a one-year term for failure to purchase a $50 gambling stamp, and ordered to pay the syndicate's ten-percent wagering tax on a gross 1952 income of $371,530.16 from the numbers racket."[6] Miller asked Sou if he had anything to say.

"I just can't see where there is any willful intent here (to evade the tax) to save my life, your honor," Sou replied.[7]

When Sou's attorney announced he'd file an appeal to the Sixth Circuit

6. Gene Graham, "Numbers Kingpins Get Fines, Sentences," *Tennessean*, July 7, 1955, 19.

7. Graham, *Tennessean*.

in Cincinnati within ten days, Miller agreed to let Sou remain free, pending appeal.

Helen was relieved Sou wasn't going to jail—yet. She felt this jury had failed to understand that playing the numbers was a way of life in colored communities. That playing the lottery provided poor folks with something they generally otherwise lacked—*hope*.

Hoss had watched Little Richard perform at the Era numerous times. When Gene received a pre-release of Richard's record "Tutti Frutti," he loved it so much, he called John, Hoss, and Gab into the studio for a listen.

"His original lyrics were much better," Hoss said. Gene played the record again and Hoss sang the Era's version over the recording: "Tutti Frutti, good booty. If it's tight, it's alright, if it's greasy, makes it easy." He rubbed his index fingers and thumbs together and added, "Greasy makes it easy. 'Cause you know, just a touch means so doggone much."

"That's a spiel that'd have hair grease flying off the shelves," Gab speculated. "What're the chances of Little Richard pitching Royal Crown?"

"Pretty good, I 'spect," Gene said.

When Little Richard heard Gene proclaim on air that "Tutti Frutti" is gonna be a huge hit, he called Gene.

"Next time you're nearby, stop in," Gene told Richard. "Boss'll hire you as a pitchman."

Gene and Richard recorded a commercial for Royal Crown Hairdressing, inspired by the spiel Hoss ad-libbed while filling in for Gene. When Hoss announced on air, "Royal Crown, just a touch means so much. Pick some up on your way out for on your way in," the switchboard had exploded with complaints.

It was commonly understood in advertising and broadcast circles that WLAC dominated late-night programming, with an unprecedented fifteen million nightly listeners. Yet even Gab was surprised by how many white teenagers tuned their transistors to 1510 to listen covertly "under the covers." The teens' parents were okay with Pat Boone's "Tutti Frutti," but the "under the covers" crowd preferred Little Richard's original recording. WLAC's mail-room noted teens ordered both. Boone's would be shipped to their home, while Richard's went to a friend's or "their auntie's house."[8] Boone's record was for display. Richard's was played.

In November, the duplicate orders helped Randy reach his goal of a million records sold in a single month. He intended to sell his company, though he'd concluded the next step in maximizing the value would be to move the business from Tennessee.

Little Richard had reached a similar conclusion and had returned to Macon, Georgia, where he'd become a star attraction. Whenever he was indisposed or overbooked, Richard hired James Brown to impersonate him and "the audience didn't know the difference."[9] Serving as Richard's understudy helped Brown hone his showmanship skills, but he wanted to be a star in his own orbit. And he knew WLAC was where to go to make it happen.

"I didn't have any sort of strategy figured out, but I did know which radio station I wanted . . . WLAC in Nashville," Brown said, as "WLAC was all we ever listened to."[10]

WLAC was strategic, because unlike most jocks, Gene, John, and Hoss actually listened to dubs and demos. Often, only after they aired a demo was the record pressed. As a result, WLAC virtually presided over the development of R & B. Other popular jocks, including Alan Freed and Wolfman Jack, copied their playlists. According to Hoss, "Alan Freed called Gene Nobles at night and ask him what to play."[11]

When Brown delivered the demo that launched his career, it wasn't his first attempt at WLAC. In 1952, security had refused to let him into the station, so he'd waited outside for John or Gene to emerge. Gene spoke to James but passed on his gospel demo. Brown then waited for John. When the station signed off, Brown asked the security guard when John would leave.

8. "Rock and Roll; Renegades; Interview with Hoss Allen (Part 1 of 2)," Open Vault, https://openvault. wgbh.org/catalog/V_00F1B92CD5EA469EAD5EF13B601F7AEC.
9. Smith, *Pied Pipers*, 55.
10. James Brown and Bruce Tucker, *James Brown, the Godfather of Soul* (London: Fontana/Collins, 1988), 52.
11. "Rock and Roll; Renegades; Interview with Hoss Allen (Part 1 of 2)," Open Vault, https://openvault. wgbh.org/catalog/V_00F1B92CD5EA469EAD5EF13B601F7AEC.

The guard pointed to a tall white man on the sidewalk. "Just missed him."

"That old white guy's John R?" Brown exclaimed. John had walked right past him, because, like most WLAC listeners, James assumed John was Black. John wasn't interested in Brown's gospel tune either, yet he offered to listen to anything else James submitted.

"He took more interest in me than anybody else did, which is why he will always be number one in my book when it comes to disk jockeys,"[12] Brown stated in his biography.

Neither Gene nor John gave Brown the big break that launched his career. That honor went to Hoss. In February 1956, while filling in for Gene, Hoss pulled "Please, Please, Please" from Gene's reject pile and broadcast the unusual gospel hybrid. John, having remembered the singer, stayed on the record until it hit. James Brown, the young man who'd later come to be known as the "Godfather of Soul," was grateful and, years later, went out of his way to repay John's kindness.

12. Brown, 53.

17

ROLLIN' STONE

Many civic leaders below the Mason-Dixon are of
the opinion that [Negro radio] will do more for
lowering Jim Crow barriers than flowery oratory.

—*PITTSBURGH COURIER*

By 1956, Tennessee's governor was on the Democratic Party's radar as a future
senator or vice president. When President Truman visited Tennessee the year
before, he'd encouraged Frank Clement to seek higher office. During his visit,
the Prisonaires had entertained Truman and his daughter, Margaret. She had
even accompanied the singing inmates on the piano.

After four Prisonaires were pardoned and released, the group's name was
changed to the Marigolds. Johnny Bragg recruited a new inmate-member, Hal
Hebb, Bobby's older brother. The Hebb family had advanced from playing
spoons and washboards on street corners to performing at the Opry, a Black
Nashville version of the von Trapp family singers. Ernie expanded his recording
businesses, creating an R & B label, Excello, with Ted and John as producers. John produced the Marigolds' "Rollin' Stone" record for Excello. One of
Excello's biggest fans was a British teenager named Mick Jagger. He regularly
ordered records from WLAC and later named his band after Muddy Waters's
R & B song of the same name.

When Sou watched his house band perform "Rollin' Stone" at his club, he hoped that he wouldn't someday watch the original singers perform it in the state pen auditorium. His attorney had assured him he'd win the circuit court appeal. Until that happened, he couldn't relax.

On March 5, Sou's anxiety soared to the bleachers when tipped off bettors hit a jackpot destined to break every numbers banker. Nashvillians had played the numbers the same way since Bill James brought the lottery to town during the Depression. A banker would bet a player they couldn't guess the last three digits of the butter and egg closing quote from the Chicago commodities market published weekdays in the *Banner*. On this day, local gambling bankers paid 600-to-1 odds for a correct guess. Unfortunately, no one advised the bankers that the Department of Agriculture ordered a change in how the quotes were reported. Round numbers rather than digits were ordered, making "000" the last three numbers of the March 5 quotation. This information was closely held and kept secret from the numbers bankers. However, someone had tipped off local bettors. Naturally, Sou suspected Jimmy Stahlman.

He explained the consequences to Kat. "For every $175 bet on triple zero, we owe the winner $105,000. It'll bankrupt all of us."

"What're you gonna do? Paper's out soon and they'll be showin' up to collect."

"Me, Shorty, Teddy Acklen, and the other runners are gonna meet outta town. We'll be back soon's we figure it out," Sou said. "Everybody's closing for the day. I'm going home to warn Funny and pack. We gotta hightail it out 'fore someone shoots us."

"Where're y'all going?" Funny asked Sou when he explained the situation.

"Better if you don't know."

Funny was furious Sou left her at home with the fallout. She unplugged her phone, which brought "winners" to the door. She considered going to her aunt's, but Nashville was such a small town, she couldn't stay hidden long. She had no idea where Sou had gone, and the damn man took his pearl-handled revolver with him.

The runners bankers met in Kentucky to discuss a solution.

"Tipped off bettors ain't winners, they's cheaters," Shorty said.

"The Feds done it to ruin us," Teddy said.

"Let's refund all bets from yesterday," Sou said. "Can't keep the losers' bets if we don't pay the winners.'"

"They ain't winners!" Shorty reiterated.

After hours of discussion, it was decided that each house would refund triple zero bets on the basis that the tipoff made the bet "illegal."[1]

Sou returned home to an icy reception. He tried to reassure Helen, but she hadn't slept and was furious. "Did you notice the police parked across the street while I's gone?"

"I figured they'd bet triple zero and wanted their money like everybody else."

"Funny, you know they's on the payroll. I had 'em there to guard you and the baby."

She stormed out of the house and went to her aunt's.

Sou returned to the club, where Kat was overly interested. When Sou told Shorty that Funny wasn't speaking to him, Kat spread the *Tennessean* on the table, nestled beside him, and pointed to the headline: "Bettors Get Tip On '000' Break Numbers Game."

Sou scanned the article, then was distracted by an adjacent headline: "1st Grade Plan for Mixing Seen." Sou read the report that Nashville schools would integrate "next fall, starting with first grade and moving up the grades in subsequent years."[2]

Sou hoped he wouldn't be in the state pen when school integration occurred, as it was something he'd have to see to believe. Recently, Z. Alexander Looby had asked if Sou would send Harriett to a white school. Sou wouldn't. However, he left those decisions to Helen. She was an incredible mother who'd achieved the impossible. She'd raised Harriett in a segregated, racist community without their daughter even realizing racism existed. Harriett lived in the sheltered bubble of "Black Belle Meade," where Helen planned to keep Harriett until she left for college. To enroll their daughter in a white school now would be akin to throwing her under the school bus.

One night at the Elks Club, Sou asked Charles Johnson, the president of Fisk University, what he expected would happen when Tennessee integrated the schools.

1. "Numbers Racketeers Resume Business," *Tennessean*, March 21, 1956.
2. Gene Graham, "1st Grade Plan For Mixing Seen," *Tennessean*, March 8, 1956.

"I'm not worried about the ordinary white people," Johnson told Sou. "I'm worried about the Bourbons. In this state they're the ones who are unreconstructed."[3]

"The Bourbon Hypocrisy," Sou said. "Jimmy Stahlman, John Sloan, and that bunch."

"Precisely," Johnson agreed.

After a week of stone-cold silent treatment from Funny, Sou gave in to Kat's advances and immediately regretted it. Kat began plotting how she might become the next Mrs. Bridgeforth. She might have had better luck if not for the unexpected trauma a few weeks later that threw Funny back into Sou's arms.

From the perspective of the dark-eyed junco, the area along North Jefferson Street known as Black Belle Meade would appear a happy, peaceful, matriarchal society, where a daily ballet of women in housedresses tended spring flowers, pushed baby carriages, watched toddlers ride tricycles, and minded students studying on expansive front porches. It was unexpected and frightening, then, when this domestic tranquility was interrupted by a squeal of tires, women screaming, and a child's cry. Helen bolted outside to discover Harriett had been hit by a car. Helen called her aunt, a funeral director, who drove her ambulance to the scene, picked up Harriett, and transported her to Vanderbilt Hospital. Sou rushed to the hospital to be with his wife and daughter. Funny fell into his arms. She was comforted. He was forgiven.

A few weeks later, with Harriett in a cast and on crutches, Helen stopped at H. G. Hill for a few groceries. She rarely shopped in white grocery stores, but it was getting late. She knew the market where she regularly bought steaks would be closed by the time she reached Jefferson. Harriett was hungry and Helen was tired. She grabbed what she needed for Sou's dinner, plus a few luxury products Black grocers didn't carry. The checker tallied the total: $21.20. Helen had one $20 bill in her wallet, which she gave the clerk.

"I'll write a check for the difference."

"Hill don't take checks from *coloreds*," the cashier said. "Put somethin' back."

"I don't wanna *put something back*," Helen argued as she scribbled on a check. "You got my $20. Here's the $1.20. Call your manager."

3. Halberstam, *The Children*, 213.

"He ain't comin' to *you*. Take that to the cage and see if they'll accept it."

Harriett hobbled behind Helen as she went to the service counter to speak to the manager. "I've spent $21.20, gave the cashier twenty, and here's the check for the difference."

Helen argued with the manager until he agreed to call her bank. After a brief phone conversation with a banker, he jotted Helen's driver's license on the check, followed by "Colored woman in cream colored jacket and skirt, brown belt, brown handbag, brown and beige shoes. WITH CRIPPLED CHILD." Helen never again shopped at H. G. Hill.

A few nights later, Helen noticed traffic backed up on Jefferson Street. She surveyed the long line of cars, noting nearly all were full of white teenagers. She couldn't fathom what so many young whites were doing in this exclusively Black neighborhood. She walked to the end of her lawn and spoke to the couple stopped near her mailbox. "What're y'all doing here?" she asked the boy in the driver's seat.

"We're going to a concert at A&I," the boy said. "Little Richard, Fats Domino, Ruth Brown, Clovers, Cadillacs—they're all there."

Helen raised a brow. He hadn't answered her real question—why would these *white* kids think they'd be welcome?

The pretty girl exclaimed, "A&I's student council sent an invite to the white colleges in town, to promote school integration."

"Ahhh," Helen said. "Which college y'all at?"

"We're in high school," the girl said. "My sister's at Vanderbilt and told us. Steve's lookin' to hire a colored band to play fraternity parties, so we thought it might be a good place to find colored musicians."

"You could just stand outside the colored nightclubs. My husband owns the New Era."

"Sou Bridgeforth?" the boy asked. "He sends runners to my daddy's trucking business. I'm Steve George. This's my girlfriend, Kaye Duff."

"Well, y'all enjoy the concert. Hope there's no trouble." As Helen walked back to her porch, she wondered what their parents would think. It was an altruistic gesture from A&I's students. The long parade of white teens lining up to attend was inspiring. Yet Helen suspected these students' parents wouldn't accept integration as easily.

Richard told John, Gene, and Gab about the integrated concert, how A&I had overflowed with students from each local college, who made no attempt to segregate. Rather, they danced, sang, communed, and enjoyed a happy, once-in-a-lifetime moment they'd someday tell their grandchildren about. A generation later, they'd reminisce about the night Little Richard and Fats Domino unified a once-divided people, inspiring the city's progressive youth to believe that the democratic ideal of Athens was within their grasp.

Following his performance at A&I, Richard recorded this commercial for Gene and Strickland's hair care products at Specialty Records in New Orleans:

> Slippin' and a slidin' Gene Nobles with that good word on Royal Crown
> Hairdressing. Everywhere I go—and I go just about everywhere—girls are
> really going on about that Royal Crown Hairdressing, even Long Tall Sally
> use it! You know somethin', Gene, I goes for the girls with that Royal Crown
> look, 'cause, man, um, she's got it.[4]

Helen read about the A&I concert in her neighborhood newspaper: "The large audience was composed of college students from all of the educational institutions in the city and was therefore a veritable picture of what the future holds in store for 'racial integration. . . . The young people are taking desegregation in stride.'"[5]

The success of an integrated concert gave Helen hope; however, she intended to keep Harriett safely ensconced at St. Vincent's as long as possible. She couldn't imagine white parents of first graders embracing integration as effortlessly as college students.

On May 15, Sou received the long-awaited news from Ward Hudgins that the US Sixth Circuit Court of Appeals had overturned Sou's conviction. In the appeal, Hudgins had stated that Sou and his runners were "illiterate and ignorant men and depended entirely upon their attorney for advice."[6] Sou told Funny this was his best bluff—ever!

---

4. Richard Penniman, Art Rube, Royal Crown Hairdressing ad, recorded in 1956. Bonus track on *Night Train to Nashville*, compact disc. Country Music Foundation, 2004.
5. "Tremendous Interracial Audience Hears 'Rhythm In Blues' Artists at A&I," *Nashville Globe and Independent*, April 24, 1956.
6. US Court of Appeals for the Sixth Circuit, 233-F.2d 451 (6th Cir. 1956).

He'd described himself as "country" and stated that as a "plowboy from Alabama," he "didn't know no better." The Feds bought his defense. Nashville's reporters did not.

The editor of the *Tennessean* called on the Internal Revenue Service to explain "the curious maneuver" Sou had "pulled off," described as a "devious scheme" that would "baffle anyone except those initiated into the mysteries of the relationship between the Internal Revenue Service and the gamblers." The editor called it a "bizarre episode."[7]

Normally humble, Sou boasted to his wife, "I went nine innings with the Feds and beat 'em at their own game! Woman, as you like to say, *that ain't nuthin'!*"

At the end of May, Eddie returned from college and surprised Gab with the news he'd proposed to Anne Duff. A student at Vanderbilt, Anne was the oldest daughter of their family physician, Dr. Price Duff. As both the bride's and groom's families had been in Nashville over 150 years, the large extended families resulted in dozens of showers and engagement parties. The *Banner* and *Tennessean* covered Anne and Eddie's wedding events with as much falderal as they'd covered Grace Kelly's to her prince.

Randy Wood was the only close business associate of Gab's to miss the wedding, because he'd just relocated to California. Gab was sorry to see Randy go.

Governor Clement expressed how nearly everyone felt. "I am sorry to see him leave Tennessee," Clement said. "But I'm proud to see him succeed."[8]

Hoss was the only person happy about Randy's departure. After years of man-on-the-street reports, reading news from the wire services, and entertaining his afternoon housedress brigade, Hoss was ready for prime time. He wanted what Gene and John enjoyed—symbiotic relationships with musicians, producers, advertisers—so he could leave his mark on music. Gene had announced he'd retire when Randy sold. Hoss started counting the days.

To prepare for Gene's departure, Gab gave Hoss the transitional 8:30 p.m. spot.

7. "Baffling And Then Some," *Tennessean*, May 21, 1956, 6.
8. Hawkins, *Shot in the Dark*, 178.

Randy had moved Dot Records to Los Angeles to give his record company a California value. It worked. In LA, the offer doubled *and* Randy maintained ownership of his retail concern, Randy's Records. Gene flew to LA on December 26 to sign the sales agreement.

Randy had proven the concept of geography as destiny, Gab thought. He considered Randy's path from Gallatin to Los Angeles and how without the proximity to WLAC, Randy wouldn't have become a multimillionaire. Gab wondered how Nashville's plan to desegregate public schools would intersect with geography as destiny. Already, white families were fleeing the city for the suburbs. Some, like Christine, feared interaction with Blacks would negatively impact the health of white students. Others, many without school-age children, moved in fear of their home's value declining in neighborhoods where Black students attended.

Despite intense pressure from concerned parents, the KKK, and White Citizens' Councils, Mayor West and Governor Clement upheld school integration. In the days leading up to the first day of school, Clement grew worried. A group of militant segregationists, led by John Kasper, had threatened a violent uprising. West and Clement were warned that Kasper's activists had threatened to visit every Black family with children enrolled in a white school.

Frequently, when troubled, Clement would walk to the nearby home of his personal physician and friend, Dr. Price Duff. Sometimes they'd get drunk together; more often, Duff would be called on to sober up the governor for an event. In early September, Clement sought refuge on Duff's sleeping porch. Over whiskey, he shared his concerns with his physician friend.

"Kasper's group's been calling families of colored kids who enrolled. They're saying they're gonna beat the kids to death, throw acid on 'em, hang 'em, and burn down their houses. Threatening *six-year-olds* with deadly violence! Christ almighty, Price! Can you imagine?"

"Yes, I can," Duff replied matter-of-factly. "Have you forgotten I liberated two German concentration camps? I've seen the evil that racial hate begets. *Sunt lacrinae rerum*," Duff said, repeating the Latin phrase he'd heard in Buchenwald.

"A tragedy of life? Yeah, for Germans, but this is Tennessee, where folks are rational!"

"Hah!" Duff exclaimed. "Rational people don't hate for reasons of race, and you're naive to think irrational people will act rationally."

"I've ordered police be at all the integrated schools, but I'm not sure even that's enough."

When Clement left, Duff filled his medical bag with extra supplies. His office was near Jones Elementary and down the street from Fehr Elementary. Both had enrolled colored students. As he drove to the office the next morning, Duff saw angry segregationist protestors lining the streets. He hoped the heavy police presence would keep the children safe.

Harriett was at St. Vincent's Catholic school for colored children, when nineteen first graders were forced to walk past throngs of angry racists screaming racial epithets while holding signs that read "KEEP OUR WHITE SCHOOLS WHITE."

"It was sheer madness," Helen told Sou. "At Fehr, five hundred whites protested. They pitched glass bottles at coloreds and set cars afire. Nooses were strung along Church Street. Some folks even hung an effigy."

"Let's hope that's the worst of it," Sou said.

The "worst of it" came just after midnight as "a hellish explosion" tore through Hattie Cotton Elementary School, where five-year-old Patricia Watson had attended earlier. Few Blacks were surprised by the maliciousness of the whites determined to keep their schools white.

Most white Nashvillians experienced cognitive dissonance over the Hattie Cotton bombing. They couldn't reconcile their belief that Nashville was a cordial, cultured, racially moderate city *and* the location of the country's first school desegregation bombing. This became Nashville's "Emmett Till moment," causing most whites to shift sides in support of school integration. The city remained calm for six months until the Jewish Community Center announced they'd welcome biracial group meetings and, in response, were dynamited. Following the explosion, the likely bomber called the *Tennessean* and stated, "This is the Confederate Underground speaking. We just blew up the center of integrationists in Nashville."

The *Tennessean* also reported that Rabbi William Silverman received a similar call:

"We have just dynamited the Jewish Community Center. Next will be

The Temple and any other nigger-loving place or nigger-loving person in Nashville."[9]

Helen went to extreme lengths to protect Harriett from the sting of racism. She made sure Harriett always ate and used the bathroom before they left the neighborhood. In the spring of 1959, Helen took Harriett to Donelson to get her Girl Scouts accessories. On the way home, they stopped at a drugstore. As Helen shopped, drawn by the smell of grilled burgers, Harriett sidled over to the lunch counter. She was hungry. There were a few empty stools, so she sat down and waited. After a while, feeling like the waitress was ignoring her, she announced, "I want to order a cheeseburger!"

"We don't serve coloreds," the waitress snipped.

"You think I don't have money?" Harriett placed a five-dollar bill on the counter.

"I said, we don't serve coloreds!"

"What's my skin color have to do with a cheeseburger?"

Helen heard her daughter's voice and rushed over. "Come on," Helen said. "Let's go."

"That biddy says I can't have a cheeseburger 'cause I'm colored," Harriett complained.

"Yeah, it's like that in white places."

"Say what?" Harriett exclaimed. "I'm ten and you're just now telling me?"

Several diners laughed. "They must be from up north," the waitress snarked.

"That's right," Harriett said. "North Jefferson. Black Belle Meade." She snatched her bill from the counter and waved it. "Guess someone there'll get this big tip."

On Monday, December 16, Harriett hurried home, excited to finish decorating the Christmas tree. The day before, after she and Helen returned from church, Sou had gone with them to pick out a Christmas tree at the roadside stand near the Melrose shopping center. It was one of the few traditions they

9. "Rabbi Told U.S. Judge To Be Shot," *Tennessean*, March 17, 1958, 1.

had. Harriett knew her parents didn't have a normal home life due to her father's schedule. They rarely dined together as a family. Usually, Harriett and Helen ate early. Hours later, Helen would make a meal for Sou, arrange it on fine china, wrap it in foil, place it in a basket with cloth napkins and silver flatware, and deliver it to the Era. Harriett had never been inside her father's club as he insisted she abide by the rules. Just like everyone else, she wasn't allowed inside until she was twenty-one.

Harriett worked on the tree all afternoon and finally finished it after dinner. When her mother left to deliver Sou's meal, Harriett plopped onto the couch to watch Erskine Hawkins on *The Nat King Cole Show*. Harriett had met Hawkins when he'd come by the house while performing at the Era. It annoyed Harriett she had to watch her father's friends on television like everyone else. The next morning, she went into Sou's bedroom to tell him about seeing Hawkins on Cole's show but found the room empty.

"Where's Daddy?" she asked Helen.

"Police station," Helen said between sips of coffee.

"Again? How many times they gonna arrest him for somethin' that won't stick?"

"Daddy wasn't arrested. There's a shoot-out at the club last night. Gambler lost money shooting dice, then pulled a gun on the cashier to get it back. Now you know why Daddy don't want you at the club."

"Did Daddy shoot him?"

"Of course not! Go get dressed for school."

"Who did? One of the policemen Daddy pays?"

"Girl! You're too smart for your own good. Go get dressed and moving or Santa might leave you a lump of coal instead of that Pez candy and transistor you asked for."

"Oh please," Harriett said. "Like you'd want a stupid kid."

Helen laughed. Everyone said Harriett had a world-class sense of humor. To Helen's mind, that trumped Sou's financial genius and her literary brilliance.

18

YAKETY-YAK

E. G. "Blackie" Blackman spent much of his twenty-eight-year career at WLAC defending his deejays.

—WES SMITH, *THE PIED PIPERS OF ROCK 'N' ROLL*

Hoss had manned the 8:30 p.m. time slot for several years as he waited for Gene to retire. In February 1959, that moment finally arrived. A few weeks earlier, Gene had been on air when his daughter, Nikki, experienced a life-threatening appendicitis attack. Unfortunately, no one could be located to take over for Gene. John was out with Margaret, his new girlfriend, and Hoss couldn't be reached. Gene woke up Gab, who got out of bed to take the call in the kitchen.

"Where's Della?" Gab asked.

"No idea. Martha Jean at WDIA might know. She carries messages between Hoss and Della Reese. Otherwise, you could try asking someone at the Era. He's not there. I already checked."

Gab switched on the radio, poured a glass of milk, and took two chocolate chip cookies from the jar. He sat at the breakfast bar, nibbled on cookies, and watched the moon's reflection flicker over Old Hickory Lake. The music stopped; Gene's voice came over the air. "My daughter, Nikki, is in surgery right now. Please pray for her."

"Dadgummit, Hoss," Gab mumbled. If he called the Era to ask if they knew where Della was, it could tip them off to the relationship, which would surely get Hoss banned from the club, not to mention give the brass-knuckled, gold-teeth-sporting gangsters of Booker Street an excuse to beat him up. Gab decided to let his sleeping hound dog lie.

When the station signed off for the night, Gene went to the hospital.

"We got all the money we'll ever need," his wife said. "It's time you put family first."

Gab confronted Hoss the next morning. "Where the hell were you last night?"

"With Ted," Hoss said. He handed Gab a page of sheet music. "Check it out."

Gab glanced at the page. "A jingle? Sing it."

"Whether you're a husband, a kid, or a wife, you need White Rose in your everyday life. . . . White Rose, White Rose, White Rose Petroleum Jelly."

Gab loved it so much he forgot he'd summoned Hoss to chew him out for being unreachable while on call. "It's fabulous," Gab said. "Be even better with a real singer. You can't carry a note in a shot glass."

A few days later the mailroom was inundated with cards and gifts for Nikki. Gene was so moved by the audience's thoughtfulness, he offered to replace Hoss as the late-night backup.

Gab worked to minimize the financial fallout from Gene's departure. John's protégé, Alan Freed, had captured some of WLAC's white listeners. Freed was getting Gene's playlist and repackaging it as "rock-'n'-roll as a way to sell black music to white teenagers."[1]

Gab consistently worked to keep his research up-to-date. Many of the core advertisers who'd supported Hoss's afternoon shows had switched to WLAC-TV. Using Lloyd Warner's social class system, Gab developed a method for differentiating his audiences, which rotated with the clock. The upper- and middle-class audience that had tuned in to Hoss in the afternoons didn't follow him to 8:30. They watched television instead. Hoss's 8:30 audience was diverse and lower on the economic scale. John followed Hoss, and the audience again shifted. John's audience was heavily Black, as Freed pulled away many

---

1. Smith, *Pied Pipers*, 6.

of John's white under-the-covers listeners. John's audience stayed with WLAC when Gene took over. As the night progressed, the audience expanded, adding college students and shift workers. Then, when Freed signed off, white teens returned to WLAC en masse.

Gab did not take for granted how significantly his jocks bonded with their listeners. The songs they played—including their theme songs, the products pitched, the jingles, their trademark expressions and repetitive phrases, along with the ambient sounds, like the Tarzan yell on Gene's broadcast—were a sort of lyrical version of the front-porch storyteller. Millions of lonely people connected via WLAC, becoming a like-minded community that recognized each other by the unique cultural vocabulary of a deejay. Gab believed that the stories his jocks told, whether in music or commentary, stories originally directed to a previously neglected audience, all contained a moral. Gab needed to make sure the moral didn't change with the narrator.

"You got some big-buckled shoes to fill," Gab told Hoss. "I need you to hold on to Gene's audience while simultaneously making 'em yours."

"How do I do that?" Hoss asked.

"First, let's take a look at who and where they are." Gab pulled the map of WLAC's coverage area off his wall. Beside it, he placed a spreadsheet that cross-referenced the 1950 census data with the locations of the COD orders. Because orders were addressed to the deejay, Gab knew who listened to each show.

"With the late-night crowd, never revert to your news announcer voice. That guy is not who Gene's audience wants to hear. His listeners felt like they were eavesdropping on a party. Now, you're the host. Make it sound like you've just come from the Era, it's after hours on the wrong side of town, and the audience are some friends from the club who followed you home."

"Got it. I'll use my midnight club chatter, like 'it's git-down time.'"

"Perfect! Do it like that and you'll own the night."

On February 9, 1959, Hoss switched on the microphone and midnight yakked. In his deep, honey-molasses voice, using the Black idiomatic intonation he'd come by honestly, he welcomed Gene's fifteen million fans to his party: "Bless your heart, honey. It's git-down time with the Hossman, and I'm down for Royal Crown."

Strickland sponsored Hoss's show. Little Richard pitched their Royal

Crown Hairdressing, and Earl Gaines sang the praises of their White Rose Petroleum Jelly. The catchy jelly jingle Ted composed became so popular, Hoss produced it as a record that sold like jelly.

Hoss peppered his chatter with street expressions he'd heard from childhood or picked up at the Era. The more "midnight" Hoss yakked and the more R & B he played, the more he drank. The more liquor Hoss consumed, the more he devolved into the street ruffian that prompted his mother to send him to boarding school. As soon as the microphone switch flipped, like the parable of the werewolf, Bill, the Beau of Belle Meade, *became* the Hossman—a wild-ass, blues-loving, dice-shooting, heavy-drinking, skirt-chasing Black man.

A decade would pass before Gab comprehended how destructive it was for Hoss to live as a white man by day and a Black man at night. Gab would later identify an early-warning sign he wished he'd heeded. After having watched Della on *The Ed Sullivan Show*, Gab confronted Hoss about their rumored affair.

"Are you messing around with Della?"

"Depends. Who're you asking?"

"*What?* I'm asking *you*, Bill Allen."

"No! Bill's faithful to Nancy."

"Then why all the chin wag 'bout Della?"

"Ahh, well, she's *hot-cockled* Hoss."

"Jiminy Crickets!" Gab barked. "What the hell, Hoss? Get outta my office!"

By the time Hoss replaced Gene on air, most tentpole stations had emasculated their deejays with a Top 40 format. Gab adamantly refused to deviate from WLAC's proven formula. Not only had Gene created personality programming, he'd introduced a new genre to millions. Despite pressure from his L & C overlords, Gab supported John and Hoss wanting to play dubs and demos. WLAC *created* hits, he insisted. No self-professed radio guru from Omaha was gonna tell Gab's jocks what forty songs they could play in a mind-numbing shuffle.

Gab stood in the boardroom of Dudley and Mountcastle's phallic structure—the L & C tower—facing the executives, defending his deejays. "No station in the country receives the mail we do!" Gab insisted. "Those orders put the neon *L* and *C* letters atop this tower! Y'all send out press releases bragging about the ten thousand letters a month that come into this mailroom, most of it for my jocks. You realize that'll stop if we start doing what everyone else does."

The board begrudgingly agreed to let the late-night R & B broadcasts continue.

At thirty-one stories, L & C's tower was the tallest building in the South. It was twice the height of Nashville's first skyscraper, the Stahlman Building. In addition to being the city's landmark location, the tower also served as the city's weather vane. The *L* and *C* changed color based on the weather report. When the tower opened, WLAC radio moved into the insurance company's previous location adjacent to the tower. Gab suspected the Bourbons didn't want colored musicians and record producers loitering in their marbled lobby.

The station's relocation put the 50,000-watt peepers out of business. It also put Gab and Tom Baker under the same roof. The sales departments of WLAC television and WLAC radio operated from the same location. The Katz Agency in New York represented both entities, and while they were supposed to share information, the rivalry between Gab and Tom was too entrenched. Gab felt Baker attempted to undermine him. He suspected Tom had suggested the change to a Top 40 format. Occasionally, complaints from White Citizens' Councils that WLAC's broadcast drove whites down "to the level of the Nigra" were mistakenly routed to Baker.[2] Gab had his suspicions that Baker didn't want WLAC-TV's reputation sullied by WLAC radio's demographic.

He'd just managed to hold on to his jocks' personality programming when Gab was ambushed by a challenge to the station's pay-for-play strategy. Because of their massive audience, WLAC moved the needle on records. Gene and John had pushed demos to press and bumped records up the charts. They'd parlayed their influence into partnerships with their sponsors—Gene with Randy, and John with Ernie—and the station owners (past and present) approved of the symbiotic relationships. Like waiters and bellmen, everyone knew the money was in the tips. When Gab first launched the late-night COD sales of baby chicks, the announcer received a percentage of each per-inquiry sale. After Gene and John perfected the huckster's art, they made more money than the station's accountant, who put an end to the jocks' commissions. Fortunately, no one took

---

2. "Segregationist Wants Ban on 'Rock and Roll,'" *The New York Times*, March 30, 1956.

issue with record producers making up the difference. As long as the mailroom overflowed with COD orders, no one cared which song a deejay plugged or produced or what musician he managed. For ten years, music producers had been slipping "dead presidents" into record sleeves and dropping "one-hundred-dollar bills into wastebaskets and no one thought anything of it."[3]

However, in 1959 a glut of new records was released on the market, but because of the new format, only forty songs were broadcast on most stations. Hundred-dollar bills were no longer enough to motivate a top jock to move his needle onto their vinyl. Color televisions, all-expense-paid vacations, cars, swimming pools, or other perks, such as those described in *Billboard* magazine where producers took "New York models on the road to entertain deejays," were expected.[4]

John depended on these financial perks to provide for his three children, ex-wife, soon-to-be-new wife, her two children, and the son they would later have together. Now that he was in a supportive relationship, John had time to produce records for Ernie at Nashboro and Excello. Like Ernie, John was fair and kind, and he enjoyed nurturing talent. This was particularly evident in his relationships with musicians James Brown and B.B. King, plus his protégés, Alan Freed and Robert Smith, aka Wolfman Jack.

Hoss enjoyed the lifestyle perks. Money had never concerned Hoss, as he and Nancy both came from wealth. What Hoss craved was fame, liquor, sex, and leaving his mark on music.

In mid-May, Gab was already frustrated and feeling undermined when his Waterloo began. Todd Storz, the radio entrepreneur and mastermind of the Top 40 format, invited most of WLAC's deejays to the Second Annual Radio Programming Seminar and Pop Music Disk Jockey Convention in Miami. Within minutes of the invitations hitting the mailroom, all the jocks started lobbying Gab to go.

Gab told John and Hoss if Gene covered for them, they could attend. They discovered Randy had already invited Gene, along with Governor Clement and Pat Boone, as his guests. None of the other jocks would cover because everyone wanted to go. When the nonstop bickering over the event escalated, Gab called Storz for more information.

3. Smith, *Pied Pipers*, 29.
4. Smith, 29.

"Why'd you invite every yakety-yaker we got? I'm feeling like Captain Bligh. Whoever I keep here's gonna mutiny."

"With the size of John and Hoss's audience," Storz said, "they're at the top of every VIP list. The perks for those guys are over the top. Send them. They'll have the time of their life."

"Yeah, that's what I'm afraid of," Gab said. He asked Storz for a list of seminars and took notes. After hanging up, Gab underlined the events he expected Hoss and John to attend: "Radio Reps Are Salesmen Too," "Promotion Men Can Work for the Deejay," "Too Many Releases," "News Should Be New," and "What's Next Mr. Music Man?" When he gave John and Hoss the green light, he handed them his list of required events. Because Gab had heard of Storz's "cocksman" reputation and history with prostitutes, he asked John to keep tabs on Hoss.[5]

"Be prepared to bail him out of jail, just in case," Gab said.

"You're overreacting, Blackie," John replied. "I lived in Miami. There's bigger sharks to snare than Hoss there."

On May 28, Hoss and John were met by a chauffeur at the Miami airport's baggage claim. A bevy of beautiful women waited at a nearby luggage carousel.

"Where's the beauty pageant?" Hoss asked loudly.

"Them's the hookers in town for the convention," the driver whispered.

"What? Miami suddenly got a hooker shortage?" Hoss asked.

"Too few locals to tickle the jocks' cocks," one of the women replied as she walked by.

Hoss's face lit up. "Well, alrighty! It's *git-down time*, Miami-style!"

"You can have mine too," John deadpanned.

"Mighty white of you," Hoss said in his Black vernacular. "Come on, John. Live a little."

The driver loaded their bags into the trunk of a convertible Cadillac. In the car, he handed John a newspaper. "*Miami Herald* says you're off to 'greatest talk session since the erection of the Tower of Babylon.'"[6]

The Americana Hotel's flamboyant lobby was dominated by an enormous glass-enclosed terrarium filled with orchids, a parody of a tropical oasis. "It's

5. Marc Fisher, *Something in the Air: Radio, Rock, and the Revolution That Shaped a Generation* (New York: Random House, 2007), 14.

6. Jack Anderson, "Deejays Meeting At Beach," *Miami Herald*, May 28, 1959, 22.

like Fred Harvey and Carmen Miranda birthed a hotel," Hoss pronounced. "Only the monkeys are missing."

The registration clerk smiled. "Well, he tried."

"Tried what?" Hoss asked.

"To have monkeys. The designer wanted them, but the owners overruled. Your name?"

"Bill Allen."

The clerk slid a brass key and an envelope full of funny money across the counter. Hoss read the key's engraving: "1959 Pop Dee Jay Convention Capitol Records."

"That key's your VIP access to Capitol's penthouse hospitality suite," the clerk said. "This million dollars is for gambling at RCA's lanai suite. You can use your winnings to bid on items at Saturday's auction." She handed Hoss a program with the list of prizes: "A Studebaker Lark, Expense Paid Trip for Two to Europe, $500 Worth of Botany Clothes, RCA-Victor Color TV, RCA Mark III Stereo."[7]

"Holy payoly!" Hoss exclaimed. He placed the key, funny money, and program in his pocket then handed a dead Hamilton to a bellman. "Take my luggage to my room and unpack for me, would ya?" he asked.

John shook his head and stepped to the counter.

"What?" Hoss said to John. "You know I'm gonna be too drunk to do it myself."

"As if you knew how to use a hanger," John joked.

"Catcha later, gators," Hoss said. "Hossman's down for some Royal Crown."

"Was that the Hossman?" the clerk asked. "Oh. My. God. Here, I thought he was colored. Is he married?"

"Yes, but he's never let that stop him from doing things he shouldn't."

As John carried his bag to his room, unpacked, and called Margaret, Hoss visited the poolside lanai suites. Sexy girls in skimpy bikinis showered him with attention as faucets dispensed martinis, and record producers slapped him on the back, claiming, "Without you, we'd be dead."[8]

---

7. Second Annual International Radio Programming Seminar and Pop Music Disk Jockey Convention program.
8. "Disk Jockeys: The Big Payola," *Time*, June 8, 1959.

John opened his door to room service. "I didn't order anything," he said. He took his glasses from his pocket to look at the tray the gal held.

"Don't you recognize me?" she asked. "From baggage claim?"

John noticed how the woman was dressed. "You must have the wrong room," John said. "Bill's next door."

"Aren't you John Richbourg? You're on my call sheet."

"Look, I'm newly engaged. You're an attractive woman, but this's not my thing." He took the tray, closed the door, and opened the invitation taped to the bottle on the tray. It offered an excursion to Havana, Cuba. The RSVP requested he select his preferred mode of transportation: "Private Plane or Yacht." He called Margaret. She encouraged him to fly to Havana.

Hoss also went to Havana. He chose to travel by yacht and was pleasantly surprised to find it manned by an all-female crew who stripped naked as they entered Cuban waters. Onshore, Hoss rendezvoused with John and the other VIPs at a nightclub brothel. John kept his word, allowing Hoss to leave with *two* ladies.[9]

Hoss and John returned to the Americana Saturday morning. They slept through the afternoon sessions, including the auction. At 7:00 they made their way to the ballroom, where Randy welcomed 2,500 guests to dinner. Governor Clement spoke about the radio industry's contributions to keeping America and the world free.

At 8:30 the entertainment started with the warm-up acts: the Lon Norman Orchestra, the Kirby Stone Four, Anita Bryant, Catarina Valente, the Jordanaires, Tommy Thompson, Cathy Carr, Pat Boone, Connie Francis, Jimmie Rodgers, Dodie Stevens, Connie Russell, Lloyd Price, Patti Page, the George Shearing Quintet, Peggie Lee, Alan Dean, Chris Conor, Richard Otto, and Vic Damone.

Then the dance floor was cleared, drinks replenished, and an old-fashioned Southern barbeque buffet featuring spareribs was offered.

At 2:00 in the morning the headliner, Count Basie and his orchestra, took the stage. Basie performed three sets. Between the second and third, the barbeque was removed and the staff set up for breakfast. During those eight hours from Randy's welcome speech to the breakfast buffet, the 2,500 deejays and

---

9. Smith, *Pied Pipers*, 36.

500 other assorted guests (musicians, press, and prostitutes) "consumed 2,000 bottles of bourbon."[10] The army of prostitutes that worked the evening's event had been given one proviso: "at the height of the man's arousal, the prostitutes were to extract a promise that the jock would play the latest record pushed by a particular company."[11]

The *Miami News* was delivered to the Americana and stacked beside the coffee buffet. As Hoss poured a cup, he glanced at the paper's headline: "For Deejays: Babes, Bribes and Booze."

He picked up several copies.

"That headline's gonna ruin us!"[12] Hoss said as he dropped the papers on the table. He, John, and Gene read the article that began:

THE DISC JOCKEYS, here from cities throughout the United States and Canada, were given the greatest buttering up since Nero was persuaded he was a fiddle virtuoso. There were expensive prizes, free liquor around the clock in at least 30 suites, and girls, imported and domestic.[13]

John, having attended the "News Should Be New" seminar, announced, "This'll be all over the wire services before we leave."

Gene lightened the mood. "Y'all hear who bought all the auction items? . . . The hookers!"

Hoss downed the remainder of his Bloody Mary and tossed his napkin on his plate. "I gotta go. I'm not going home without gifts for Nancy and Blackie."

Hoss went to the office early Monday, hoping to control the fallout from Miami. "We saw 'Super Hombre' in Havana," he told Gab. "His pecker's as long as from here to Chicago."[14]

"Really, Hoss? That's what you got outta the convention?" Gab said. "Was that the most interesting thing that happened?"

"Well, no. Saw Alan Freed throw his wife into the pool for flirting with

10. Fisher, *Something in the Air*, 82.
11. Fisher, 82.
12. Smith, *Pied Pipers*, 37.
13. Haines Colbert, "For Deejays, Babes, Bribes and Booze," *Miami News*, May 31, 1959, 1.
14. Smith, *Pied Pipers*, 36.

Mitch Miller. The female yacht crew got naked, and speaking of peckers, I brought you this." He handed Gab a sketch of seven dogs urinating on a wall. "It's called *Dirty Dogs of Paris*, by Boris O'Klein."

Gab read the caption below the sketch: "Taken from the Men's Room at Jamaica Inn's English Pub on Key Biscayne, Miami, Florida."

"Thanks, Hoss, I've got the perfect place for it."

Gab hung the print over the toilet in his master bathroom. Christine thought the picture vulgar and wouldn't allow her grandchildren to use that bathroom. Gab laughed about how Hoss brought home a canine penis-envy sketch, while John brought a copy of the *Miami News*.

"Hurricane-strength bad news's coming from Miami, Blackie," John warned, and he was right. The Miami article was broadly syndicated.

On June 8, *Time* magazine published the story, "Disk Jockeys: The Big Payola." *Time's* article was soon followed by others in *Newsweek*, *Life* magazine, *Billboard*, *Variety*, *Cash Box*, and more. The *New York Daily News* and *New York Post* ran accounts of the prostitutes scoring the top prizes at the auction, including one about a "New York hooker driving back to Manhattan from Florida in a new Cadillac convertible purchased from her earnings at the convention."[15] These salacious details attracted the attention of the FCC, the Manhattan District attorney, and the US House of Representatives. Congressman Oren Harris opened an investigation into the Miami convention and the industry's payola practices.

On Monday, November 23, Gab was summoned to the tower's boardroom to again defend his deejays. Gil Dudley, Paul Mountcastle, Truman Ward, F. C. Sowell, and other top L & C executives were waiting when Gab arrived. No one looked happy to see him.

Sowell started the inquiry. "Robert E. Lee at the FCC has threatened to revoke the broadcast license of any station whose deejays took payola. What do you plan to do about it?"

"Tell your jocks what WABC told Freed," Baker said. "Don't let the door hit you in the ass.'"

Gab felt like Napoleon at Waterloo. He needed time to think. What he

---

15. Smith, 35.

wanted to do was throw it back on them for their corporate greed. If they'd just paid his guys the commissions they'd deserved, this pay-for-play scenario might've never been necessary. The easy solution, what Gab knew Baker had likely presold the board on, was to fire all the late-night personality deejays and replace them with announcers who'd spin Storz's Top 40.

There was no way Gab would agree to that. He had too much invested in his programming and his jocks to go down without a fight.

PART 3
THE 1960S

Something happened in Nashville that didn't
happen any other place in America.

—CONGRESSMAN JOHN R. LEWIS

19

JAILHOUSE ROCK

He [Elvis] wanted to sing with us, but they
[Parker] wouldn't let 'im. See back in those
days it was the Whites and the niggers.

—JOHNNY BRAGG

State law prohibited Governor Clement from seeking another term. Before leaving office in January 1959, Clement pardoned Johnny Bragg. Johnny had spent half his life behind bars, having served "fifteen years, eight months, and twenty-one days"[1] of a 594-year sentence for six rapes he "likely didn't commit."[2] While incarcerated, Johnny had entertained President Truman, numerous senators (including Lyndon Johnson), multiple governors, movie stars, and recording artists, and he had made a hit record. Johnny's fondest memory occurred on December 21, 1957, at the governor's mansion, where Elvis sang "Just Walkin' in the Rain" and Johnny sang "Jailhouse Rock."

Governor Clement had Johnny's song royalties held in trust, which enabled Johnny to leave the Tennessee State Penitentiary with a sizable fortune. His grandmother, Parthenia Jordon, welcomed him home with a celebratory meal of turnip greens, dumplings, corn, stew beef, and chicken.

---

1. Warner, *Just Walkin'*, 188.
2. Warner, 13.

In the year since he'd been freed, Johnny had traveled the Chitlin' Circuit and opened for Ray Charles in Nashville and for Sammy Davis Jr. and Frank Sinatra in Las Vegas. To commemorate his success, Johnny bought a 1957 peach and white convertible Mercury Monterey. When he cruised down Charlotte Avenue, he'd attract the type of attention Satchel Paige had in his gray Cadillac.

On January 18, 1960, Johnny drove his Monterey to the Era. He entered the club looking like a member of the Vegas Rat Pack. Sou watched Johnny, thinking if Johnny knew Nashville like Sou knew Nashville, he'd have stayed in Vegas. In this town, like most Southern cities, Johnny's flashy vehicle was strike one. His sharp, dark blue suit, cashmere overcoat, starched dress shirt, gold cuff links, black bowler hat, and patent leather shoes, strike two. Johnny sidled to the bar and flashed a big wad of dead presidents. Strike three.

In Vegas, Johnny might have been part of the Rat Pack's entourage, but to a certain faction in the local police force, Johnny was a colored ex-con thumbing his wealthy nose at them, the modern-day equivalent of a free Black Tennessean in 1860, when the legislature proposed free Blacks choose from three options: leave the state, be imprisoned, or voluntarily return to slavery. Jordon Stokes Sr. argued against this proposal, stating, "I deny, Sir, utterly deny, that the Legislature can stride into the courts, cancel all the decrees of emancipation, disregard its solemn compacts or agreements with liberated slaves, and drive them as a herd of cattle out of the State."[3]

Apparently, Stokes didn't share Stahlman's opinion that Andrew Jackson was "the greatest character developed in American history," because that's precisely what Jackson did to the Creek and Cherokee Indians. Prior to the Battle of Nashville, wealthy landed gentry had controlled the city. Since Reconstruction, Nashville (like most Southern cities) was controlled by oligarchic politicians and businessmen. These Bourbons, the Stahlmanesque elites, accumulated generational wealth by paying white workers seventy cents for every dollar workers in other parts of the country were paid. And they exploited their Black workers by paying them half of what Southern whites received. As Washington journalist I. F. Stone explained:

---

3. Jordon Stokes, *Republican Banner*, March 18, 1860, 2.

To the outside world it must look as if the conscience of white America has been silenced, and the appearance is not too deceiving. Basically, all of us whites, North and South, acquiesce in white supremacy and benefit from the pool of cheap labor created by it.[4]

The same tribal thinking that had many Tennesseans in 1860 believing freed Blacks should be expelled, imprisoned, or voluntarily returned to slavery still existed—albeit in a more evolved version—a century later. When Johnny flaunted his wealth in 1960, this was the modern-day equivalent of a Black man flaunting freedom in 1860. It was unacceptable in certain circles because it led coloreds to "forget their place" and, worse, enabled them to aspire to something better. Hence, it came as no surprise to Sou when the *Banner*'s lead headline the following day proclaimed, "'Walkin' in the Rain' Composer Jailed."

"Here we go again," Sou told Shorty. "What's it been, twenty years since Bill James forgot his place? Someone musta thought we need remindin'."

"Damn!" Shorty exclaimed. "You's right. Exactly twenty. Same street corner. Only thing's changed is the names of the drunks and unemployed men loiterin' there."

"Whatcha talkin' 'bout?" Kat asked.

"Bourbon-swillin' hypocrites run the guy outta town that got me into numbers," Sou said. "He was puttin' on pants, steada stayin' in Black boy knickers," Shorty clarified.

"You know that *Banner*'s article's twenty-seven paragraphs long?" Kat said. "I counted. Lotta space for a minor hit-and-run, ain't it?"

Sou read the lengthy article. According to the *Banner*, when Johnny left the Era, a black car sideswiped his Mercury and kept going. Johnny chased the car for four miles, then lost it briefly before finding the car pulled off to the shoulder near Gallatin Road and Trinity Lane. A young, white, blond female driver told the police, who were conveniently parked nearby, that her purse had fallen off the seat and she'd pulled over to pick it up, and while she was parked, Johnny confronted her. Minutes later, the police arrested Johnny. He was charged with breach of peace and violation of an automobile registration

---

4. John Egerton, *Speak Now Against the Day*, (New York: Alfred A. Knopf, 1994), 618.

for having one plate on his car registered to another of his vehicles. They cuffed him and took him to jail.

"What a coincidence! Shades of Mary Davenport," Sou exclaimed as he noticed the photograph and recalled the past interracial scandal. "Middle of the night and a *Banner* photographer just happens to be there to snap a photo of Johnny's arrest."

"So, y'all are sayin' the Bourbons set him up?" Kat asked.

"How many young white women come by here at closin' time?" Sou asked. "Speed away, then pull over and wait for the colored guy chasin' her?"

"With doors unlocked and window open to the cold 'cause her pocketbook fell!" Shorty added. "Why'd it fall anyways? Ain't no sharp turns 'twixt here and there."

"Put that-a-way, seems obvious," Kat said.

Later that evening, Kitty shared the scuttlebutt Bobby overheard at the police station. "Says they ain't lettin' Johnny out," Kitty told Sou. "Police stuck him in a lineup. Him in that fancy suit, everybody else in prison stripes. They brung in four women said they was robbed or assaulted by a colored guy. All four fingered Johnny. Bobby said they's just hopin' least one happened when Johnny got no alibi."

"I warned him," Sou exclaimed. "Said no colored ex-con gets away with showing off round here. That's just waving red flags at a bull in heat. He didn't listen."

"Apparently, one woman claimed Johnny robbed her of $2.50. Another said he took $6.00. All claimed he assaulted 'em. Ha! We seen the womens chasin' Johnny. If he assaulted somebody, it's cause he had to beat her off with a stick. He ain't assaulted nobody and he sure ain't snatched their lousy eight bucks! He gives double that to bums each day, so *please!* He's supposed to sing with me at the March of Dimes Caravan, Friday. Now Johnny's behind bars for being rich, and I'm left raising money for po-folks my own damn self!"

"Who's producing the Caravan?" Sou asked.

"Morgan Babb over to WVOL. He's known as Happy Jack on air."

"Tell Babb to call me if he needs help replacing Johnny on the ticket," Sou offered.

Morgan "Happy Jack" Babb turned to Henry Edwards, a gospel singer and host of WVOL's Sunday morning show, to fill Johnny's concert slot. Edwards recruited one hundred local gospel singers from churches, Fisk, A&I, and the American Baptist Theological Seminary.

While Johnny pondered his fate in the county jail, Gab worked overtime to keep Hoss and John out of it after having admitted they'd taken payola.

F. C. Sowell told reporters two of WLAC's employees "admitted receiving money to plug certain records" and had believed perks for play was common practice.[5] They hadn't realized they'd done anything wrong. "Now that they have been made fully aware this is contrary to the principles of good ethics, they can be depended on to adhere to all rules governing the matter," Sowell explained.[6] He also claimed management was unaware anyone had received payola and he hoped this would conclude the matter.

It didn't. On February 10, 1960, Edward Eicher of the Americana Hotel testified before the congressional committee investigating the payola scandal. When Oren Harris, a Democrat from Arkansas, questioned Eicher, he learned Randy had paid for Pat Boone and his wife and former Tennessee governor Frank Clement and his wife to attend the convention.

"Maybe I'd better stop now," Harris said upon hearing his fellow Democrat had benefited from the scandal. This caused "a roar of laughter in the hearing room."[7]

Eicher added, "The governor found it a most dignified and proper convention."

"So, why'd the bar bill exceed the food costs at the barbeque breakfast?" Harris asked.

"Bourbon costs a bit more than eggs," Eicher replied.[8] "And they consumed some 2,000 bottles of it between midnight and breakfast." Eicher's comments were repeated in newspapers throughout the country.

The following day, Eddie Blackman and Noble Blackwell were in the break room at WVOL, drinking coffee and sharing the newspaper. WVOL was the all-Black-format radio station previously known as WSOX. The station,

---

5. "Two Nashville Radio Employees Admit Payola," *Tennessean*, December 18, 1959, 1.
6. "Two Nashville Radio Employees Admit Payola," 18.
7. "Payola Lists Boone, Clement," *Tennessean*, February 11, 1960, 1.
8. "Payola Lists Boone, Clement," 2.

launched by Ernie's nephew Cal, was sold to the Rounsaville radio chain. Noble was one of the original teenage announcers Ted Jarrett had recruited to the station. Hoping to one day own his own station, Noble had moved to the business side. Eddie Blackman had been recruited to WVOL from a station in Clarksville. As Gab's son, Eddie was on a first-name basis with virtually every white advertiser in the city.

Following Jim Crow traditions, WVOL's Black advertisers worked exclusively with Noble, while the white advertisers worked exclusively with Eddie.

"That convention was wild," Noble said after reading Eicher's testimony in the *Tennessean*. "You think they'll call your dad to testify?"

"Nah," Eddie said. "John R, or Hoss maybe. L & C's so connected I'm sure they're callin' in favors. Considering Gil Dudley was Eisenhower's campaign finance chair, he'll wrestle a way outta that mess."

The program director, Morgan Babb, came to the break room to refill his coffee. "Don't forget we got our monthly staff meeting tonight," Babb said. "Eddie, you'll be pleased to know I found a place willing to serve even you." The men laughed. "Y'all come to Wood's Barbeque at 5:30. It's on Charlotte next to the New Era."

"Thank goodness," Noble said. "No offense, Eddie, but I'm sick of that white bread at the airport. Say, Happy, d'you see the article about the deejay convention? Wonder why Randy didn't invite us?"

"Gee, I wonder," Happy said. "Maybe us colored jocks should have a convention of our own. Anyway, about the convention—I just got the latest from LAC's news desk." He switched to his news announcer voice and read: "Mr. Eisenhower said in response to the payola hearings, 'public morality's involved when people using the airwaves, under government license, use the privilege just for personal gain.'"[9]

"Guess Dudley's not as close to the prez as you thought," Noble told Eddie.

By the time Eddie arrived at Wood's Barbeque, Congress had proposed making payola a criminal offense. They granted the FCC power to take a station off the air temporarily for illegal or unethical activities. As the WVOL employees gathered at the table, the station's manager brought up this news and

9. Paul Healy, "Payola Issue One of Public Morality, Ike," *Baltimore Sun*, February 12, 1960, 1.

issued a warning against accepting gifts of any kind. "Not so much as a pack of cigarettes, or it's grounds for termination," he warned.

Eddie stifled his laugh. *WVOL's 5,000 watts hardly warranted payola*, he thought. At least he enjoyed the work of selling advertising. He even dealt with some of his dad's old *Banner* clients. Sometimes it annoyed him how often his customers wanted to talk about Gab and WLAC. Eddie told Gab that he might as well be working for WLAC as often as he had to discuss the station, their ads, and rates. Gab wanted to hire Eddie for the same reason WVOL had—because Eddie already knew everybody, was experienced at sales, and understood the business. But L & C wouldn't allow it. Nepotism, they'd said. When Eddie argued that Jimmy Ward worked there, Gab said Jimmy'd been hired before L & C bought the station.

Eddie told Anne he sometimes thought he'd have to leave Nashville to make something of himself. In this "Who's your daddy?" town, Eddie had always been compared to Gab, which was burden enough, especially on the golf course, where he'd never once beat his father. Now he also had to contend with his larger-than-life, war hero father-in-law. Between Gab and Dr. Duff, Eddie felt like a caddy, always trailing several paces behind.

Fortunately, Eddie loved his job and got along well with his coworkers, most of whom were colored. He especially liked Noble. Eddie had never known a contemporary colored man and would never have imagined being friends with one. In Eddie's world, this never happened. Hoss was the only white person Eddie ever knew who had a close friend who was colored.

Eddie was glad to see that Wood's Barbeque featured traditional Southern cuisine. The only integrated dining spot in town was at the airport. And in trying to be more continental, that place didn't do Southern well. Eddie had never been in a colored restaurant before, so he hadn't known what to expect. He worried there'd be pig knuckles, fatback, or chitlins on the menu, which he could now see and smell was ignorant on his part. If the food was half as good as it smelled, he'd want to come back, with Noble, of course.

While Eddie and Noble enjoyed the same taste in food, their taste in music diverged. Noble liked the R & B music Ted Jarrett and John R produced. Eddie preferred Pat Boone's records to Little Richard's, and Happy Jack liked gospel. Noble went off on a tangent about how Boone and Elvis had stolen Black music and were now making far more money from their remakes than the original artists would ever make. Noble used Big Mama Thornton, a regular act at the New Era next door, as an example: "You know she got one check for $500 for writing the song 'Hound Dog,' but Elvis's making millions from it."

"I did not know that," Eddie said. "And yeah, that's not right."

Of the twenty-plus employees of WVOL, all but two were at the dinner. Of the twenty in attendance, only Eddie and the manager were white. Eddie glanced around and noted there was one additional white guy in the place, seated with a group of Fisk students. When Eddie got up to order his meal at the counter, a meat and three sides (pulled pork, coleslaw, mac and cheese, black-eyed peas), the white guy followed.

"What're you doing here?" he asked Eddie.

"I'm with my coworkers at WVOL," Eddie replied. "You?"

"I'm a student at Fisk," the man said. "Name's Paul LaPrad."

"You attend Fisk?" Eddie said, blurting his astonishment. "So you're not from around here, are you?"

"Indiana, by way of Chicago," LaPrad said. "Obviously, you are."

"Yeah, my family's been here forever. I'm Eddie Blackman," he said as he picked up his tray. "Good luck to you, Paul."

"You know him?" Noble asked as Eddie returned to the table.

"Nope," Eddie said. "Had no idea whites went to Fisk."

"But you do know school integration's been mandated, right?" Noble teased.

"Ha, ha," Eddie said. Of course, he *knew*. It just never occurred to him that a white guy, even one from Chicago, would *choose* a Southern Black college. As often as Eddie'd been called a "nigger lover" while walking downtown with Noble, he couldn't imagine what it must be like for Paul LaPrad. He wondered if anybody'd warned LaPrad to keep a baseball bat in his car, just in case he caught the KKK's attention. Folks thought the KKK targeted only coloreds, but they also loved making examples of whites who dared to cross the color line.

The next day, Gab called Hoss and John into his office. "Not a penny. I mean it! Not even lunch. With what's going on in Washington, y'all might be forced to choose between being promoters and deejays. Your reign as the saviors of radio's over." Gab still had the *Variety* magazine article that posed the question, "Deejay: Performer or Puppet?" John and Hoss were performers who consistently received over three hundred new dubs, demos, and record releases each week. And they listened to as many as possible, mostly on their own time. To Gab's knowledge, no one else did that, which is why the other—in his mind, lazy—jocks copied their playlists. John had become the tastemaker, the hitmaker of the entire R & B genre. And for what? So grandstanding politicians could brand him a shyster? So the board demand Gab fire him? So the whole country's forced to hear the same forty songs because that's what Storz had "scientifically" determined?

Gab wasn't worried about Hoss. His *Hoss Allen Presents* shows at Sulphur Dell and the state fairgrounds were extremely popular. Hoss could work as a concert promoter and emcee and do well. However, John was different. John did the work of listening to the music because he believed in the genre and its musicians and should be able to support his large extended family doing it.

Hoss and John had taken payola, which was bad enough, but as a record producer, John had *given* payola. Not only was John's livelihood in jeopardy but he stood to be criminally charged.

While Gab worried about John, Christine worried about Gab. She wanted him to take the partnership offer from the advertising agency, as she feared Sowell's press releases had been worded so if WLAC were sanctioned, Gab's neck would be on the chopping block. Gab didn't believe it'd come to that, although he did admit that after this latest fiasco, the general manager title he'd been promised when Sowell retired would likely go the same way as his promised television career.

"It's okay," he told Christine. "Titles never meant a hill of black-eyed peas to me, anyway."

With the completion of the L & C tower, Life and Casualty Insurance had become *the* white shoe firm in town. The board made it clear they felt Gab's nighttime broadcasts put a black mark on the company's reputation after they'd been forced to order a censorship committee; the Peeping Toms made a mockery of their Christian values, and now the FCC had reclassified a standard industry practice as bribery. Gab knew taking the Noble-Drury ad agency offer would be in his best interests. But he couldn't bring himself to do it. He was all that stood between L & C's board, a wholesale firing of his deejays, and a change in programming to Top 40. In good conscience, Gab just couldn't let that happen.

He reminded himself that he was *Blackie Blackman*, the first person to recognize "the great commercial potential in this black music, and in this colored audience that no one had ever tapped."[10] The powers that be hadn't liked it, and he'd "taken a lot of kidding about it on the golf courses and in the country clubs."[11] And now, he owed it to his audience, his advertisers, and his deejays to fight back. When Christine pleaded with him to leave WLAC, he told her how on Gene's last day, they'd all gathered in the large studio and he'd given a speech.

"Told a *story*, you mean?" Christine said.

"Christine, you're a first-generation Southerner. I've got seven generations on ya. You know how the Bible says sins of the fathers carry forward to the third and fourth generations? Well, that's how it is with us. Southerners are born with three to four generations of stories bound up in us just waiting to get told."

"Okay, so let's hear it then."

"I called Gene 'The Little Engine That Could.' Said he was a master conductor who'd transported a lyrical cargo along an 'overhead' railroad. Told 'em all how Harriet Tubman used music to carry messages on the Underground Railroad, and we do it in the sky. Not as heroes, not even for the right reasons. See, each order we receive represented a passenger who rides the rails with Gene. From the orders, I know where folks boarded. Now, it don't matter if that was in Georgia or Indiana, or even on a ship out to sea. Everybody's ridin' that night train to Nashville together, feeling the drumbeat of the wheels and the pitch in the whistle—"

"I get it, Galbreath. Whyn't you go put a few generations' worth of stories into a book?"

"Well, because I can't type or spell."

"You got a dictionary and a pencil."

"And you got a frying pan," he teased. "When's there gonna be some chicken in it?"

Gab had a love-hate relationship with chicken. He loved the taste, but

---

10. Broven, *Record Makers and Breakers*, 99.
11. Broven, 99.

he'd come to hate the blowback from thousands of unhappy baby chick customers. One lady complained one of the chickens attacked and killed her dog.
Sometimes they were shipped to the wrong address. Usually they died, but that
was better news than if they lived, because they were said to be "the flyingest,
queerest chickens" anyone had ever owned.[12]

Gab had become a victim of his own success. Innovators, entrepreneurs,
and con men thought if WLAC could sell millions of chickens, then why not
any number of possibilities? As a result, Gab was spending entirely too much
of his workday weeding out product pitches. His salesmen were supposed to
screen the callers and try out the products before passing them on to Gab for
approval and pricing. This was so Gab didn't waste his time while people like
Barry Gordy, who tended to show up unannounced, waited in the lobby. Gab's
secretary ushered in his first product pitch salesperson of the day.

"Gab, this is Sam Moore," Rats said.

Gab looked at the young man holding a Bible. "How-do, Sam," Gab said.
"Have a seat."

Sam placed the Bible on Gab's desk. "Mr. Blackman, I've been selling
Bibles door-to-door for the past year, trying to make enough money to pay my
way through college."

"How's that workin'?"

"Not so good. Nearly every door I knock on, folks tell me they already
got a Bible."

Gab stifled a laugh. "Did nobody tell ya, this is the Bible Belt?"

"What everyone tells me is they bought their Bible on WLAC. I got to
thinkin' the only way I'm gonna make enough money to stay in college is if I
sell my Bibles on WLAC."

Gab picked up the Bible, flipped through it, then pulled his own Bible
off the credenza. He placed the two Bibles side by side. They looked identical.
He opened each to the first page of Genesis. "Your Bible is identical to mine,"
Gab said.

"As it should be," Sam answered.

"You think? Then let me ask you: Why would I discontinue doing business

---

12. Smith, *Pied Pipers*, 94.

with a longtime, consistently faithful advertiser to sell the same product for you instead?"

Sam thought for a few moments, but unable to come up with a reason, picked up his Bible and turned to leave. "Well, thank you for seeing me, Mr. Blackman."

Gab liked the earnest young man and decided to teach him a lesson. "Hold up, Sam. There's a correct answer to that question. You just haven't found it yet."

"What is it, sir?"

"Bring me a *better* Bible. Not the same thing I've been selling for years. Something better. Then I'll consider it. And on your way out, tell Rats to send in Mr. Gordy."

John came into the office with Barry Gordy. After they spoke about Gordy's new venture, Motown; the artists Gordy had contracted; and the records they were producing and wanted WLAC to sell, Gordy left and John stayed. He handed his paycheck to Gab.

"Look at this, Blackie. Could you live on this? Can't make my house payment, car payment, furniture payment, hell, I can barely feed my wife and kids, and now Margaret's pregnant with number six. Legal warned I'm about to receive a summons to appear before the FCC. Am I expected to pay for my own attorney now too?"

Gab was sure the station would provide John an attorney, but he didn't think relying on L & C's attorneys would be in John's best interests.

"I get it and I'm on it," Gab said. John needed his own attorney, and it was time to rally the troops. This situation warranted calling in that chit he'd been holding on to from Ernie. Gab paid Ernie a visit and afterward drove to Warren Paint and Color Company to see his brother-in-law, Joe Warren, and Joe's brother-in-law, retired brigadier general Harold A. Nisley.

Joe's condescending personality rubbed Gab the wrong way, but being related to the wealthy Warrens had its perks. And the perks Gab valued didn't involve flying on Joe's plane or cruising the Cumberland in his fancy Chris-Craft, which occasionally he did at Christine's insistence. Fortunately, the FAA had grounded Joe for flying drunk, and now that Gab had his own boat, all Gab had to worry about was Joe crashing his boat into Gab's dock. The perk

Gab most appreciated was how Joe always knew whose string to pull to make things happen. And if Joe didn't know, Nisley did. Nisley had attended West Point with Eisenhower and General Omar Bradley and served as Bradley's chief ordnance officer in World War II. After the war, Nisley helped Gil Dudley with Eisenhower's campaign. And if those connections weren't good enough, Joe's father and Jordon Stokes's mother were brother and sister. Gab's best shot of sidestepping any legal problems related to payola was to seek advice from Joe and Nisley. Joe's influence was local. Nisley's was in Washington with a direct line to the Oval Office. Gab knew how to work Joe, as he and Jimmy Stahlman were cut from the same pelt. Gab hated playing the lickspittle, but it worked—every damn time.

Later, Gab told Christine he'd gone to Warren Paint and genuflected to get her sister's husband to make calls on John's behalf.

"Ouch. What about Hoss?" Christine asked.

"Hoss's in better shape and can take care of himself," Gab said. "You'll get a kick out of what Nisley heard when he called Washington though. Said shortly after the congressmen heard about the junkets to Havana, they immediately flew there to investigate."[13]

"Of course they did," Christine said. "Men are so predictable."

Had Johnny Bragg solicited Ernie's advice, as John did, the suggestion would have been the same—to call Jordon Stokes—and things might have turned out differently. A century after they'd defended the rights of free Negroes, the Stokes's third generation still worked to make Nashville a more equitable city. Unfortunately, Johnny wasn't a Stokes client. His first trial ended in a hung jury. He was retried and found guilty of assaulting and stealing $2.50 from the woman who'd sideswiped his car. His attorney suggested an appeal, but prosecutors promised Johnny that if he dropped his appeal, he'd serve only six months. Johnny dropped the appeal and was sentenced to five to ten years. Johnny was indeed guilty—of flaunting his wealth. Little wonder he would think that "back in those days it was the whites and the niggers."[14]

13. Pat Anderson, "'60 Festival To Be Irreproachable," *Tennessean*, September 25, 1960, 33.
14. Warner, *Just Walkin'*, 179.

20

WE SHALL OVERCOME

The most powerful segregationist in Nashville . . . was
not, as in many Southern cities, a politician or a sheriff,
or a judge, or the head of an all-white segregationist
movement; it was newspaper man James G. Stahlman.

—DAVID HALBERSTAM

Paul LaPrad thought Johnny Bragg's version of life in the South, "the whites
and niggers," just "seemed so wrong to him" he felt compelled to do something
about it.[1] An Indiana farm boy, Paul came to Nashville from Chicago. He'd
first attended Manchester College, then spent a summer traveling Europe,
where he'd visited several German concentration camps. When Paul returned
to the States, he worked in Chicago and saved money to continue his education.
Like Dr. Duff, LaPrad had drawn a parallel between the way many Southerners
viewed Blacks and the way many Germans viewed Jews. This prompted Paul
to take a bold step and attend a Black college, where he could get involved with
social programs and make a difference. He applied to three schools and was
delighted when he received an acceptance letter from Fisk. On campus Paul
met Diane Nash, a beautiful coed also from Chicago.

---

1. Halberstam, *The Children*, 132.

When Diane first arrived in Nashville the previous fall, a date had taken her to the Tennessee State Fair, where the *Hoss Allen Presents Caravan of Stars* was in concert. There, she encountered the loathsome signs on the entrances of the restrooms that read: *WHITE ONLY* or *COLORED*. Having never seen this before, Diane felt humiliated. As she became more familiar with Jim Crow customs, she appreciated that the fairgrounds had "colored restrooms" as most downtown stores did not. Nor would they allow colored women into their dressing rooms. The finer department stores had bathroom attendants who monitored the facilities. And while the store clerks would politely accept money from Blacks for their purchases, including lunch from the counter, waitresses—like the bathroom attendants—monitored who was permitted to sit at the counter. Coloreds were instructed to eat on the sidewalk and "pee in the alley."[2] When Diane voiced her frustration about this to Paul, he invited her to join a group of student activists intent on showcasing the "major problems of segregation and the need for genuine integration."[3]

The student protest workshops were led by James Lawson, a Methodist missionary minister and graduate divinity student at Vanderbilt who'd served prison time as a conscientious objector to the Korean War. Following his release, Lawson did missionary work in India, where he became immersed in the philosophies of Mohandas Gandhi. Upon Lawson's return to the States, he recognized the similarities between Gandhi's and Dr. Martin Luther King Jr.'s teachings. He joined the Fellowship of Reconciliation, an international pacifist Christian organization, with the intention of founding a peaceful protest activism in Atlanta. However, Lawson soon realized a peaceful protest would have a better chance of success in Nashville. The city's population was more racially moderate; Nashville was home to four Black colleges, Fisk, A&I, American Baptist Theological, and Meharry Medical School; and the city's mayor, Ben West, was moderate-to-liberal, as was the governor. And perhaps most importantly, the city had a progressive daily newspaper, the *Tennessean*.

Beginning in the fall of 1958, Lawson conducted weekly talks on the

---

2. Mielczarek, Natalia, "Jefferson Street was 'Mecca' for sit-in movement," *Tennessean*, June 24, 2004.
3. James M. Lawson, interview by Robert Penn Warren, March 17, 1964, Who Speaks For The Negro? The Robert Penn Warren Civil Rights Oral History Project, Louie B. Nunn Center for Oral History, University of Kentucky Libraries.

Ghandian model of nonviolence. Each Tuesday night, in a modest redbrick church, Clark Memorial Methodist, near the Fisk campus, Lawson lectured on a diverse set of philosophies. He began his teachings by establishing that justice was the one universal value on which all the world's major religions agreed. And if one accepts the enlightened premise that all individuals, regardless of race, gender, color, or creed, should be treated impartially, with fairness and equal justice, then Jim Crow segregation is oppression and therefore a form of tyranny.

These informal talks would eventually become workshops that instructed students how to peacefully protest in order to bring attention to the injustice of segregation. They would not teach nonviolence merely as an expression of passivity but rather as an expression of love—Christian love, as taught by Jesus. Lawson taught what Jesus had—that when one turns the other cheek, hatred is exposed as one-sided.

In India, teaching the same values from the Hindu culture, Gandhi had successfully deployed the yogic practice of *satyagraha* (Sanskrit for "truth + insistence") in his nonviolent civil disobedience. Yoga, a spiritual discipline rooted in Hinduism, contains both a mental and a physical component. In yoga (Sanskrit for "union") one works to align the body, mind, and spirit. The physical movements in yoga—commonly practiced in the West—are referred to as *asanas* (Sanskrit for "pose + posture + sitting"). In following the Ghandian model, Lawson taught his students to hone their inner strength (*satyagraha*) while maintaining (*asana*) a pose of sitting with good posture. The students came up with their own English interpretation of *satyagraha*: soul force. By activating their soul force as they sat, the students could rise above the destructive cycle of racial hate and anger. They could suffer while simultaneously forgiving the person inflicting the suffering on them. From the Christian perspective, they were following Jesus's example.

"You are all *someone*," Lawson told his students. "You are all children of God. You have within you the greatest qualities, human nobility. True children of God do not reap anger or violence on others."[4] In this way, Lawson taught them to embrace all of humanity.

---

4. Halberstam, *The Children*, 78.

To prepare the student protesters for the inevitable suffering he knew they would endure, Lawson began with the verbal abuse he knew they'd encounter. "Every flinch at the word *nigger* only serves to reaffirm its poisoned power. But that word does not define *you*," he insisted. "It defines the person using it."[5]

The educated and well-mannered white residents of Nashville provided fertile ground for a civil rights advance, in part because they viewed radical segregationists as low-class and ignorant. Most Nashvillians believed the use of the N-word defined the person saying it, not the person it was said about. In gracious Nashville, the racial terminology one used indicated their social and economic status. "Style meant everything in expressing racial differences, because the presumption of white superiority remained unquestioned."[6] Well-mannered children were taught from an early age that only "common" people (what ill-mannered people called "poor white trash") would permit such a vitriolic word to cross their lips.

Lawson's goal was to create a "beloved community" in the city of Nashville. Not a utopia, but a place where the intangible "barriers between people gradually came down and where the citizenry made a constant effort to address even the most difficult problems of ordinary people."[7] His words resonated with students, including one future legendary congressman, then a student at American Baptist, John R. Lewis. After studying with Lawson, Lewis vowed to make building a beloved community within this diverse country his life's work.

Following months of preparation, reconnaissance trips, and trial runs, the public phase of Lawson's activism began Saturday, February 13, 1960, when 114 Black students and ten white students—men dressed in coats and ties, women in stockings and heels—walked with dignity and purpose through several inches of snow. From First Colored Baptist Church they proceeded to and through the Arcade (a covered mall alleyway) to the city's central retail corridor of Fifth Avenue North. The soul force of the students was evident with each perfectly postured step they took. At 12:30 p.m., they splintered into smaller groups and entered the Woolworth's, McClellan's, and Kress stores and purchased assorted sundries. Having established themselves as customers, they

---

5. Halberstam, 79.
6. Houston, *Nashville Way*, 22.
7. Houston, 22.

practiced an *asana* with *satyagraha*. Engaging their soul force, they sat with perfect posture and politely asked to be served.

At Kress's, the manager immediately closed the counter. At McClellan's, a game of musical chairs commenced after Black students took the seats of departing white patrons, and the manager instructed waitresses to signal to waiting white customers so they took the vacated seats first. When the protesting white students thwarted this endeavor, McClellan's closed the counter.

At Woolworth's, John Lewis recounted, "one waitress stopped dead in her tracks, 'Oh my God,' she said to no one in particular, 'here's the niggers!'"[8] Police arrived shortly thereafter. They informed the manager they couldn't stop the demonstration unless an incident occurred. After an hour, the Woolworth's counter also closed. The students continued to sit peacefully until 2:30. The following day, the *Tennessean* reported:

> An estimated 100 students—about 90 of them Negroes—went on a two hour sit down strike at Nashville variety stores yesterday after waitresses refused to serve them.... "We just got tired of having no place to eat when we shop downtown," said Miss Diane Nash. "So we decided to do something about it." ... Paul LaPrud, [sic] one of the white Fisk students in the group, said the waitress and managers at each store "were courteous, but not particularly nice."[9]

Meanwhile, at the *Banner*, Jimmy Stahlman instructed reporters *not* to cover the story of the student protestors. Despite having the ideal reporter on staff, one who might have written a Pulitzer-worthy account—Robert Churchwell—Stahlman threatened to fire any reporter even in the vicinity of the protestors. Instead, David Halberstam, a twenty-two-year-old reporter at the *Tennessean*, covered the story extensively. Halberstam later wrote an extraordinary book, *The Children*, about the student protestors. In his book, Halberstam states, "He [Stahlman] took the sit-in as a personal challenge. He might not be able to stop Blacks from voting and he might not be able to stop

---

8. John Lewis with Michael D'Orso, *Walking with the Wind*, (New York: Simon and Schuster Paperbacks, 1998), 95.
9. James Talley, "Lunch Counter Strikes Hit City," *Tennessean*, February 14, 1960, 10.

the integration of the city's schools, but he had a lot of influence downtown, both with the mayor and with store owners, like John Sloan . . . Stahlman had decided one thing—that Jim Lawson was a sworn enemy."[10]

During the initial sit-in protest, Lawson's students "had complete protection from the Nashville police."[11] They protested again on February 18 and over 200 students participated.[12] On Saturday the 20th, with 340 protesters, they were able to expand the protests to two additional stores, Walgreens and Grant's. At this point, Stahlman's patience ran out. He rallied the city's power brokers and pressured Mayor West to arrest the protestors and Vanderbilt's chancellor to expel Lawson.

Word of this reached Lawson. He heard that Stahlman had prevailed upon Mayor West to acquiesce to a chilling arrangement that allowed white hecklers a few minutes alone with the protesters, uninterrupted by police. Lawson was informed Stahlman "had used leverage with city officials to let the cops and the white marauders have one good shot at the black activists."[13] It had been overheard in the mayor's office that "violence against the students was likely to take place, and there would be a large number of arrests of the Black demonstrators."[14] Lawson let the student protesters decide if they wanted to continue with the planned demonstrations. When the student leaders voted to proceed, John Lewis created, mimeographed, and circulated five hundred copies of a list of dos and don'ts protestors should follow.

On February 27, Big Saturday, as it would come to be known, mobs of white teens lay in wait for the student protestors. As had been suggested, the police vanished on cue. The white mob's initial target was the "traitorous, nigger lover" Paul LaPrad. He was yanked off his stool, punched by many, savagely kicked by one. On the floor, to avoid internal injuries, Paul curled into a fetal position as they'd practiced. He placed hands over the back of his head to assume the yoga position known as praying child. In this posture, Paul was

10. Halberstam, *The Children*, 121.
11. Lawson, James M., interview by Robert Penn Warren. March 17, 1964, Who Speaks For The Negro? The Robert Penn Warren Civil Rights Oral History Project, Louie B. Nunn Center for Oral History, University of Kentucky Libraries.
12. Houston, *Nashville Way*, 93.
13. Halberstam, *The Children*, 127.
14. Halberstam, 127.

able to maintain eye contact with the tormentor who kicked him repeatedly. A United Press photographer and a television crew documented the incident. Later that night it was broadcast nationally. The footage showed Paul LaPrad, "bloody and bruised and silent, pulling himself back on to his chair."[15]

When the police returned, LaPrad was arrested for disorderly conduct but not the whites who'd perpetrated the violence on him. LaPrad sat alone in a dirty, wire-caged paddy wagon, waiting to be taken to jail. He knew his fellow protesters would soon join him in the wagon when he heard them sing "We Shall Overcome."

Guy Carawan, the resident musician from Highlander Folk School, where Rosa Parks and Martin Luther King Jr. spent time, had taught the students this song. Pete Seeger, a Highlander regular, composed "We Shall Overcome" by cobbling together the old hymn "I'll Overcome Someday" and a song Black union organizers used in the 1940s, "We Will Overcome." The students sang this song as they were arrested. They sang it in the dingy paddy wagons. They sang it in the city jail. The song was a cry for justice.

By late afternoon, eighty-one protestors had been arrested: seventy-seven Blacks, including Diane Nash and John Lewis, and four whites. They were crammed into tiny cells, each meant to hold three to four prisoners, now housing fifteen to twenty. Police stopped arresting students once the mayor realized the city jail was full. There was no more room at the inn.

Many of the students were beaten. Several had cigarettes put out on their backs. They'd been spit on. One was thrown down a flight of stairs. Others had hot coffee, ketchup, or mustard poured on their heads. All were called vulgar names. And what had they done to deserve this treatment and be crammed into an overcrowded jail?

Sit.

They'd taken a seat at a store's lunch counter.

On February 28, Eddie Blackman walked through the mix of snow and sleet to retrieve his Sunday morning newspaper from the holder beneath his mailbox. By the time Eddie reached his front door, he'd read the headline and studied the corresponding photos.

---

15. Lewis, *Walking with the Wind*, 100.

"Holy shit, Anne!" he said as he stepped out of his shoes and into the living room. "Remember that Fisk student I told you about? The one I talked to at Wood's Barbeque?"

"Yeah," Anne said. "The guy from Chicago?"

Eddie showed her the front page. "That's him!" He pointed to the photograph of a young man curled into a fetal position and read aloud the caption: "Paul LaPrad, white student at Fisk University, doubles up under blows from another white student at McClellan store. LaPrad is a leader in the demonstration against lunch counter segregation in Nashville stores."[16]

Anne and Eddie read the article together in silence. The *Tennessean* reported:

> "You haven't seen anything yet," said Earl May. "We're gonna fill their jails. That's a promise . . ." Luther Harris said last night, "police abandoned the Negroes when they were in danger. It was the most scandalous thing that's happened in the South since Emmet Till. I wouldn't really have expected this in Nashville. The police just pulled out and left us unprotected."

Anne, who'd majored in sociology, was shocked. "Why would police arrest him and not the guys who beat him up? That's just ridiculous!"

Across town, Sou Bridgeforth read the same article and fumed. Luther Harris was his own godson. Sou suspected Stahlman, the puppet master, had given West his orders. "Stahlman jerked the mayor's chain," he told Helen. "Now Luther's lucky his head didn't get bashed in."

"Don't you know it. Stahlman and that lowdown snake in the grass Sloan. They're in it together. Heard Sloan's closed their luncheonette and dining room soon as a couple colored students walked into the store." Helen was still furious over their refusal to issue her a charge-a-plate in her name.

---

16. James Talley, "Massed Police Halt Sitdowns At Food Counters," *Tennessean*, February 28, 1960, 1.

"Churchwell said not only would Stahlman not let him cover the protests, he also said if he was anywhere near 'em, he'd be fired."

"I'm surprised the *Banner*'s not spouting off about it, calling the protestors communists," she said. "Didn't think Stahlman was capable of keeping his opinions to himself."

"He's not. He'll brand the students 'communist agitators' any day now. I had money delivered to Looby for the kids' bail and legal expense."

Helen kissed him on the cheek. "You're a good egg, Bridgy."

"Thanks, Funny, but Looby said the students didn't want to be bailed out. Bail was set at one hundred dollars. No one paid it, so West reduced it to five and still no one bailed out. Finally, West had the students released into the custody of Fisk's president."

"You sure I can't talk you into coming to church this morning? It's bound to be mighty interesting."

"Nah, I got some things to think on, and the quiet will do me good."

All professional gamblers of Sou's keen ability share a common trait. They're proficient, even brilliant at reading people. Sou'd never met Stahlman in person and had no desire to, yet he read him as astutely as he did a balance sheet; James Stahlman was a man of strong opinions whose narcissism led him to believe his opinions were facts. Anyone who didn't share his opinion, he considered an idiot. Yet Sou understood that men like Stahlman—who refused to read anything or listen to anyone unless it confirmed what they already believed—were the true idiots, because they were deliberately ignorant. This trait made Stahlman predictable, and predictable people made gamblers like Sou rich.

Sou saw James Lawson and his students as men and women of goodwill and pure hearts. From Sou's perspective, Stahlman, Sloan, and even West had yet to realize that willful ignorance is no match for righteous goodwill. If Vegas offered odds on this war between the students and the powerful, Sou would bet the house on the students. He believed that in the end, good would triumph over evil, and before Harriett got to high school, she'd enjoy a cheeseburger at Cain-Sloan's lunch counter.

On Monday, Z. Alexander Looby walked with the student protestors from First Colored Baptist Church to the Davidson County Courthouse, where they were tried for disturbing the peace. Judge John L. Harris not only ignored Looby's argument for the students' defense, he spun his chair around so Looby couldn't make eye contact with the judge as he spoke! "Eventually Looby threw up his hands. 'What's the use?' he said, cutting short his comments and returning to his seat."[17]

While Looby grew increasingly frustrated by the charade of a trial, two thousand Negro supporters outside the courthouse sang in support of the students.

Judge Harris declared all students guilty of disorderly conduct. Each was given the choice of paying a fifty dollar fine or spending thirty days in the county workhouse.

Diane Nash stood and spoke for all the students: "While we graciously thank the people who made the fine money available to us, we cannot find it in our hearts to go against the moral principles we hold dear. We feel that if we pay these fines, we would be contributing to and supporting the injustice and immoral practices that have been performed in the arrest and conviction of the defendants."[18]

The entire country watched the news reports later that evening, showing the Nashville student protestors being returned to jail. And making Sou's words manifest that Nashvillians called their jail the workhouse for a reason, the brave, dignified college students were forced to labor outside in subfreezing cold, on slushy streets. After they were photographed picking up trash and shoveling snow, telegrams overwhelmed the mayor's office. The dispatches came from all over the country—many from notable people such as Eleanor Roosevelt and Harry Belafonte.[19]

Frustrated, the mayor called Gab. "Y'all got credibility with coloreds and the merchants, and you know Jimmy. I'm searching for a workable way outta this. Help me, Gab."

"Listen, Ben, you held yourself out to be a friend of the Negro. I can't see any way puttin' those kids in jail and makin' 'em work as street sweepers does any good. You're gonna have to decide. You're either a friend of the coloreds, or of Jimmy. You can't be both."

17. Lewis, *Walking with the Wind*, 103.
18. Mac Harris, "2 White Coeds Freed on Bond in Sitdowns," *Tennessean*, March 2, 1960.
19. Lewis, *Walking with the Wind*, 103.

"Jimmy's working to get Lawson expelled. He sent a reporter to Ohio to dig up dirt on him. Thinks if he cuts the head off the snake and runs him outta town, that'll end it. But in the event it gets worse, he sent someone to Fort Campbell to buy rifles and ammunition. Larry Brinton had to run around town buying out all the surplus stores' metal helmets, bulletproof vests, and mace. Said it's to protect the *Banner* in case the students attack. They locked it all in that closet by Charlie's office."[20]

Gab didn't know whether to laugh at Jimmy's stupidity or cry over his brutal arrogance. "Nuthin's changed. The *Banner*'s still got guns at the ready for killing Negroes."

"Guess so. He thinks he can hold 'em off till the cavalry comes from Fort Campbell."

"For criminy sakes, Ben. You gotta know the only way this ends is by integrating the counters. Ask yourself: When that day comes, which side do you wanna be on?"

"I get it, Blackie, but if I'm on the side of integration, Jimmy'll see to it I'll never be governor. You know that's been my goal since Central High. I'm putting together a biracial panel to mediate between the merchants and students, to try and take the heat off me."

"Don't put me on it. With this payola thing, I got problems enough of my own."

"I'm askin' the leaders of the local colleges. Actually, the reason I called is I may need a back channel to your network in New York. I don't trust the local TV guys. Not like I do you. When the time's right, if it's filmed from the proper perspective, the outcome of this fiasco could be favorable for both me and the students."

"Just lemme know when, my friend. And in the meantime, stay outta the line of fire of that crackpot *Banner* army."

---

20. Halberstam, *The Children*, 199.

21

I'LL TRY SOMETHING NEW

I came to Nashville, not to bring inspiration, but
to gain inspiration from the great movement
that has taken place in this community.

—DR. MARTIN LUTHER KING JR.

On Friday, March 3, Mayor West announced the creation of a biracial committee. Meanwhile, five blocks down the street, four Nashville police sergeants walked disrespectfully—"hats on heads and cigars in mouths"[1]—through First Colored Baptist Church's sanctuary, to "roughly arrest" James Lawson. He was charged with "conspiring to violate the state's trade and commerce law" by organizing the peaceful protests.[2] A United Press International staffer photographed the officers and Lawson as they emerged from the church. In the widely circulated picture, a sign on the church marquee clearly announced the topic of Rev. Kelly Miller's upcoming Sunday sermon: "Father, forgive them."

Lawson's arrest provided Stahlman and John Sloan, members of the Vanderbilt Board of Trust, the ammunition they needed to persuade Chancellor

---

1. Houston, *Nashville Way*, 106.
2. "Student's Cases To Go Before Grand Jury," *Nashville Banner*, March 4, 1960, 8.

Branscomb to kick out Lawson. After Branscomb ordered the dean of the Divinity School to expel Lawson, four hundred white faculty and staff of the university temporarily resigned in protest. Lawson's arrest and expulsion resulted in a scathing story about the school's treatment of him in the *New York Times.*

Diane Nash testified before West's biracial panel. She made clear that no form of token desegregation would be acceptable to the students. The following day, Harvey's manager, Greenfield Pitts, and John Sloan testified. They adamantly maintained their position that integrating the counters "would hurt business."

"Hurt their twenty-five-cent cheeseburger business? Ha!" Helen exclaimed at bridge. "That's nuthin' compared to what we spend downtown! Let's hit 'em where it really hurts!"

In Black Belle Meade, at bridge tables and baby showers, garden clubs and prayer meetings, a quiet movement began among the neighborhood's affluent matrons. "Don't Buy Downtown," became their slogan, and their strategy quickly gained traction.

Helen was one of the movement's most vocal supporters. "Turn in your charge-a-plates at any store that won't serve coloreds," she told everyone. "Hit 'em with your pocketbooks."

The retail corridor along Fifth Avenue North and Church Street became a ghost town after Rev. Kelly Smith and other preachers urged their congregations to use their economic muscle to support the student protestors by boycotting the merchants. Easter was on the horizon, and it had long been an important shopping season for Nashville retailers. Because sporting new clothes for Easter Sunday was a long-standing tradition, stores were loaded with spring dresses, hats, gloves, and shoes. "No Fashions for Easter" became the theme of the season. Between the merchant boycott, the white flight to the suburbs, some whites' fear of shopping downtown during the protests, and sympathetic whites boycotting the stores in support of integration, the student protestors had placed the merchants in a financial stranglehold.

Woolworth's advertisement of Easter baskets, Harvey's promotion of gingham-checked cotton dresses, Cain-Sloan's sale on bone-colored shoes, and Grant's store window signs offering plush stuffed Easter bunnies did not have the desired results. The city's buses, stores, and eateries were empty. Downtown was deserted.

Gab hung up from a call with Greenfield Pitts of Harvey's who'd phoned to let Gab know the store was putting a temporary hold on their radio ads.

"Blackie? Got a minute?" John asked as he stepped into Gab's office. "My car was just repossessed. Pretty soon my house and furniture'll be gone too. Me, Margaret, and the six kids'll be lucky if we're not homeless."

"I got a solution. I've asked for legal to sign off—"

"Hey, Pop," Eddie interrupted. He stood in the doorway. "I was downtown and thought I'd stop in."

"Come in," John said. "I was just telling your dad my car was repossessed and my house's likely next. I'm sure he'd rather talk to you."

"Probably not," Eddie replied. He took the chair John vacated.

"You here to order baby chicks for your children?" Gab teased.

"I thought that was your thing, Pop. Paula and Brett will love getting chicks from you. I was downtown trying to make some sales, but things are so bad, I could roll a bowling ball down the sidewalk on Fifth and not hit a single soul! You know most of my pay's commission and nobody wants to advertise on Black radio while they're boycotting the stores. I'm gonna be in the same position as John soon. If this doesn't end, I'm worried they'll have to lay me off. I don't know what to do!"

Gab should have seen this coming. Eddie had been hired because he knew all the white merchants and understood advertising. But with the boycott, it didn't pay to advertise. There was nothing Eddie could do to change the dynamics of the market. He was trying to sell an unsellable product. Gab leaned back in his chair and tried to think of a solution that didn't involve him financially supporting his son, which he'd vowed, for reasons he believed were in Eddie's best interests, that he'd never do.

"You know," Gab said, thinking out loud, "Anne went to Vanderbilt. At the moment, it'd be easier for her to make money than you. She should work and you should just hold on until the market corrects. Which it will."

"Pop! You're seriously telling me I should force my wife to get a job?"

"Isn't that why one gets an expensive education? What'd she study?"

"Sociology." Eddie read the question in his father's expression. "I guess it's the science of human relationships in society and consequences of humans' behavior."

"Leave it to Vandy to label that 'science,'" Gab said. "There's gotta be some practical application to it. Let me make a few calls, see what I can do. Keep your chin up, son."

A few weeks later, Anne Duff Blackman was named the human resource manager of IEI, James Pugh's radio electronic capacitor manufacturing concern. Anne practiced her applicant interview skills by carefully selecting the ideal nanny for her children. Aggie, a kind, vivacious, and resourceful Black teenager, was hired. When Anne discovered Aggie was participating in the student protests, Anne went to Warren Paint and talked Eddie's uncle Joe into giving her paint, cardboard, and wooden stir sticks. Anne and Aggie then turned the Blackmans' family room into a protest sign factory.

The student protestors waited three weeks for the mayor's committee to release their findings. Eventually, they grew frustrated and determined the merchants were delaying the process to extend the truce. To force the panel's response, the students resumed their protests.

On Friday afternoon, March 25, 120 students left First Colored Baptist Church intent on taking a seat at the lunch counters in Woolworth's, Grant's, Kress's, Walgreens, Harvey's, Cain-Sloan's, Moon-McGrath's, and McKlellan's. At Cain-Sloan's, when a few students tried to enter the fancy Iris dining room, they were met by the manager. John Sloan came to deliver his response to the students personally.

"We don't have to serve you, we won't serve you, and I have to say that not only is it the store's policy not to serve you, but as the head of this store I personally believe in the policy."

A fortuitous coincidence occurred that day. The local press had agreed to a news blackout during the truce period, so press coverage was usurped by a CBS news crew from New York, who just happened to be in the First Colored Baptist Church at the time the students resumed their protests.

Chief of police Douglas Hosse accused the CBS crew of having snuck into town like "thieves in the night."[3] The crew filmed the protests and broadcast

---

3. Tom Flake, "Bi-Racial Group Back Where It Started: Sarratt," *Nashville Banner*, March 26, 1960, 2.

the scenes nationally. Governor Buford Ellington and the *Banner* accused CBS of having orchestrated the protest.

"I have learned that the sit-in demonstrations by the Negro students in downtown Nashville were instigated and planned by and staged for the convenience of the Columbia Broadcasting Service," Governor Ellington said.[4] He further explained, "WLAC-TV was as shocked as I to learn of this dangerous, trumped-up news story and the network's part in it." The governor called for a thorough investigation into the CBS news fiasco.

Jimmy, perhaps suspecting Gab tipped off the network, used his editorial page to call for Congress to "now turn an investigative eye on the Columbia Broadcasting Service crew whose visit to Nashville—by the oddest of circumstances—occurred just in time to photograph that breaking of the sit-in truce."[5]

Mayor West responded to Jimmy's editorial bluster. "I regret very much that this has happened. The whole matter is in the hands of the committee of outstanding citizens. I do not care to comment further."[6]

Gab read Jimmy's comments and laughed. "A congressional investigation? Jimmy musta forgot that freedom of the press doesn't just apply to newspapers," he told Christine.

Following the panel's recommendation that the lunch counters be segregated into sections—one for whites, one for Blacks, and one integrated—the students continued their protests. They believed "token integration" with "restricted areas" missed the moral point completely. On the Monday following Easter, they returned to sit at the lunch counters (which were promptly closed). They then picketed in front of the stores, at Memorial Square, and in front of the city courthouse with signs that read: "Let's Break Bread Together," "Make Nashville Great—Desegregate," and "Dignity Before Dollars."

White segregationists soon followed to protest the student protestors. The whites carried signs that read: "Throw Coons Out" and "We Don't Like Jungle Bunnies."[7]

4. Flake, *Nashville Banner*, March 26, 1960, 2.
5. Flake, 4.
6. Flake, 4.
7. David Halberstam, *Tennessean*, April 12, 1960, 1–2.

At the courthouse, students prayed and sang beneath the mayor's office window.

After "a long afternoon of jeering and pushing in Memorial Square," several demonstrators were beaten by whites.[8] Racial tension again heightened throughout the city.

Then, as Sou would say, "the worst" happened on the morning of April 19, when someone hurled dynamite from a car into the home of Z. Alexander Looby, attorney for the student protestors. Looby was unhurt, but the damage to his home was extensive.

That morning, the student protestors sent a telegram to Mayor West. He was informed "they" would be coming to see him. "They" turned out to be over three thousand student protestors from the colleges and from Pearl High. From the A&I campus to the city courthouse, the students walked silently. Many carried mimeographed pages that read, "We shall let our complete silence be our only speech."[9]

As the first students reached the courthouse, the silent army became a singing army. Guy Carawan, "the old-fashioned troubadour" from Highlander Folk School, played his guitar and led the protesters in singing, "I'll Overcome Someday." With each verse, more protestors arrived and joined the protesters in song.

When the news announcer alerted Gab that thousands of students were headed from A&I to the courthouse to confront the mayor, Gab dashed to the executive balcony. The sight of thousands of dignified students, three abreast, stretching across the city was a sight he would never forget. Through the ever-present binoculars, he could see Ben West come out from the front stoop. Ben stood stoically, awaiting the students.

The deck was quickly crowded with L & C executives who stood shoulder to shoulder as they watched history in the making.

"What's that they're singing?" someone asked. No one in the crowd could identify the music, but they all knew it was reminiscent of an old Negro spiritual.

---

8. Halberstam, *Tennessean*, April 12, 1960.
9. David Halberstam, "Crowd Told Decision Is Up to Stores," *Tennessean*, April 20, 1960, 1–2.

"Too bad Hoss isn't here," Gab said. "He'd not only know it, he'd sing it authentically."

As the students approached the courthouse they sang: "We are not afraid. We are not afraid, today. . . . We are not alone, we are not alone, today."

West recognized the pretty coed Diane Nash, the Reverend C. T. Vivian, and the expelled Vanderbilt divinity student James Lawson, the snake whose head Jimmy and his group of staunch segregationists had been unable to sever. As a sign of respect, Ben removed his hat.

Reverend Vivian read aloud the prepared statement. He accused the mayor of "steadfastly ignoring the moral issues of segregation, refusing to speak out against the injustice of segregation, not using the moral weight of his office to speak out against violence, and encouraging violence by letting the police use their authority with partiality."[10]

Initially, Ben defended his record, but Reverend Vivian and Diane Nash pushed back. They pressed him to take a moral stand rather than hide behind legal excuses.

"Do you believe segregation is moral?" C. T. Vivian asked.

Ben looked out at the sea of faces, most of them colored. This was the moment Gab predicted would come. The time Ben could no longer hide behind tradition, legal statutes, and biracial panels. He had to choose sides: Jimmy's, which paved a path to the governor's mansion; or the students', which followed Jesus's Sermon on the Mount, the Golden Rule.

"No," Ben said. "It is wrong and immoral to discriminate."

Diane Nash appealed to the mayor's humanity. She asked him to use his office to end racial segregation.

"I appeal to all citizens to end discrimination, to have no bigotry, no bias, no hatred," Ben said.

Diane asked if he meant that to include the lunch counters. The mayor agreed it did.

The next day, the *Tennessean's* headline read: "INTEGRATE COUNTERS—MAYOR."

"Wilma Jean and her friends marched with the protesters," Kat bragged.

---

10. Halberstam, 2.

Wilma Jean, Kat's daughter, was a student at Pearl High. "She's going to see Dr. King at Fisk tonight."

Dr. Martin Luther King Jr.'s speech was delayed an hour due to a bomb threat received at Fisk. Eventually, the overflow crowd of four thousand heard King proclaim, "The diehards should know by now that bombs will not stop us." When the thunderous applause died down, he added, "I came to Nashville not to bring inspiration, but to gain inspiration from the great movement that has taken place in this community."[11]

Nearby, Z. Alexander Looby was overcome with emotion and wept as King praised the students.

"You have lifted the jails from badges of dishonor to badges of honor," King stated.[12] He then encouraged the students to continue their march toward equality: "Let's keep moving; let's walk together children, don't you get weary."[13]

After King's visit to Nashville and David Halberstam's excellent coverage of events in the *Tennessean*, even John Sloan begrudgingly acknowledged the student movement had gained unstoppable momentum. On May 10, Fred Harvey and John Sloan surrendered. They agreed to voluntarily integrate their counters. *Time* magazine dubbed them "pocketbook integrationists."

By late May, all of Nashville's downtown lunch counters were integrated; however, the city's restaurants, theaters, hotels, public pools, and golf courses remained segregated. Most Nashvillians lauded the integration decision and took pride in claiming "the Athens of the South" was the first Southern city to desegregate. History has defined Athens as the birthplace of democracy— the first city where each citizen was allowed an equal voice in governing the society. Even with the integration of Nashville schools, government properties, and lunch counters, the city still had a long way to go to live up to the ideals of its namesake.

Helen had never been in Cain-Sloan's new store, but when she heard John Sloan had surrendered and integrated his lunch counter, she had to see for herself to believe it. The whole town knew "Sloan didn't like Black people, and

---

11. Gary Fullerton, "King Delayed By Bomb Scare," *Tennessean*, April 21, 1960, 1.
12. Houston, *Nashville Way*, 117.
13. Houston, 117.

he showed it. C. T. Vivian called Sloan a 'man in a suit and tie with the soul of a redneck sheriff.'"[14]

Helen picked up Harriett from school and took her straight to Cain-Sloan's lunch counter for cheeseburgers. She later told Sou that she'd rubbed it in a bit to the waitress, complaining that the burgers at Sloan's were not much better than the five-cent Krystals, and she still had no intention of shopping at Cain-Sloan's.

John Richbourg had also sworn off Cain-Sloan's. He watched with a sinking heart as repo men carried away his furniture.

"At least they left the mattresses," Margaret said. "I hate to think of the kids having to sleep on the cold floor."

John called a family meeting. "Look, kids, we're going through a bit of a rough patch. We're all gonna have to pull together and work to get us through this."

Margaret, her daughter Patty, and John's daughter Lelaine worked as waitresses, while John's son Johnny and Margaret's son Barry delivered papers, mowed lawns, and pestered neighbors for odd jobs. Ellen, who was a senior in high school, babysat her baby brother and served as a surrogate mother for her siblings. Everyone pitched in and pooled their earnings.

After Gab had convinced the L & C brass that turning John into a vendor, letting him sell something he alone owned, would have no impact on the billboard charts, he told John.

"You got so many pictures of musicians, stories of you and the musicians, how you discovered the musicians, you get it. Whataya say let's create a souvenir booklet to sell on air? Lots of photos and a few paragraphs of narrative. We'll advertise it as John R's scrapbook."

John wasn't as convinced as Gab that his scrapbooks would sell like baby chicks, but he was desperate and willing to try anything.

"Let's get some samples printed in time for Hoss's concert at the Dell," Gab said. The concert Hoss was promoting had become a sore subject. Hoss's laissez-faire attitude about payola and his failure to grasp what constituted a conflict of interest left management fuming. Hoss insisted that because the

---

14. Halberstam, *The Children*, 212.

concert was contracted before the deejay convention, he couldn't remove his name from advertising, withdraw from the event, or tamper his on-air enthusiasm for artists who performed at events he sponsored. Gab warned if the FCC filed another complaint, Hoss would lose his job.

"Get photos and we'll print the final books after," Gab told John. "Who's he got on tap?"

"Bunch of folks he knows from the Era. James Brown, Etta James, Joe Tex, Bea Ford, Baby Lloyd, Bobby Marchan, Ron Holden, Nat Kendrick, a few more. I can't remember 'em all. Oh, Harvey Faqua and the Moonglows."

"'Sincerely,'" Gab said. "Love that song. Make sure you get a photo of that really good-lookin' guy in Harvey's band Hoss says all the ladies love. That should help sell some."

"Marvin Gaye? Yeah. Good idea."

Gab received notice from L & C's legal department that they had concerns Hoss had violated the conflict of interest clause in his contract. In addition, they feared Hoss's drinking had become a corporate liability. With the television station adjacent, too many employees hovered around to witness his drunken misbehavior. Gab had repeatedly confronted Hoss about his drinking. At first, he said he never drank on air; then, when caught in the act, he claimed he couldn't be the Hossman unless he'd had a few.

Shortly after Hoss had taken over for Gene, a box was received in the mailroom addressed to the Hossman. When Hoss opened the box, he discovered a faded, threadbare housedress along with an order for records. One of Dave's apprentice engineers used the dress, a wooden hanger, and a broom to create a scarecrow. The employees said they could always tell when Hoss was drunk, as he would dance around the studio with the scarecrow, proclaiming, "Send no money, friends, just your name and a dress."

In November, when the L & C board again raised concerns that Hoss had become too much of a liability, Gab delivered the bad news. "I'm sorry. You're a hell of a pitchman and a darn good disc jockey, but your lack of discipline and ethics undermines your success."

Hoss called Leonard Chess at Chess/Checker Records in Chicago. "I'm fired," Hoss said. "I need work."[15]

---

15. Broven, *Record Makers and Breakers*, 120.

Leonard Chess gave Hoss a job as an A&R man, more out of gratitude for what he'd done for Chess Records than what they believed he could do. Chess knew John well enough to know that John would play what Hoss promoted, as would Gene when he filled in. Chess provided Hoss an expense account for entertaining program directors, with the goal of getting Chess releases on their short list of forty songs. In addition, Hoss was to be Chess's southern region talent scout. Hoss shared the good news of his new position with Gab.

"Can't think of anyone more qualified than you to drink and chase women on someone else's dime," Gab said. "Congratulations, my friend. I'm happy for you."

Hoss's final day on air at WLAC was December 17. Before he left the office, Gab asked Hoss if he wanted to take the housedress scarecrow home with him.

"Nah, I'm leaving her for Hugh," Hoss said. "I warned him it can get pretty lonesome here at night and she's good company."

Hugh "Baby" Jarrett was hired as Hoss's replacement. Also from Gallatin, Hugh was well known at WLAC. He'd been a member of the Jordanaires, a gospel and studio vocal backup group that often performed on the station. The Jordanaires backed Elvis on his records and had toured with him. After returning to Nashville, Hugh took one of John's courses at the Tennessee Broadcasting School, then got a part-time gig at WHIN in Gallatin.

Hugh was younger than Hoss and more like Alan Freed than John. Jimmy Ward, Truman's son, had suggested Hugh would appeal to Elvis's audience—a younger and more diverse demographic. With Freed no longer broadcasting in WLAC's coverage area, Jimmy believed Hugh could bring back white teens Freed had pulled away. Gab felt WLAC at night had become an integral part of Black culture and that switching gears could cost their core audience. What Gab wanted to do was hire a Black deejay, but the board wasn't there yet. He decided to let Jimmy Ward prove himself. At least the kid didn't ask for Top 40.

Gab split the evening time slots between Hugh and John. Hugh played Freed-type rock and roll, while John broadcast only Black R & B. The night-time audiences had become racially diverse. Gab knew that ultimately the market would rule. Whichever deejay received the most orders, and for which records, would tell Gab what genre the audience preferred.

Herman Grizzard—the voice of Sulphur Dell baseball—took WLAC's final hour. Herman replayed John's playlist, sprinkling in a few traditional gospel songs.

If the orders for rock and roll outpaced those for R & B or gospel, Gab would concede that Jimmy Ward had been right. Then he'd work to adjust the product and advertiser mix to reflect rock and roll's audience. Gab already knew whites ordered race records and coloreds ordered Elvis, which was a neon-lit sign of the times, but that didn't mean WLAC should relinquish its identity as the powerhouse station that had launched R & B. That was Gab's claim to radio fame, and he wasn't willing to surrender so easily. He was sure John's program would outsell Hugh's, and when it did, he'd have the data to back up his hypothesis as correct. Perhaps then he'd be able to convince the board to let him hire a colored announcer.

22

HIT THE ROAD, JACK

Great stories happen to those who can tell them.

—IRA GLASS

In January 1961, Hoss hit the road as the southern sales rep and talent scout for Chess Records. Leonard Chess had hired him to entertain disc jockeys and scout for talent they could discover or poach from other producers. Hoss was eager to begin this new phase of his career.

With Hoss gone, Gab had concerns that Strickland might pull their sponsorship. Hugh's show featured a rock and roll playlist that was targeted toward a younger, whiter demographic than Hoss's show had pulled in. Hugh found creative ways to insert blue comedy into his chatter, often using petroleum jelly as the punch line. He took Gene's sexual double entendre a step further, ensuring Strickland's loyalty. White Rose Petroleum Jelly became a trendy status symbol among teens who felt a jar in the glove box represented their rebelliousness.

Hugh played a lot of Elvis records, and with each intro of "Don't Be Cruel," "Jailhouse Rock," or "Hound Dog," he reminded listeners that he was the bass singer who'd backed Elvis on those songs.

On Tuesday evening, February 21, after reviewing the mail orders Hugh had received—and finding them reduced considerably from Hoss's—Gab finally left the office. As he turned left onto Church at Fourth Avenue, he noted a long line of student protesters that extended a full city block from the box office of the Tennessee Theatre. Another equally long line extended from the Loews Theatre. He drove past Seventh Avenue and still the line of protestors continued. At Eighth Avenue, they stood in line at the Paramount Theatre. He stopped at the red light and watched the students. They would approach the ticket window, attempt to buy a ticket, be refused, and then rejoin the queue at the end. On the opposite side of Church Street, Gab noticed a group of teen-aged white troublemakers in the parking lot. These ducktail-haired hoodlums threw rocks, tomatoes, and eggs at the students standing in line while nearby policemen stood idly by.

As Gab drove home, he wondered how long before the theater owners understood that once the *Brown v. Board of Education* ruling became law, there was no going back. Sooner or later, the South would either embrace integration or risk a second civil war. Those who clung to the magnolia-scented past were like turtles in a shell, blind to the reality that humanity evolves. Perspectives shift; refusing to recognize that they had changed was a fool's folly. Nothing ever stays the same—not even the past.

Gab recalled the minstrel performances he'd done at the Belmont Theatre years ago. Back then, he'd laced up his dance shoes and strutted across the stage in blackface and tuxedo, never envisioning the time would come when whites and coloreds sat side by side in a theater—*and* that he'd call that progress. When he pulled into his carport, he caught a whiff of fried chicken and decided not to mention to Christine what he'd seen outside the theaters. He understood Christine's worldview had to evolve at her pace, not his. He stepped into the utility room off the carport and removed his galoshes and heavy winter coat. He glanced at the toilet in the corner, which Christine had insisted be installed exclusively for use by their Black domestic, Lucy. The toilet was tangible evidence that Christine was still nestled snugly in her Southern turtle shell.

On Sunday night, March 12, Hoss and Ted Jarrett had planned to meet at the New Era but changed their minds when they saw police outside the club load men into a paddy wagon. Hoss made a U-turn and passed one of the club's regulars on the sidewalk. He rolled down the window to ask what happened.

"Bunch of us was shootin' dice," the man said. "Thought nuthin' of the cops watchin' us, seein' as how Sou pays 'em. One yells, 'THIS IS A RAID!' Then we's like, 'Naw . . . you ain't raidin' us,' but they done did! Few guys got cuffed. Cops didn't bother comin' after us runners."

"You need a ride someplace?"

"Nah, just gonna wander till they reopen. Hit a lucky streak and since I ain't on the wrong side of the bars I's figurin' it ain't ended yet."

At Sou's home a mile away, Helen cleared the Sunday dinner dishes. The phone rang, Helen answered, then told Harriett, "Go tell Daddy the club's been raided."

Harriett looked up from her homework. "Daddy!" she yelled. "Era's raided!"

"Dang it, girl! I coulda done that. Show some respect. Daddy's not a dog you yell at."

"But, Momma, I'm givin' my homework the respect you told me. Which you want?"

Helen tossed a dish towel over her shoulder and went to find Sou. She heard the shower running and stepped into the bathroom. "Did you hear the baby? Club's been raided."

Sou pulled the shower curtain aside. "Yeah. Come join me in here. Shower's nice and hot and so am I."

"I see that," Helen said. "But sorry, Bridgy, I gotta finish cleanin' and help baby with her homework so's she can get into a top college."

"Well, okay. I'll go bail out my gamblers and pay the cops. Won't be home till daylight."

The fines and bail Sou paid on behalf of the players was a necessary expense in his operating budget. The injunction against his operating a gambling concern had no teeth, so the raid, paddy wagon, and subsequent news articles were primarily for show.

When Sou arrived at the club, Kat was all in his face with her boobs and legs and sashaying fanny. He sent a runner to bail out the gamblers and went home with Kat. If Helen had any idea Kat and Sou were involved, she'd only made a few snarky comments—unlike before when she'd immediately kicked him out and filed for divorce. Shorty suspected Sou's wife had accepted that philandering was part of the nightclub lifestyle. Sou justified his being with Kat, thinking if Funny were as concerned about his needs as she was about Harriett's college options, he wouldn't be tempted to get those needs met elsewhere.

A week later, on Monday, March 20, Kat called in sick to work.

"She ain't sick her ownself," a waitress told Sou. "She took Wilma in."

"In where?" Sou asked.

"For a *procedure*."

The way the girl said *procedure* told Sou he didn't want the conversation to continue. Later that evening, Kat came in. "Why're you here?" he asked. "Isn't Wilma sick?"

Kat grabbed a tray from behind the bar and snaked past Sou without a reply.

Later, after Sou closed the club and went home to bed, he was awakened by his wife. "Your whore's on the phone," Helen barked as she shook him awake.

"Who?" he said.

"Kat. You know damn well who!"

Sou was tempted to tell Funny to hang up on her. What the hell was Kat thinking? She knew better than to call him at home in the wee hours. Funny threw the receiver at him.

Through the receiver, Sou could hear big, gulping sobs even before he had the phone at his ear. "What?" he said, impatiently.

"It's . . . Wilma . . . Jean," Kat wailed. "She dead!"

"*Dead?*" he repeated. "Sweet Jesus, I'm so sorry. What happened—"

"Come here now. I need you to talk to the police." Kat hung up before Sou could say anything else.

Sou glanced at his wife. The look on her face showed that if she didn't know about his involvement with Kat before, she did now.

"Now, Funny," he said gently, "I know you're upset. Wilma Jean's dead and Kat's hysterical. I gotta go."

"The back-alley procedure, which was the source of the barbiturate, won't be reported." Sou came home at noon and told his wife, "Wilma Jean's death will be reported as an 'overdose of barbiturates and alcohol.'"

Rumors circled someone had slipped a mickey into Wilma Jean's drink at the Era. Wilma wasn't old enough to be in the Era, nor had she been there; however, Sou advised the staff not to dispute the story out of respect for Kat.

Sou confessed his affair with Kat to Funny, and an icy silence ensued at home. He promised to end it, but Funny wasn't interested in hearing anything he had to say.

Helen read Wilma Jean's obituary in the newspaper and called her aunt for advice.

"I don't wanna go to the funeral," Helen said. "But I don't want him there without me."

"Listen, sis, Kat's worked for y'all for years and the patrons love her. You don't have to go, but Sou does. Let her have him this one day while she buries her only child."

Helen knew this was right, but the thought of her husband with his mistress in a church infuriated her. She called Sou's cousin, who was also her doctor.

"Be the gracious Mrs. Bridgeforth," she advised. "Stay home, do small things you enjoy, and just let the day go by."

On Saturday, Helen pinned a carnation onto Sou's suit jacket. "Don't humiliate me, Bridgy," she said.

"I promise."

When Sou left, Helen called a white cab driver. She gave him money and instructions to go to Candyland (which didn't serve coloreds) and buy her five pounds of turtle pecan candies.

While Sou, his employees, regular patrons, and most of Helen's friends went to Olivet Baptist Church for Wilma Jean's funeral, Helen sat alone at her kitchen table and tried to read.

She had no idea how much time had passed until Harriett interrupted.

"Momma, you okay?"

As Harriett reached for the box of chocolates, Helen realized she'd mindlessly consumed half a box of turtle candies.

"Nah, but I will be after I get some fresh air." She pushed the box to Harriett and then stepped outside. It was unusually warm and sunny; her daffodils and hyacinths had exploded in full bloom.

"It's a mighty fine day to be buried, Miss Wilma Jean," Helen said as she snipped a handful of flowers. She carried them into her kitchen and placed them into a crystal vase. As she carried the bouquet to the living room, the phone rang.

Harriett thought she'd heard her mother cry out. She turned down the volume on her record player and heard wailing sobs. Harriett returned to the kitchen. She found her mother sitting on the floor, slumped against the wall, phone in hand.

Harriett took the phone from her mother. She heard her auntie's voice come through the handset: "Helen! Did you hear me? I said put him out! You gotta put the man out!"

"She'll call you back," Harriett said. She sat on the floor and wrapped her arms around her trembling mother. "What happened, Momma?"

"This is what you call an 'existential crisis,' baby."

"An exis . . . what?"

"We gotta do what your auntie says and put your daddy out."

"Put him out like a dog? You said—"

"I know what I said, but this is different."

"It's because of that slutty waitress Kat, isn't it?"

"No honey, this is about me and you."

"Me? How's it about me?"

"Your father is the only man I've ever loved. Probably the only man I ever *could* love, but as much as I love him, I love you more."

"I love you, too, Momma, but what's that got to do with puttin' daddy out?"

"You know how I said I was just gonna let the day go by. Be the gracious Mrs. Bridgeforth at home while I let Kat have your daddy for one day. I told him to go to the funeral and all I asked was that he not humiliate me in front of God and everybody. He couldn't even give me that."

"Huh?"

"It'll be all over town tomorrow, so you might as well hear it from me. At the conclusion of Wilma's service, when Kat went to kiss the casket goodbye, she became so overwrought she fainted. Collapsed right there at the altar. Daddy picked her up and carried her outta the church like a bride."

"*My daddy?*" Harriett repeated incredulously.

"Your father."

"Are you kidding me? My daddy's never carried anything heavier than a biscuit, and that includes me!"

Helen laughed through her tears. "Baseballs are heavier'n biscuits."

"Okay, so Daddy's never carried nuthin' heavier than a baseball. He sure ain't gonna carry trash to the curb."

Helen laughed. Thank goodness for her daughter's wicked sense of humor. Together, they piled Sou's clothes, jewelry, pearl-handled pistol, and autographed baseballs into suitcases and baskets. Helen called cab number sixty-eight (reserved for Sou's use only) and told his driver, Henry Kimbro, to deliver Sou's belongings to the New Era. Kimbro finished loading the last laundry basket into the trunk when the locksmith pulled up. Instead of driving to Twelfth and Charlotte as instructed, Kimbro delivered Sou's belongings to 337 Arena Place—Kat's home.

A week later, Helen learned Harriett had been right. Sou hadn't carried Kat out of the church. The deacon who'd worked the service told Helen the pallbearers had carried Kat out. Sou had been one of several and he'd only held on to Kat's big toe. Had Helen heard this from the get-go, she may not have thrown him out, as she'd built her life around William Sousa Bridgeforth. She also knew that if she forgave him, Sou would come home.

But Helen had spent the last week really thinking about what she wanted for Harriett. The world was changing. Women like Diane Nash were the future. Helen wanted Harriett to emulate Diane, the woman who'd stood up to Ben West and his powerful allies, James Stahlman and John Sloan. How could Harriett be expected to do that if her own mother couldn't stand up to her misbehaving father?

What Helen wanted for Harriett was a good education, a loving family, and worthwhile work that would give her a sense of dignity and her life meaning. The more Helen thought about what she wanted for Harriett, the more she realized it wasn't too late for herself. When Harriett left for college, Helen would dust off her old dreams of being a college librarian. There was no reason she couldn't work at one of the nearby colleges, where she'd be surrounded by her passions: education, great literature, and the empowerment of a new generation of women.

The Diane Nash generation.

23

STAND BY ME

[In Nashville] everybody knows how to play
guitar. You walk down the street and people
are on their porch playing guitar. That's where
I learned to play, really, in Nashville.

—JIMI HENDRIX

Following the fallout from the deejay convention, Gab spent much of the next year developing a plan for WLAC to maintain its late-night R & B programming and immensely profitable per-inquiry sales strategy. On February 8, 1962, Gab was presented a sales and marketing award for having created a sales stratagem designed "to guard against disc jockeys accepting money to favor numbers record manufacturers particularly wanted to push. He sold five leading record manufacturers in New York and Chicago on the idea of sponsoring programs five nights a week for broadcasting their own selections."[1]

Gab's strategy was soon adopted as a broadcast industry standard.

While Gab felt honored by the recognition of his peers, the award he received paled in comparison to the gratitude John expressed after his *Soul Book* sold over one hundred thousand copies. As with the infamous WLAC

---

1. "Midstate's 46 Top Salesmen, Saleswomen To Be Honored," *Tennessean*, February 8, 1962, 8.

baby chicks, as well as Randy's and Ernie's records, the station and Gab earned a small percentage of each transaction.

To become a vendor, John had created a business, JR Enterprises. JRE handled the printing and distribution of *Soul Book*. The enterprise operated from a butcher block coffee table in the family room where John's four middle children worked as mailroom clerks. Each day after school, Lelaine, Patty, Johnny, and Barry would stuff copies of *Soul Book* into envelopes, address them from the COD orders, bundle the outgoing orders by state, then pack them into boxes they'd load into John's quirky Ford English car and deliver to the post office.

After Gab was nationally recognized for finding a workable solution to the industry payola crisis, he was named vice president by the L&C board of directors—the same title that Tom Baker held—and was given a raise. To celebrate, Gab decided he would fulfill one of Christine's lifelong dreams and take her on a three-week tour of Europe. A few days before Gab was set to depart for vacation, John asked him to lunch.

John wanted to drive and said he needed Gab's opinion about something. They drove out Hillsboro Pike to the edge of Belle Meade. John turned onto Chickering Lane and pulled into the driveway of an impressive, beige-brick estate home.

"I'm thinking of buying this place for my family," John said. "A year ago, I was bankrupt, had lost everything—even my furniture was repossessed. Today, I have the wherewithal to pay cash for this place."

Gab was near to tears as he walked through the spacious contemporary home. He was so touched by John's sentiment. "You've gone from Rags Richbourg to Richy Richbourg in no time," Gab said with amusement. "It couldn't have happened to a better guy. I can't tell you how happy I am. Buy it!"

"Thanks for standing by me, Blackie," John said. "I told Margaret, the first folks we're having over'll be you and Christine. In the meantime, the Realtor left this for you and me." John opened the fridge. He pulled out pimento cheese sandwiches, corn chips, and lemonade. The humble meal was one of the most memorable lunches of Gab's career.

Sou had grown so accustomed to Helen bringing his dinner to the club each evening he'd forgotten how to order for himself. He didn't even know what temperature he liked his steaks. Rarely would he realize how hungry he was until Helen arrived. And whatever she brought turned out to be exactly what he wanted.

"Life's a hell of a lot easier with a wife and no mistress than the other way 'round," he told Shorty.

"Well, don't go thinkin' 'bout marrying your mistress," Shorty advised. "All that does is create a job vacancy."

"I'm not gonna marry Kat."

"Then you best convince Helen not to divorce you. And soon like."

Sou requested that Helen come to the club Tuesday, since Kat and the house band took Tuesday nights off. "I want to make sure you and Harriett have everything y'all need," he said on the call.

As a show of good faith, Helen brought Sou dinner. She made his favorites, arranged them on the fine china he preferred, and wrapped the plate in tinfoil. When she arrived at the Era, she placed the meal in front of him and sat quietly while he ate.

Sou put down his fork and reached for Helen's hand. "Is there anything I can do to get you to reconsider?"

"I'll always love you, Bridgy, you know that. But this life of yours"—she twirled her hand to indicate the club—"it doesn't work for me. I'm exhausted from the ups and downs and the dramas of it all."

"What if we didn't divorce? What if I let you enjoy all the financial benefits of being my wife? You can have the home and I'll continue to pay for everything. You'll be free to do whatever you want. Just don't divorce me."

"If you think I'll have a change of heart, I won't."

"I'd rather things stay just like they are."

"Meaning you don't wanna marry Kat." Helen picked up the dinnerware. "Okay, Bridgy, but I'm not bringing you dinner anymore, and the next time I come here, it'll be with a date."

"Ouch," he said, feigning he'd taken a shot to the chest.

As Helen turned to leave, he added. "Hey, Funny, one last thing: What temperature do I like my steaks?"

She didn't turn around or answer. Sou felt as if she'd ripped out his heart.

"She was always too good for me," he told Shorty. "She's just the last person to know it."

On their Tuesday nights off, the New Era's house band would book other gigs in other places and bill themselves as the Imperials. In the spring of 1962, a few of the Imperials traveled fifty miles north for a regular Tuesday gig in Clarksville at the Pink Poodle Club, a favorite of soldiers stationed at Fort Campbell. The Imperials' Johnny Jones was a well-known studio musician that most pickers in Nashville considered the best guitar player in the city. This designation was quite the honor, as at the time "half of all American recordings were issued from Nashville."[2]

Among the soldiers who came to the Pink Poodle on Tuesday nights to watch Johnny Jones play were two guitar-playing airmen attached to the 101st Airborne, Jimi Hendrix and Billy Cox. Jimi sat up front, mesmerized by Johnny's talent. When Jones took a break, Jimi asked if he could hold Johnny's guitar. Johnny left his amp on low, went to the bar, and while the jukebox played, left his guitar with Jimi. It was the first time Jimi had ever picked the strings of a decently made and impeccably tuned guitar.

Johnny later said of that night, "When he [Jimi] flipped around and put it on upside down, that's when I got a cold chill."[3]

Jimi and Billy formed a band that first played on the base and later in and around Clarksville. Whenever they could get away, they'd head to the New Era Club to watch Johnny Jones. Billy had met Hoss there several years before. Billy had told Hoss how, when he was a boy, he'd built a crystal radio from a wood box and some parts he'd ordered through the mail, following instructions he'd found in a library book. When Billy finally got the radio to work, the first sound he'd heard was Hoss saying, "I'm down for Royal Crown."

After that conversation, Hoss invited Billy to the regular Saturday afternoon jam sessions he hosted at King Studios. The sessions would last as long as five hours, with Hoss hoping he'd find a few minutes he could edit into a demo and sell. One Saturday, Billy brought Jimi to meet Hoss.

Hoss plugged Jimi into the soundboard and asked him to "play a New

2. Steven Roby, Brad Schreiber, *Becoming Jimi Hendrix*, (Boston: DaCapo Press, 2001), 31.
3. Roby and Schreiber, 20.

Orleans rhythm, a simple four-four." Jimi's guitar screamed. "Hey, man," Hoss said. "Just give me a good straight four." Again, Jimi's guitar screamed. "Cut that mother off! Cut him off the board," Hoss yelled.[4] Later, he played back the recordings and erased all of Jimi's riffs. Hoss had no clue how the young picker thought the noise he created could be mistaken for music.

Jimi manipulated an early discharge from the service. He worked odd jobs while he waited for Billy to get out. Once Billy was discharged in October, they rented a house in Clarksville and, with bass guitarist Alfonso Young, formed a band, the King Kasuals. They played gigs around Clarksville and in small circuit clubs. When they weren't booked, Billy and Jimi headed to the New Era to see Johnny Jones. Jones, like Jimi, couldn't read music when he started playing guitar professionally. After Ted Jarrett discovered Jones, he taught him to read music. Jones shared what he'd learned from Ted with Jimi. When Jones told Billy the Del Morocco in Nashville was looking to hire a house band, the King Kasuals auditioned and got the job. Billy, Jimi, and Alfonso moved to Nashville, where they were allowed to live rent-free above the hair salon in the adjoining space.

In the year he played at the Del Morocco, Jimi honed his skills and hung out at the Era with Jones. He'd walk the mile from the Del Morocco to the Era with his guitar slung over his shoulder. He'd sleep with it on his chest.

In August, when Hoss returned from the road, he sought to record a blues song Jones had written. Jones insisted that Jimi be allowed to record it with him. Hoss was again unhappy with Jimi's unconventional style. He went ahead and had the record pressed, and even got John to play it, but it never caught on and wasn't released. In November, Hoss had a third chance to recognize Jimi's exceptional talent. Jimi had garnered a significant following, and professional pickers from Jefferson Street to the Ryman agreed Jimi had phenomenal talent. Yet Hoss couldn't hear it. When he recorded Frank Howard and the Commanders performing a song Billy composed, Hoss turned down Jimi's microphone, cutting him from the recording.

While he was in Nashville, Jimi learned more than just mastery of the guitar. Coming from Seattle, Jimi hadn't experienced community-sanctioned

4. Roby and Schreiber, 18.

racism before. He was introduced to Jim Crow and subsequently joined the student protests.

On Black Friday 1962, John Lewis and his student nonviolent protest group distributed seven thousand leaflets to the college campuses in Nashville. The leaflets read in part:

> For over two years we have sought to negotiate with the major business establishments, the Chamber of Commerce, the restaurant association, and individual owners and managers. After this long period of time, without any major advances, the hope of many that negotiations would bring about a change had grown dim. We have no choice but to again witness in a dramatic yet loving fashion that segregation is an evil we cannot and will not support.[5]

Hoping to repeat the success they'd had in disrupting the 1960 Easter shopping season, the student activists resumed their nonviolent protests, targeting restaurants.

Diane Nash's group saw the struggle for civil rights as a moral issue. Segregationists saw the struggle as "Negroes versus Caucasians." Most white college students saw the struggle as an attempt to bring the "Old South" into a new era—the Kennedy era. The protests were an attempt to create a "New South," one that embraced President Kennedy's progressive agenda. Segregationists wanted to hold on to the "Old South," best exemplified by the segregationist agenda of Alabama gubernatorial candidate George Wallace.

The student protesters returned to the sidewalks, this time with more white activists. A few Blacks would attempt to enter a segregated restaurant like the B & W cafeteria, Tic Toc, Cross Keys, the Krystal hamburger chain, Candyland, or the Wilson Quick Pharmacy. They would then be arrested, bailed out, and returned to do it again. Jimi Hendrix and Billy Cox sat with the protesters. After a few Sundays of sitting on sidewalks, they decided to be proactive. They entered a diner displaying a "Whites Only" sign, took a seat, attempted to order, and were promptly arrested. Teddy bailed them

---

5. Larry Daughtery, "Downtown Sitins To End Fisk Rally," *Tennessean*, November 24, 1962, 2.

out of jail and got the charges dropped, then deducted the expenses from their earnings.

For all the trouble Vanderbilt gave the protesters, including having expelled James Lawson, Sou found it ironic that Vanderbilt's Greek Week would conclude with Hank Ballard and the Midnighters performing exclusively for Vandy students at the newly opened civic auditorium. Ballard was one of Sou's most popular acts, and the auditorium was located where his former clubs stood. The whole thing rubbed Sou the wrong way. It felt as if the city had nefariously and legally stolen a business he'd created.

Sou complained to Gorgeous George about it. George was the promoter and Ballard's cleanup man—a cross between an emcee and a stand-up comedian. George had come into the New Era Club with Aretha Franklin, who'd been a frequent performer at the Era. While at the club, George mentioned he needed a guitar player to back his band. Jimi happened to be at the Era, as he was most afternoons, jamming with Johnny Jones.[6] Sou introduced Jimi to George, and a few days later, Jimi left to tour with George's revue.

Gab read the article about Vandy's Greek Week in the *Tennessean*: "A door-to-door solicitation of funds by fraternity freshmen for the Nashville Symphony Orchestra initiates the annual program today . . . among the highlights of the week will be an all campus dance at the Nashville Municipal auditorium . . . featuring Hank Ballard and the Midnighters."[7]

Gab clipped the news article so he could show it to B.B. the next time he came to town. It was written proof that the toffee-nosed snobs wanted the common folk to pay for their symphony.

Gorgeous George returned to Nashville in May—this time with Sam Cooke, Little Esther, the Drifters, Jerry Butler, Dee Clark, the Crystals, Johnny Thunder, and Dionne Warwick. It had become customary for any R & B act to swing by WLAC while in town, though this pit stop wasn't as successful as it once had been. With Hoss on the road for Chess, Gene working only occasionally, and Hugh attracting white teens, the musicians felt the station was turning its back on their Black audience. Gab acknowledged that Hugh didn't sell anywhere near the R & B records Hoss and Gene had.

6. Ann Wallace, "Blues Greats at Festival," *Leaf-Chronicle*, August 4, 2006, 42.
7. Frank Sutherland, "Greek Week Opens At VU," *Tennessean*, March 31, 1963, 14.

As Sam Cooke made his way to Fourth and Church, he noted the crowd that blocked the street and sidewalks in front of the B & W Cafeteria and Cross Keys Restaurant. The two restaurants, on either side of Sixth Avenue North, had their entrances blocked by fifty arm-linked protestors. When Sam arrived at the station, he complained about the way the city was treating the protestors and requested Gab put Hoss back on the air.

The following day, Gab read the morning paper and realized why Sam had been upset. The front page of the *Tennessean* showed a photograph of a patrolman who'd lost his temper and had to be removed from the scene by a superior officer. Page 2 featured a heart-wrenching photo of fifteen-year-old Ewing Ella Bigham lying unconscious in the street after having been struck by a patrolman's billy stick.[8] While some whites in the crowd disputed that patrol officers hit girls with billy clubs, Harriett Bridgeforth can confirm that's exactly what some police did.

On another occasion, Harriett and a friend skipped class at Pearl High to join the protesters. Harriett was sitting with the protestors when an officer walked through the crowd swinging his billy club to and fro, hitting whoever was in his way. That day, it happened to be Harriett's friend. The girls left the scene traumatized to the extent that nearly sixty years later, Harriett can still describe the location, size, and color of her friend's wound.

In April, Nashville switched from a city to a metropolitan government. This brought a new mayor, Mr. Beverly Briley, and new countywide adminis-tration. West had given up on becoming governor, especially since Tennessee had changed the term-limit laws, a move that allowed Frank Clement to return to the governor's mansion. When the protests resumed, Briley created a perma-nent biracial committee to address any future problems.

As Ben West left office, he stated, "Their [the students'] battle is won here. We're going too slow for some and too fast for others, but we're moving right along all the time."

The following week, Governor Clement escorted President Kennedy to Vanderbilt. The president addressed the students in reaction to the previous week's protests:

---

8. "Injured During Melee," *Tennessean*, May 11, 1963, 1–2.

A special burden rests on the educated men and women of our country to reject the temptations of prejudice and violence, and to reaffirm the values of freedom and law on which our society depends. Certain other societies may respect the rule of force—we respect the rule of law. . . . He (the educated citizen) knows that law is the adhesive force in the cement of society, creating order out of chaos and coherence in the face of anarchy. He knows that for one man to defy a law or court he does not like is to invite others to defy those laws which they do not like, leading to a breakdown of all justice and order. He knows too, that every fellow man is entitled to be regarded with decency and treated with dignity.[9]

The president's remarks had a sobering effect, and no further protests occurred that year.

New York Herald Tribune writer Charles Portis said it best: "Nashville has had its bombings and street battles, but it's a city that cannot abide unpleasantness . . . it values peace and quiet."

---

9. Wayne Whitt, "JFK Told Nashvillians To Ban Bias, Violence," *Tennessean*, November 23, 1963.

24

SHOTGUN

Sales Manager and Vice President Blackie Blackman
rode herd on the deejays by monitoring a twenty-
four-hour-a-day master tape of their on-the-
air performances, known as Blackie's Bible.

—WES SMITH

Hoss and Etta James had known each other for years by the time they each signed on with Leonard Chess in the summer of 1960. They'd met when Etta came to town with the Top Ten Revue following her 1955 release of "Wallflower," popularly known as "Roll with Me Henry." Etta had written and recorded the song, which Georgia Gibbs covered, changing the lyrics from "roll with me" to "dance with me." Despite having recorded her original composition, Etta had been required to label her record as a cover of Georgia's. Shortly thereafter, Georgia covered LaVern Baker's "Tweedle Dee," and Little Richard's song "Tutti Frutti" was similarly appropriated with changed lyrics.

In the ensuing years, Hoss had seen Etta perform many times. He'd witnessed her manic restlessness, the ups and downs and weariness of living out of a tour bus. Add to that the frustration of seeing someone else benefit financially from her original work, while she lacked the wherewithal to do anything about it. This life had taken a toll on Etta's body and spirit. Up close, needle marks had left her wrists looking like road maps. Hoss couldn't help but compare Etta to Della and think that the only thing they had in common was the fact that their stage names had been created by splitting their first names in two. Jamesetta became Etta James; Delloreese became Della Reese. Or he compared Etta to Gladys Knight, who at fifteen years old had the same confidence, grace, and ambition that drew him to Della in the first place.

Hoss voiced to Leonard Chess his concerns about Etta's unhealthy lifestyle. Chess advised Hoss to clean up his own addictions and not worry about Etta's. "Get a handle on your drinking before you end up dead, or kill someone else," Chess warned. Hoss had heard that before—from Gab—but felt both men were being overly dramatic.

Soon after Hoss's conversation with Leonard, Etta was hospitalized for her drug addictions. She got clean, and the next time he saw her, she looked amazing.

In the spring of 1963, Hoss had a rude awakening. He awoke in a gutter with no memory of how he'd gotten there. His wallet was gone and he'd obviously taken a few punches to the ribs. It wasn't the first time he'd awakened without knowing what had happened, but it was the first time he'd passed out in an alley. He feared life on the road had him following in Etta's footsteps. Nancy had run out of patience and threatened divorce.

When Chess had offered him the job of an A&R man, Hoss thought it "sounded awfully glamorous."[1] Yet living as the musicians did, he discovered the road was more demanding and destructive than glamorous.

In May, the *Nashville Tennessean* magazine featured a short story about Hoss's famous ancestor Hugh Rogan: "Rogan's life story—and love story— were epics in Tennessee history, told to sleepy children in the nighttime stillness of frontier log cabins."[2]

Rogan was Davy Crockett before Crockett was born. Many children donned their coonskin caps to play Davy Crockett on the wild frontier. At Miss Nannie Berry's preschool in Hendersonville during the summer of 1963, Eddie Blackman's daughter, Paula, and her kindergarten classmates played Hugh Rogan rather than Davy Crockett. They learned to recite the legend of Hugh Rogan: "They never molded a bullet that could kill Hugh Rogan."

---

1. Broven, *Record Makers and Breakers*, 111.
2. Hugh Walker, "The Raw Irishman," *Nashville Tennessean*, May 5, 1963, 10.

"How brave was Hugh Rogan?" asked the teacher.

"Brave enough to sneak through Indian lines to get coals to start a fire so a dying man could see to write his will."[3]

The magazine story was illustrated with pictures and contained a photograph of Charles Rogan Allen, Hoss's son, in front of the stone house Hoss's great-great-great-grandfather had built in Sumner County. The article gave Gab an excuse to call Hoss. During their lengthy chat, Hoss confessed the road had gotten to him and he planned to get sober at a rehabilitation hospital. He said that what Gad had predicted would happen, had happened. Hoss had gotten drunk regularly, been beat up, and knew he needed to turn his life around.

"If I get sober, and commit to staying sober, would you consider rehiring me?"

"Get sober, then let's talk," Gab said. "I know you can do it."

Gab had never been happy with Hugh's show. It was popular with teens, and his Hugh Baby Hops and Funtown Dances were well received, but Hugh's revenue fell short. Sometimes deejays would start thinking they were in the music business and Gab would have to remind them that they were in the *advertising* business. John understood it; therefore, everything John pitched sold. Even the gimmicky weight gain tablets he marketed as "Weight On" sold like baby chicks. Six months later, he'd relabel the same tablets as "Weight Off" and sell even more. From mufflers to socks, razors to Bibles, John created revenue. Conversely, Hugh's show sold records but little else. Gab had given up trying to find products to sell white teens. They didn't buy items COD because they had easy access to everything in stores, unlike rural Blacks who listened to John and didn't have the luxury of shopping at local retailers—if those even existed.

When Gab told his secretary to send in his next appointment, a young man carrying a leather satchel came in and sat down.

"Hello, Mr. Blackman. Remember me?" he asked.

"I know we've met before, but—"

"I'm Sam Moore." He pulled a huge Bible from his satchel and placed it on Gab's desk.

---

3. Walker, *Nashville Tennessean*, May 5, 1963.

Gab glanced at the massive tome. "The door-to-door Bible salesman!"

"Right. After you told me to come back with a better Bible, I went home to Lebanon and spent two years gathering beautiful color photographs and creating family history pages. This is the prototype. I wanted your feedback before I put them into production."

Gab ran his finger along the Bible's binding, noting how the cover and fore edge were embossed in gold. The frontispiece plate depicted a beautiful scene of Jesus with some of his followers. He turned to the end and noted the page number: 1198. "This's definitely a better Bible," Gab said. "Just one question, what's the retail price?"

"If I can print enough in bulk, I should be able to get it down to twenty dollars."

"Twenty!" Gab exclaimed. "That's seventeen dollars more than our listeners can afford."

"You said better, not cheaper," Sam said.

"Look, this's absolutely better. I'd be proud to own it, proud to sell it, proud to give them as gifts. But the price. I don't know that I can make that work. Let me think about it."

"Why don't you keep this over the weekend? Show it around. See what folks would be willing to pay. I'll come back Monday."

Gab did as Sam asked. He showed the Bible around the office and at his church. Everyone agreed Sam's Bible was superior to anything on the market and well worth the lofty price. As Bibles go, this was a masterpiece. Gab told Christine he wanted to sell it but didn't know how he could.

"Twenty dollars is just too much. Our listeners will buy anything if it's priced at three dollars."

"Too bad you don't offer layaway," Christine said.

On Monday, Gab told Sam, "I've got an idea. Let's offer the Bibles for $19.95. We'll ask for $1.95 down and six monthly payments of $3.00 each. When the final payment is received, we'll ship the Bible. This will provide you working capital to help offset the costs and allow our listeners to buy something they'll be truly proud to own. Deal?"

Sam and Gab shook on it. It was the beginning of a long partnership between Royal Publishers Inc. and WLAC—and an even longer friendship between Sam Z. Moore and Gab Blackman. Over the years, WLAC sold hundreds of thousands of Sam's "better Bibles."

Weeks later, Gab received a formal complaint from the FCC accusing Hugh of using "improper and suggestive language."[4] Normally, this would be cause for alarm, but in this instance he took it as a godsend. He'd tired of the complaints from Christine, her church friends, and some advertisers regarding Hugh's broadcast of comments about sending five-gallon drums of White Rose Petroleum Jelly to Belmont, an elite girls' college, and to Ft. Walton Beach. The FCC echoed Christine's complaint that Hugh's comments were "vile and tasteless."[5]

The commission threatened to revoke WLAC's license if they didn't exercise tighter control over their deejays. Gab thought it was long past time to let Hugh go, yet taking a chance on Hoss was risky. He reached out to Nancy, who put him in touch with the facility where Hoss had been treated for alcoholism. Assured that Hoss was now sober, Gab recommended bringing him back.

Jimmy Ward admitted that targeting white teens had taken the station in the wrong direction. The timing worked out fortuitously for Hoss because both WLAC-TV and WLAC radio broadcast the March on Washington, DC, and Dr. Martin Luther King Jr.'s "I Have a Dream" speech.

Those events helped Gab and Jimmy persuade Gil Dudley—who held the title of president of WLAC—that the station that had pioneered R & B programming needed to honor its legacy, especially since so many musicians wanted Hoss back. Gab had felt increasingly guilty about having fired Hoss. It was not lost on Gab that he had been partially responsible for Hoss's problems. After all, Gab had directed Hoss to create an on-air atmosphere of a bawdy party, and in doing so, he had inadvertently encouraged the drinking and immoral behavior. Rehiring Hoss would demonstrate the station's commitment to the music, the musicians, and their cause. And it would offer Hoss a chance at redemption. Dudley agreed to let Hoss return, provided Gab monitor him to ensure Hoss stayed sober on air.

Gab and Dave Binns determined that in order to "maintain tighter control," Binns would install a monitoring system to record every minute of WLAC's

4. Smith, *Pied Pipers*, 91.
5. Smith, 91.

broadcasts. Hoss was rehired with the understanding that if the tape—which came to be called Blackie's Bible—ever showed evidence of Hoss being drunk on air, the door would hit him in the ass before he knew it.

On Tuesday afternoon, September 17, 1963, Hoss stopped by the New Era to tell Sou he was returning to WLAC. As he walked into Sou's office, he interrupted Shorty, who had been talking about Cassius Clay. The previous night, one hundred spectators had crowded the Jefferson Street sidewalk to listen to Clay recite a braggadocio's poem about a mythical fight between himself and Sonny Liston.

After Shorty concluded the tale, he added, "Clay then said he was just passing through on his way from Miami to Louisville, and asked folks what other fighter would come to a country town like Nashville and speak to the little people."[6]

"Country town?" Kat exclaimed. "Did he not see those letters atop the L & C tower? What *country town* has a skyscraper?"

"Anyways," Shorty continued, "he signed some autographs and said, 'You think Liston's gonna sign autographs? He can't even write.' A few folks walked off. Clay yelled, 'Wait, nobody leaves when Clay is talkin'!'"[7]

"I hope Liston knocks him out first round," Kat said.

"You'll have to place that bet with Nathan Bellamy," Sou said.

"I warned ya about him, didn't I?" Shorty asked.

Bellamy had set up his own numbers bank and partnered with Sou's nephew, Wallace Bridgeforth, and two other runners, John Gant and Edward Brown. Together the three friends had come up with an ingenious twist on the numbers game. Hoping to siphon Sou's business for Bellamy, they created a rolling numbers bank, a paneled van equipped in the back with "two adding machines, an electric fan, ice chest, and chairs."[8] They'd drive this decked-out van through town like it was an ice cream truck, selling lottery tickets like popsicles. Sou was glad Wallace's group of runners had left. The three were nothing but trouble.

A few days later, Hoss picked up Chess's A&R man, Ralph Bass, at the

---

6. Tom Powell, "Clay Wows Group, Spouts Liston Poop," *Tennessean*, September 17, 1963, 17.

7. Powell, *Tennessean*. September 17, 1963.

8. Nellie Kenyon, "Rolling Numbers Bank Seized," *Tennessean*, August 30, 1963, 10.

airport. As they drove to the Era, Hoss retold Shorty's story about Clay and gave Ralph a rundown on the New Era. Chess had long wanted Etta to record a new album but had trouble getting her into the studio. Etta was an emotional singer, like Roy Brown, who drew energy from a crowd and transformed it into an electrifying performance. It was nearly impossible to replicate that magic in a studio. Ralph noted how tears would roll down Etta's cheeks when she performed for an audience. He wanted to capture that intensity on a live album. Etta agreed to do a live recording. Ralph chose Nashville and let Etta select the club. She chose the New Era.

Hoss escorted Ralph to the club and introduced him to the staff. Ralph was impressed.

"You've got the correct atmosphere, receptive audiences, and good acoustics," Ralph said. "Perfect for a live album."[9]

"Etta's one of my favorites," Sou said. "I'm honored to help."

Etta rocked the house on Friday night, September 27. Hoss was supposed to be on air that night, but he'd gotten Gene to sub for one hour so Hoss could watch Etta's opening numbers and talk about them on air afterward. He arrived just in time to see her step onto the stage. Cat-eyed, with her hair tinted red and piled high, she was dressed in a white, off-one-shoulder dress. Her huge gold hoop earrings and the sequins on the bodice of her dress sparkled under the spotlights. Hoss noted she bandaged her wrist to cover the scars of her heroin addiction.

Behind Etta, Hoss saw that two of Sou's house musicians had joined Etta's band—drummer Freeman Brown and guitarist James Watkins. Hoss wondered if they'd be credited. Sometimes Black artists played, were paid in cash, and were never credited. Or worse, some white musician who wasn't even there received credit and royalties.

Etta called the first song "Something's Got a Hold on Me." Ralph Bass later wrote, "The band counted off the tempo and was gone! As the song progressed, Etta caught fire. . . . A groove developed. . . . She reached heights never before captured in a studio . . . and left for all posterity."[10]

To enjoy the rowdy excitement of the New Era Club on September 27 and

---

9. Ralph Bass, liner notes to *Etta James Rocks the House*, Argo Record Corp., Chicago (1964).
10. Bass, liner notes.

28, 1963, one could listen to the album recorded those nights, *Etta Rocks the House,* which many consider "one of the greatest live blues and R & B recordings in history."[11]

Etta's album was released on December 13, 1963. It didn't immediately soar to the top of the charts as Chess had expected, primarily because the country was still reeling from the assassination of President Kennedy.

On November 22, 1963, all of Nashville had been in mourning, but nowhere was the loss felt more acutely than in the Black neighborhoods. Several hundred gathered, "grief-stricken at the assassination of the man many revered as their greatest champion, stood in the pelting rain, on the steps of the state capital in Nashville, and silently prayed for the late President Kennedy."[12]

Hal Hebb—the former soldier, inmate, and member of Johnny Bragg's Marigolds—had served his time and now worked as a bouncer at Club Baron on Jefferson. Out of respect for the slain President Kennedy, Club Baron requested patrons to remove their hats. When Donald Ridley refused, bouncer Bernard Cox, wielding a shotgun, chased Ridley out of the club. Ridley lay in wait outside with plans to get even. Later, when Hal exited the club, Ridley attacked him with a knife. Numerous cuts to his abdomen left Hal nearly sliced in two. Cox tossed Hal the shotgun. Hal fired one shot. Ridley died at the scene. Hal was rushed to the hospital and died hours later.

The news of his older brother's death reached Bobby Hebb in New York. "It was so sad, such a loss," Bobby said. "I needed to pick myself up. I needed an upper. Writing 'Sunny' was therapy."[13]

When John Richbourg offered his condolences to Bobby following Hal's funeral, Bobby mentioned he'd written a new song he wanted John to hear.

"It's my version of 'Walkin' in the Rain,'" Bobby said.

John listened to the opening: "Sunny, yesterday my life was filled with rain. Sunny, you smiled at me and really eased the pain." The song was too pop for John's taste and he passed.

Bobby had learned much more from his blind parents than how to play and

11. Randy Fox, *Nashville Scene*, October 10, 2013.

12. Katherine Delmaz, *We Shall Overcome,* (Nashville: Fisk Art Museum in Association with Vanderbilt University Press, 2018), 107.

13. Tim Ghianni, "One So True To The Music," *Tennessean*, October 17, 2004, D10.

compose music. They had taught him that suffering induces resiliency. They understood that to survive the harshness of slavery, of poverty, of injustice, from the first day the first African landed on the shores of this country, music was used to express their sorrow, pain, frustration, and joy. They believed the history of African Americans is better understood through the lyrics of their songs than from any history book. In the African tradition, literature, folklore, and mythology are shared in song, not written down. The evolution from slave spiritual to gospel—from gut-bucket blues to Etta's rock and Bobby's up-tempo pop—bears witness to their experiences. Whether a plea for freedom, a call for understanding, or a recognition of one's humanity, songs teach us about life, liberty, and the pursuit of happiness. What John had failed to realize was that Bobby had written lyrics that perfectly expressed this pursuit of happiness. It's no surprise, therefore, that BMI later ranked "Sunny" the twenty-fifth most played song of the twentieth century.

By fall 1963, Gene had grown tired of retirement and returned to the air, albeit via tape rather than live. John had recovered financially and was managing artists, producing records, mentoring aspiring deejays, and spoiling his wife and children. Hoss had gone through recovery and was back on air and back at the Era, where he occasionally lapsed into his old habits. The three kings of early R & B radio had reunited to split the four peak broadcast hours between 8:00 p.m. and midnight. Herman Grizzard manned the final hour. And as Gab predicted, the 50,000-watt quartet owned the night. Their audience was vast, extending south to the Caribbean, north to Canada, from the Eastern Seaboard to the Missouri River. Their influence grew even greater. Most listeners believed Hoss and John were Black. They each had deep Southern voices; they used expressions from the streets that were common in African American culture. When coupled with the songs they played and the prointegration comments they made, it was clear that even if they weren't Black, they nonetheless shared Paul LaPrad's beliefs.

One night a listener called Hoss while he was on air. "Is you Black or is you white?" the caller asked.

Hoss broadcast the question and his answer: "Does it make a difference?"

Gab was listening at that moment and felt incredibly proud. That statement alone confirmed he'd made the right decision to put Hoss back on air.

He called Hoss. "Your soul sure came through on that one, old buddy. You said so much in such few words."

One of WLAC's longtime loyal listeners was Robert Zimmerman of Hibbing, Minnesota, a town without a single Black resident. "Zimmerman's experience of listening to Black music on WLAC led him to want to hear more and know more. That desire eventually led him to become Bob Dylan."[14] In 1963 he wrote "Blowin' in the Wind." Later, when Dylan's manager suggested he meet the Staple Singers, Dylan replied, "I've known them since I was 12 . . . I listened to WLAC."[15]

Meanwhile, Hank Ballard had fired Jimi Hendrix, who had made his way back to Nashville to rejoin the King Kasuals. Jimi, Billy, and Freeman Brown started playing in nightclubs around town. One night while playing the Era, Shorty told Billy that Sou wanted to see him. Billy went in search of Sou and found him standing beside a window.

"See the sheriff's car there?" Sou said.

"Uh-huh," Billy said.

Sou handed him a paper bag stuffed with cash. "Take this down and give it to him."

Billy did as Sou asked. A few months later, Billy read with amusement the newspaper accounts of Sheriff Jett having been indicted for taking bribes from nightclub owners. The *Tennessean* quoted Jett as saying under oath, "I've never received a dime from Sou Bridgeforth, a numbers operator, or any other law violator."[16]

"It's true," Billy teased Sou. "You never put any dimes in the lunch sacks, did ya?"

By 1964 there were more radios than people in the country. The dismal predictions that radio would die out when television signals reached every American home had been thwarted by the transistor radio and targeted programming. Because WLAC had championed race music, Noble Blackwell thought WLAC-TV might be receptive to doing the same for television.

---

14. Maureen Mahon, "What is the Most Important Innovation in the History of Rock 'n' Roll?" *Smithsonian*, February 10, 2015.

15. Andy Greene, "Mavis Staples on Summer Tour with Bob Dylan," *Rolling Stone*, May 9, 2016.

16. Nellie Kenyon, "Jett: Never Took A Dime From A Violator," *Tennessean*, June 11, 1964, 1.

Blackwell had heard how Jackie Shane, a local transgender singer, drummer, and former member of Sou's house band, was asked to appear on Dick Clark's *American Bandstand* but refused.

"No way!" Jackie told the producers. "They use our music, but they don't let our children come on!"[17]

Noble Blackwell decided to pitch a similar program with an all-Black cast. He wrote a proposal for an R & B musical variety show featuring local talent and called it *Night Train*.

Gab escorted Blackwell to Baker's office. Blackwell gave his pitch, and afterward, Gab encouraged Tom to give it serious consideration. He offered to have Hoss and John promote the show on their broadcasts. When the Noble-Drury advertising agency agreed to sponsor *Night Train*, it was greenlit and filmed in the WLAC studios. The recording took place on Tuesday nights when the musicians in Sou's house band were available to back the featured vocalists. *Night Train* was broadcast just after midnight, to air when John signed off.

Jackie Shane and Jimi Hendrix appeared on the same episode, which can still be viewed online. Jackie performs "Walkin' the Dog." Jimi plays guitar as Buddy and Stacey sing "Shotgun."

Most of the artists featured on the show's episodes also appeared at the New Era. Watching *Night Train* allows viewers to hear the music Sou, Hoss, and Ted Jarrett saw live at the New Era in the early to mid-1960s. In addition to Jackie and Jimi, the artists who appeared at the Era and are featured on *Night Train* include James Brown, Gladys Knight, Wilson Pickett, and Otis Redding.

On December 8, 1964, Cassius Clay came into the New Era with his entourage. "I'm feeling good!" he shouted. He ambled between tables, entertaining the crowd with comments: "I'm on my way to Miami to pick up a bus . . . I've changed my style but I'm still king . . . I'm twenty-two, but I'll be champ for another ten years . . . by the way, I have a new name, Mohammad Ali."[18]

"If you're a Muslim, why are you in a nightclub?" Kat asked.

"We Muslims are like everybody else—real. We're not somebody with

---

17. Rob Bowman, liner notes to *Jackie Shane Any Other Way*. Other People's Music, Inc. (2015).

18. Tom Powell, "Still King Says Clay," *Tennessean*, December 9, 1964, 39.

robes on, acting like a saint. We meet people, shake hands, come into clubs. . . . I've been invited to fifteen countries . . . I've eaten with kings."

The next day, Sou read Tom Powell's account in the *Tennessean* of Clay/ Ali at the New Era. *Finally, a bit of positive press about the club in a newspaper instead of the continual drip-drip of numbers arrests and raids*, he thought. Yet the article mentioning his club wasn't the most interesting thing he read in the paper that day. A piece about the KKK gave him hope that Sam Cooke was right and a change was gonna come:

> Sociologists and other agencies report that while a few intelligent men are attracted—usually in the moneymaking or promotional end—Klan members are, for the most part, below the average level in background and education . . . Margaret Mead, the noted anthropologist suggests that such a lack of social status may well account for a sense of insecurity and efforts to maintain supremacy by terror or violence . . . As American people, especially by those in states and areas now heavily inflicted with Klan groups, turn more and more to the processes of law, the Klans will fade out again.[19]

Sou hoped this was true. Reading the article reminded him of the night, years ago, when he and Funny had watched an opera at Fisk. He'd looked around at all the brilliant people who'd come to support such a high-brow event, and how that would have thrilled his grandmother Mary to have seen it. That night clarified for Sou that the future freedom to live equal to whites, which Negroes had for centuries only dreamed about, was visible on the horizon. He didn't know if he'd live to see it, but he sure hoped a future grandson would.

He tossed the paper in the trash and went into the club to enjoy the entertainment. He was in a good mood until he saw his beloved Funny—with a date.

---

19. Ralph McGill, "Money Making Ku Klux Klan," *Tennessean*, December 9, 1964, 17.

25

MR. PITIFUL

Ain't it a shame how white folks do the colored. First
they took Amos and Andy away from us. Then they
got a hold of Uncle Ben's converted rice. And now
they're trying to tell us that white man is Hoss Allen.

—A FAN TO SOLOMON BURKE

It hadn't taken long for Hoss to return to his old habits and haunts. On air, in
order to fully morph into the Hossman—the wild-ass, blues-loving, women-
chasing, charismatic persona he assumed when the microphone was switched
on—he had to first "get loose." Author Wes Smith described Hoss as the "wild
man who drank until he couldn't stand, then sat down to have some more."[1]
What had changed since Hoss's first stint at playing the wild Black Hossman
was that in order to stay on air, he had to hide his drinking from his bosses.

At times, Gab got suspicious. When he accused Hoss of sounding drunk
on air, Hoss argued that was his act. He was playing the host of a bawdy party.
After Gab instructed the cleaning crew to look for liquor bottles when they
emptied the trash, Hoss began stashing his empty gin bottles in a file cabinet.[2]
Jimmy Ward discovered the stash and took the evidence to Gab's office.

---

1. Smith, *Pied Pipers*, 101.
2. Smith, 101.

Gab had lined the bottles across his desk and confronted Hoss. "What the hell is this?" Gab asked. "You're drinking on air again. Aren't you?"

"No! Not at all. I've got a friend making wine and he needs the bottles. I'm just collecting and storing them."

"Really?" Gab had said, not believing a word of it. "What friend?"

"Pauline Duff," Hoss replied. "Doc Duff makes wine in his basement." Hoss knew this because he and Pauline had spent time at the same treatment facility.

Gab found it impossible to believe their family doctor made wine, but since Anne Duff was Gab's daughter-in-law, it would be easy to verify. He asked Christine about it.

"Can't you remember Paula and Brett coming over here with purple feet from smashing those grapes?" Christine said. "Price grows his blue-ribbon tomatoes to go with Sam Smith's steaks, remember? He must have decided he needed to make wine to go with them."

Gab felt guilty, but he would have sworn Hoss was lying.

Hoss had lied.

Lately, it seemed to have become a habit. He'd promised to stay sober, but he'd relapsed after having found it nearly impossible to be on air without alcohol. Gin was the magic elixir that induced the required outsize personality. When drunk, some people became sentimental, some funny, some the life of the party, some promiscuous. Bill became them all—he became the Hossman.

Gab fell for Hoss's Doc-Duff-needs-the-bottles story, but Nancy didn't. Fed up with Hoss's unreliable behavior, his drinking, skirt-chasing, and on-again, off-again affair with Della, Nancy finally filed for a long-overdue divorce.

Like Helen, Nancy craved peace and quiet and eventually found it as a school librarian.

On Sunday night, March 7, 1965, Gab was watching the movie *Judgment at Nuremburg* when it was interrupted for a special news report.

"Christine! Come look!" Gab yelled. Christine came into the den. The television showed barbaric scenes of violence directed at protestors on the Edmund

Pettis Bridge in Selma, Alabama. Tear gas choked protestors as a sea of lawmen in blue shirts, white helmets, and gas masks brought billy clubs down on the heads of kneeling, praying protesters. Gab and Christine watched in horror.

"That's the boy from here, the one with the student group," Gab said, pointing at an image of John Lewis on the screen. This was America at its ugliest.

Across town, Dr. Price Duff had also been watching *Judgment at Nuremburg* when the news in Selma interrupted. The juxtaposition of images depicted in the World War II movie—some which Duff had witnessed personally—interspersed with those on the bridge brought home the horror of being in Germany. Duff recalled he'd told Governor Clement it was naive to think that racism here was any different from the racism that nearly destroyed Germany. The ideology was the same: you're not the same level of human as me. All that kept the most radical racists from turning Selma into Weimar was that the United States was a country of laws, governed by a democratic process and not by the personal whims of an autocratic regime. Here was proof, in black-and-white and in real time, that when vigilante justice is embraced, a lynch mob mentality ensues. And once that line is crossed, it's a small step from poplar tree to gas chamber. Unnerved, Duff called the governor.

"Are you seeing this?" Duff asked.

"Selma? Yeah. No idea how Wallace thinks letting armed men beat protestors will do anybody any good. He thinks he's gonna be a Confederate hero, but all he's done is pick a fight with Washington."

Four days later, President Johnson addressed the country: "I speak tonight for the dignity of man and the destiny of democracy," he began. It was, he said, "wrong—deadly wrong—to deny any of your fellow Americans the right to vote in the country." At certain moments he said, like at Lexington and Concord, and Appomattox, "history and fate meet at a single time and place to shape a turning point in man's unending search for freedom. So it was this past week in Selma."[3]

When Sou heard Johnson's announcement that he would introduce a voting rights bill, he felt tears form. And he wasn't alone. Most of the people in the club were overcome with emotion.

---

3. Halberstam, *The Children*, 516.

Six months later, on August 6, when President Johnson signed that voting rights bill into law, John Lewis was at the White House to witness the occasion.

It had been six years since he'd first walked into James Lawson's seminars in Nashville, five years since he'd taken a seat at the Woolworth's lunch counter, two years since he'd met the late President Kennedy and spoken at the March on Washington, where Lewis recalled saying, "Men who built their careers on moral principles were all too rare in American politics."[4]

John Lewis had prophetically spoken the words that would later define his political career as one of the rarest of the rare—a politician with a strong moral compass.

While Lewis was in Washington, Gab was in Hendersonville working on a passion project of his own. Gab, along with four other members of First Lutheran Church downtown, had decided the city needed a Lutheran church on the northeast side of town. Gab volunteered to be the primary fundraiser. The first person Gab approached for a donation was Ernie Young.

WLAC had made Ernie rich. Yet Ernie wasn't the type to flaunt his wealth. He was a generous, fair-minded, devout Christian who preferred charitable giving to personal luxuries.

"How much do you need?" Ernie asked Gab.

"We've hired a pastor. With another $3,000 we can pay rent and buy hymnals and Bibles."

"Who shall I make the check out to?" Ernie asked.

"St. Timothy Lutheran. And thank you, dear friend," Gab said.

The check Ernie gave Gab enabled St. Timothy Lutheran Church to hold its inaugural service on September 13, 1964, at Nannie Berry School.

Conversely to John Lewis, any moral compass Hoss might have once possessed departed with Nancy. Their divorce was final in April 1965, and without Nancy's oversight, "Hoss was a blur, and in a blur, much of the time."[5]

Whenever he had too much to drink, Hoss lost all common sense. One of the most glaring examples happened when he made sexual advances toward John Richbourg's bubbleheaded teenage daughter when he was emceeing a high school dance. Lelaine threatened to tell John if Hoss came near her or

4. Halberstam, 454.

5. Smith, *Pied Pipers*, 109.

any of her high school girlfriends again. John was kept in the dark about Hoss's wildly inappropriate comments to Lelaine, yet she confided in Barry Kirby, her stepbrother.

After high school Lelaine went to college in Memphis. One night, shortly after she arrived on campus, she sat on a sidewalk curb to wait for a bus. A young man soon came and sat beside her. He had his transistor radio tuned to WLAC.

When John's voice came over the air, Lelaine said, "That's my dad you're listening to."

The man looked at her strawberry-blond hair and freckles. "John R's *your* dad?"

She nodded. "Yeah. John Richbourg. I'm Lelaine Richbourg."

"Wow! You sure don't look colored."

Lelaine laughed. "Why would I? My dad's white."

"No way! You're telling me this guy's white?" he said, pointing to the radio. "I don't believe it. Lemme see your driver's license."

The couple married a year later. Lelaine claimed her husband married her because that's how dearly he loved John R.

In the summer of 1965, on the heels of Noble Blackwell's success with the *Night Train* television series, Hoss decided to pitch a similar program of his own.

Gab was resistant to the idea at first because most WLAC listeners believed Hoss was Black. Hoss argued that a nationally syndicated television show would give great exposure to WLAC radio; this would in turn allow them to sell more records. Selling more records was needed because sales of the traditional R & B records had started to decline due to the British Invasion. Without Barry Gordy's Motown, the late-night programming might have given way to the Top 40 format Dudley favored.

Barry Gordy once told Gab that without WLAC, Motown might not have made it. Gab told Barry they were in a symbiotic financial relationship because without Motown, they'd be playing the Beatles, Rolling Stones, and Beach Boys, like everyone else.

Eventually, Hoss convinced Gab to let him pitch a television show. Gab called his friend Bill Graham at the ad agency that had previously offered Gab a partnership, since Noble-Drury had bankrolled shows for Porter Wagner and Ernest Tubb and had underwritten *Night Train*.

Hoss pitched *The !!!! Beat* as a televised version of a New Era stage show.

"I'll hire the New Era house band as the show's band. I've been a jock so long I know all the record producers and singers, and they all owe 'me favors from way back.'"[6]

"The problem is there's no color television studios in Nashville," Graham advised. "If you want the show to go national, it must be in color. We couldn't syndicate *Night Train* because it's in black and white. I'll find a color-capable studio and get back to you."

Graham financially greenlit *The !!!! Beat* and Hoss recruited Clarance "Gatemouth" Brown, bandleader at the Era, to be the show's bandleader. They called the musicians the Beat Boys. The first three episodes were filmed in Dallas on January 31 and February 1, with musicians Little Milton, Esther Phillips, Frank Howard, the Commanders, Lattimore Brown, Joe Tex, and Etta James. Hoss flew back to Nashville for his broadcasts, then returned weeks later to film the next episodes. Hoss was flying high, having finally realized his dream of television. He filmed twenty-five episodes of his R & B variety show, pulling in favors from top stars, such as Louis Jordon, Lou Rawls, and Bobby Hebb.

In mid-October, just prior to filming the season's final episode, featuring Otis Redding, Percy Sledge, Sam and Dave, and Patty LaBelle, Hoss received notice the show was being canceled. Devastated, Hoss turned to the bottle. By the time the cameras were set to roll, he was too drunk to serve as host. Otis Redding, who was on set to perform "Mr. Pitiful," had to guest host the episode. Those twenty-six episodes would one day be made available online. And according to critics, they stand the test of time as "far and away the quirkiest and coolest show of the decade."[7]

November found Sou feeling quite pitiful himself.

The year 1966 had been rough, as Sou had been summoned to court repeatedly. First, he'd been called to appear before a grand jury, then he'd been

---

6. Marc Weingarten, *Station to Station: The History of Rock 'n' Roll on Television* (New York: Pocket Books, 2000), 139.

7. Weingarten, 138.

subpoenaed to testify in a case against law enforcement officers charged with corruption. Once Good Jelly Jones was arrested (despite controlling thousands of votes in the city), Sou knew things would soon turn ugly.

During the previous administrations, Good Jelly was immune from prosecution. However, now that a metropolitan government had taken over, things were different. Before, when a big-money Vegas mobster wanted to take over gambling in the city, Ben West and armed patrolmen had driven onto the airport runway and denied the gangster access to the terminal. West made it clear that money gambled in Nashville stayed in Nashville.

Yet recently the new countywide government had passed an ordinance making possession of a gambling stamp legal evidence that the holder was engaged in the gambling business—which was illegal in Nashville. Sou felt that with the new administration, "a dark paranoia seemed to grip the mayor and with him the entire city."[8]

On November 28, one principled lawman decided to declare war on the numbers runners: "After a major squabble among superior officers, Metro police launched a numbers crackdown."[9] Police lieutenant R. S. Owen had grown tired of the cozy relationship between the police department and gamblers. He took it on himself to arrest all fifty-two gambling stamp holders.

"The law is being violated. It's obvious," Owen declared. "The law is on the books and it must be enforced. As long as I'm a member of this department, it's going to be."[10]

The first runner Owen arrested was Nathan Bellamy. Next he nabbed Sou, followed by Sam Sims Jr. By late in the afternoon, all fifty-two gamblers had visited jail and were subsequently all freed on bond. Then, late that evening, Sou received a phone call from Sims.

"Your nephew's partner's about to bring the wrath of God on us all!"

"Say what?"

"Process server who testified against your nephew's rolling numbers bank was shot, along with his four-year-old daughter. The bullet went through the girl's mouth and out the back of her head."

8. Houston, *Nashville Way*, 168.
9. Jim Squires, "52 Charged After Police End Squabble," *Tennessean*, November 29, 1966.
10. Squires, *Tennessean*, November 29, 1966.

Sou felt physically sick. Lottery numbers and liquor sales were intended to be victimless crimes. He'd banned narcotics, prostitutes, and weapons from the New Era and had built a reputation for running the cleanest, safest club in town. On his desk was a framed *Banner* cartoon that Funny had given him as a gag gift years before. The cartoon featured a "Law Enforcement" baseball bat, with a huge hole in the center through which three balls labeled "numbers, honky-tonks, and bookies" passed.[11] He picked it up, threw it against the wall, and watched it slide to the floor, as shattered as his marriage.

Numbers and liquor hadn't been eliminated in Nashville because no one wanted it. This was the Southern paradox—how things *appeared* was what mattered, not how they *were*. For years, local runners had bribed law enforcement to look the other way, while everyone from the police chief to the streetsweeper believed that as long as liquor and numbers stayed under local control, the city was safe. Control was made possible when a personal connection existed between bettor and bookie, between barkeep and drinker. Now, with the bigger government and violence entering the numbers business, he wasn't sure local control could hold.

Sou had what Funny called a "poolhall pity party." He cried for the little girl who'd been shot, he cried for her parents, he cried for the violence that had plagued the city, and he cried because Funny had a boyfriend.

Finally, with 1966 behind him, Sou hoped for glad tidings in the new year. He was scheduled to stand trial January 11 for his numbers arrest. Before he even made it to the courthouse, he was arrested yet again. On January 7, in a predawn raid of his New Era Variety store, the police confiscated his entire inventory of liquor—all 565 bottles! He suspected police decided they'd divvy up the bottles in case Sou went to jail and therefore their payoffs ended prematurely. He'd love to know how many of those 565 bottles found their way to Mayor Briley's personal liquor cabinet.

In April 1967, Sou caught a lucky break. The State Alcoholic Beverage Study Commission reported Tennessee's liquor laws were "the most bizarre mixture of inconsistent ordering on the law books of this land."[12] The commission's findings echoed Sou's testimony—with few teetotalers among the

---

11. Cartoon, *Nashville Banner*, April 7, 1949, 10.
12. Bill Kovach, "Liberal Laws On Drink Urged," *Tennessean*, April 8, 1967, 1.

state's adult population, it was incomprehensible that only eight of Tennessee's ninety-five counties permitted retail liquor sales, forcing drunks to drive long distances to and from counties where liquor could be legally purchased. He paid a fifty-dollar fine. Not one of the 565 bottles taken as evidence was returned.

On April 8, Dr. Martin Luther King Jr. and Stokely Carmichael came to town to speak at Vanderbilt's Impact Symposium. Dr. King gave an academic lecture in which he said it was "a fact of history that privileged groups do not willingly give up privileges. . . . Morality can't be legislated. But behavior can be regulated. Laws won't make him love me, but it will keep him from lynching me."[13]

Stahlman had tried to prevent Carmichael from speaking in Nashville. In a *Banner* editorial, he wrote about "Carmichael's 'inflammatory appeals to violence' with language 'so contemptuous as to be beyond the borderline of outright sedition.'"[14]

Carmichael stepped up to the podium, all hep-cat cool in his black beret and sunglasses, to punch back, branding the *Banner* "the modern day theater of the absurd," which brought huge roars of applause from Vanderbilt students.

"The day of white people telling Black people who they can invite to their college campuses is over," Carmichael said, referencing Jimmy's editorial protests. "Honkies can leave now, as you won't comprehend the lecture I'm about to give. The lecture is on an intellectual level."[15]

After Carmichael's "Black Power" speeches to Vanderbilt, Fisk, and A&I students, three days of unrest ensued. The protests were triggered by white police officers having beaten a Black boy. Rock throwing escalated to gunfire; violence erupted, sending mobs and riot police to Jefferson Street. In total, four hundred police officers—who had been on standby and were "ready to pounce"—blockaded the neighborhood where Helen and Harriett lived.

Helen watched as "helmeted officers with sawed-off shotguns" patrolled the street in front of her house. She told Sou it reminded her of what happened in the Mink Slide section of Columbia twenty years before.[16] She feared she'd soon see machine guns on her street corner.

---

13. Frank Sutherland, "King Warns of Cost To US in Rights Fight," *Tennessean*, April 8, 1967, 2.
14. Houston, *Nashville Way*, 168.
15. Frank Sutherland and John Haile, "Political Power for Negroes Urged," *Tennessean*, April 9, 1967, 6.
16. Larry Daughtrey, "Windy Eve Blows Into Violence," *Tennessean*, April 10, 1967, 3.

Sou realized how close she'd come to the truth when the *Banner* reported a policeman was overheard saying, "All I needed was a machine gun to mow down these niggers."[17]

With rumors circulating that after Carmichael's speech angry Nashville policemen had conducted raids on Fisk and TSU's dormitories and used tear gas on the students, Stahlman phoned Vanderbilt's chancellor Alexander Heard.

Heard asked Jimmy, "Did some event trigger this?"

"Your guest, Stokely Carmichael," Jimmy replied. "Now reap the whirlwind!"[18]

On April 14, 1967, students gathered to demonstrate at the Courthouse Plaza and condemn the police actions. Unlike previous demonstrations, this one involved a significant amount of white student protestors. Eighty protesters were arrested and thirty injured.

Although Stahlman had been unsuccessful in getting Carmichael banned from speaking, he did rile up the Bourbons enough to get the Tennessee senate to pass "a resolution condemning Carmichael and his 'racist poison,' and after his visit called for deporting him to his native Trinidad."[19] An impossibility, given that Carmichael was a US citizen and the Tennessee legislature had no such power.

In the aftermath of the Stokely Carmichael episode, Mayor Briley said, "They say I don't know them, but I know our niggers."[20]

"No wonder the protestors call the mayor and police 'Briley's Gestapo,'" Sou told Kat.

He tried to talk his daughter out of applying to white colleges. Helen and Sou wanted Harriett to attend Fisk, but Harriett was determined to be one of the first Black women in the state to graduate from a white university. When she was accepted to Middle Tennessee State University, Sou felt betrayed. He despised how MTSU displayed a bust of the devil himself, Nathan Bedford Forrest, and their athletic teams were named the Raiders, after Forrest's rebel troops. He reluctantly paid his baby's tuition and wished her all the luck in the world.

---

17. Houston, *Nashville Way*, 171.
18. Houston, 173.
19. Houston, 168.
20. Houston, 200.

Sou had anticipated there would be white backlash following Carmichael's visit. The Bourbons were still in power and threatened by the cataclysmic shift that had unraveled the social fabric holding the city together since Reconstruction.

The first indication that Sou's expected "white backlash" had been unleashed occurred when Helen, along with most of her neighbors, received a notice that her homeowners' insurance was being canceled. The second came with the announcement that the extension of Interstate 40 would cut the heart out of the Negro community. The planned highway would demolish sixteen blocks of businesses along Jefferson Street. Those blocks represented 80 percent of Nashville's Black-owned businesses. And with Jefferson Street gutted, it would turn the "majority of their residential streets into blind alleys and offering almost no access."[21]

The third came when Governor Ellington announced plans to have thousands of National Guard troops practice "riot maneuvers" along the same sixteen-block Jefferson Street corridor.

The final, tragic kiss of death occurred in Memphis on April 4, 1968.

---

21. Edwin Mitchell, "You Did Not Speak For Us," *Tennessean*, October 12, 1967, 15.

26

THE THRILL IS GONE

There are many places in America where a road or a
railroad was used to divide or segregate or remove a
neighborhood. Particularly a Black neighborhood.

—TRANSPORTATION SECRETARY PETE BUTTIGIEG

In 1962, James Lawson had relocated to Memphis to lead the Centenary
Methodist Church. He was now president of Fisk University, but he'd stayed
close to his Memphis congregants and had lobbied his fellow ministers to support the garbage workers' strike and companion economic boycott.

Hoping to bring national attention to the problem of the poor wages and
working conditions of the sanitation workers, Lawson asked Martin Luther
King Jr. to speak in Memphis. On the night of April 3, King spoke at the
Mason Temple. Against the backdrop of tornado warnings, gusts of howling
wind and thunder reverberated outside while a rhythmic clink of rain hit the
temple's roof. King's eyes filled with tears as he gave his final speech that
included this premonition:

> Well, I don't know what will happen now. We've got some difficult days
> ahead. But it doesn't matter with me now because I've been to the moun-
> taintop . . . and I've looked over and I've seen the Promised Land. I may not

get there with you. But I want you to know tonight that we as a people will get to the Promised Land. So I'm happy tonight.[1]

The next day, King was shot dead by a sniper. John was on air when the news of King's assassination crossed the wire service. John interrupted his program to broadcast the news of King's death.

Sou heard John's announcement of King's assassination and he went numb. He sat stunned, incapable of thought. He just felt an icy foreboding. Only a few weeks ago, Sou had buried his father. And now the man who'd become a father to all Negroes was gone. Without Helen and Harriett in his daily life, and Isaac and Dr. King now gone, Sou felt a sudden pang of loneliness. He wanted to reach out to Helen. Instead, Kat appeared.

Within minutes of John having read the news on air, rioters took to the streets of North Nashville. The protesters started throwing rocks at police cars. Burning and looting followed.

With Jefferson Street being demolished, Helen had been forced to move. Both her former and current neighborhoods had become a sea of steel fences topped with barbed wire.

Harriett called her mother from campus.

"What's happening there, Momma? You safe?"

"Yes, baby. I hear gunfire in the distance, but it's not directed my way."

"The governor said he's sending the National Guard there," Harriett said. "Do you want me to come home? I'm worried about you there alone."

"I'm hunkering down, baby. Don't you worry 'bout me."

The next morning, when Helen turned on the radio, she heard Stokely Carmichael proclaim, "When white America killed Dr. King, she declared war on us."

Helen glanced outside. With the bulldozers, overturned vehicles, barbed wire fences, damaged buildings, fires, and riflemen on the street outfitted in riot gear, North Nashville resembled photos of Berlin in 1945.

Gone from Jefferson Street were the numbers runners standing on street corners, the nannies pushing strollers, maids in white uniforms waiting for

---

1. Halberstam, *The Children*, 558.

buses, merchants sweeping their stoops and putting out their wares. The Bourbons were remaking the city so that "the dotted lines of the roads now replaced the WHITE and COLORED signs of the past, recasting physical space to mirror the social space of the Jim Crow era."[2]

The morning after Dr. King's murder, Jimmy Ward came into Gab's office. "We need to do something proactive, Blackie."

"Absolutely. Whatcha thinkin'?"

"We need an authentic Black voice speaking to and for our audience."

"I've been saying for years we needed a Black deejay. This is our chance, but let's not settle for a deejay. Let's hire a Black news announcer. Far as I can tell, there's not a single colored news announcer on any national broadcast. We'll be the first."

"Great idea. I'll call a friend over at A&I, see who he can recommend."

"You mean Tennessee State," Gab said, referencing the college's recent name change.

Ward called the dean of arts and sciences, Dr. Thomas Poag.

"We don't have any journalism grad students, but I got one studying speech and drama that'd be great." Dr. Poag approached his star grad student, Don Whitehead.

Don was flattered, as he had listened to WLAC's nighttime programming for many years. He'd even followed the coded messages Hoss and John R sent out over the airwaves in support of the student protest movement. When musicians like Solomon Burke or Otis Redding would call in to the station, either the musicians themselves, Hoss, or John would announce when and where those musicians planned to make themselves available to meet with fans. In reality, this was a call to action for student protestors to rally.

However, as honored as Don Whitehead was at being recommended, he didn't feel qualified for the position.

"I didn't study news," Don insisted. "I don't know anything about news."[3]

Dr. Poag persuaded Whitehead to meet with Ward and Gab. Don told them he knew nothing about news and was intending to go to New York for

2. Houston, *Nashville Way*, 242.
3. Maggie Bowers, "Whitehead First African-American in Radio Broadcasting," *Newman Times Herald*, February 21, 2016.

theater work. It took two additional meetings for Gab to convince Whitehead that being the first Black newscaster on a national broadcast was too great an opportunity to pass up. Don finally agreed to take the job. Gab said he'd schedule a press conference.

"Just one question," Don said. "What's a press conference?"

Don Whitehead became the voice of the news "on the largest radio station for nighttime programming in the United States."[4] He came on in the evenings at 8:00, 9:00, and 10:00. The first time Don sat in the broadcast booth, he forgot to switch on the microphone. Hoss stepped in, flipped the switch and walked out without a word.

Gab was listening at home when Don read his inaugural newscast. "That's him," Gab told Christine. "That's my new newsman."

"Thought you'd hired a colored."

"I did."

"That man sounds white as Martha's flour and his name's Whitehead? Why would anyone think he's colored?"

Gab laughed. "You're right. Whitehead sounds white, but he's Black. John and Hoss sound Black but they're white. And I'm their boss, Blackie, a white guy named Blackman. You can't make this up."

"Well, I couldn't. But a Southern storyteller as good as you sure could."

The next day, Gab drafted a new press release naming Don Whitehead WLAC's news, correspondence, and public relations liaison and sent it to all the papers with a photo, so it would be obvious Whitehead was a Black man.

On Don's first day at the office, Gab cautioned him to stay clear of Hoss. Gab was concerned that WLAC's resident bad boy would lead their neophyte news star astray.

However, like most people, Don found Hoss too charismatic to resist. Within weeks, Don had become Hoss's driver, personal alcohol shopper, and nightclub companion.

Gab decided that to introduce Don to their audience and show the station's support for the civil rights movement, he'd send Don on a goodwill tour of the Southern cities and college campuses. Gab told Don, in the interest of helping

4. Tamika Harvey, "Whitehead Opens Airwaves for African-Americans," *Alumni Life* 12, no. 1 (2013), 9.

to quell the unrest, Don was to both act as an inspiration to the community and ferret out positive human interest stories they could broadcast from the road.

"Look for stories that will enlighten and entertain. I think the Black college campuses are great places to start," Gab told Don. "We'll set it up so you can broadcast remotely. We'll want you to promote equal education as the key to achieving true equality. Why don't you start by visiting Jackson, Mississippi?"

Don wasn't thrilled about going to the Deep South. He'd never been there and hadn't planned to go, yet he understood the importance of the message Gab wanted delivered.

Gab gave Don use of WLAC's news station wagon, which only compounded Don's fears of traveling deep into Mississippi because the car was plastered with WLAC stickers.

"I can't believe Blackman's sending me to Mississippi!" Don told Hoss. "Pray for me."

"Sure, I'll pray for you," Hoss said. "But my prayers will only get you to Memphis. After that you're on your own."

Before leaving Nashville, Don called Charles Evers, the brother of Medgar Evers, a slain activist. Charles invited Don to attend a memorial service in Fayette, Mississippi. When Don drove into Fayette, he encountered a crowd in the city square. As soon as folks saw the WLAC stickers and realized Don was from Randy's, they were as thrilled as if the King of Mississippi, Mr. B.B. King himself, had come to town.

Don broadcast his Friday night news from the integrated church where Medgar Evers's memorial service took place. On Saturday, he came on air from Tougaloo, Mississippi, and reported on a preschool program intended to give students a "head start."

Sunday, Don drove to McComb, Mississippi, and then to Liberty, near the Louisiana border, where he reported on former sharecroppers who'd formed a co-op to get better prices for their crops, which Don stated were mostly delicious cucumbers.

Traveling from Liberty to Vicksburg, Don learned there were no markets, no grocery stores or pharmacies, no gas stations, or any type of entertainment in the rural parts of Mississippi, which explained why WLAC was so important to Black families in the area. Don had grown up in Richmond, Indiana, and had listened to WLAC because it'd been the only Black radio station in the country. Don hadn't experienced the isolation that rural Southerners did. The exuberant welcome he'd received in Fayette followed him everywhere. It now made sense.

From Vicksburg, Don reiterated the importance of an early education and how successful the Head Start program had become. He broadcast from a mobile health center that administered immunizations, provided medical care, taught prenatal care, and gave free birth control to teenage girls. He then drove to Louisiana to interview Zelma Walsh, a Black female police chief who commanded an integrated police force.

Everywhere Don went, he heard folks say, "I listen to you every night."

From Meridian, Mississippi; to Montgomery, Alabama; to Columbus, Georgia, Don listened to stories of what life was like for Blacks in the Deep South. From the first Black sheriff in Alabama since Reconstruction, to a feeder pig project, to a federal credit union, to families forced to relocate into government housing, Don shared stories of people who'd never considered they'd be of interest to a national newscaster.

Two weeks later, when Don returned to Nashville, Gab asked Don to walk to Cain-Sloan's with him for lunch. They sat side by side at the lunch counter, something that would have been incomprehensible a few years before. Gab ordered his usual pimento cheese on a biscuit. While they waited, he asked Don to tell him about his trip.

"When I left, my thought was, *What is E.G. Blackman thinking?* But it turned out to be an unforgettable and worthwhile endeavor."

"You did good," Gab said. "We got great reviews on your stories. I'm thinking you should visit every Black college in the South. You're an example of how education and equal opportunity end racism and discrimination. Someday I expect we'll see a Black man delivering the news on national television and that man will be standing on your shoulders."

Don heard the pride in Gab's voice. "I'm honored you hired me, Blackie."

"And one other thing," Gab said. "You need to keep an eye on Hoss. I'm worried his drinking's gotten out of control again. He knows staying sober's a requirement of the job. Now you do too."

Between Don's 8:00 and 9:00 newscasts, John schooled him on the finer points of being a newscaster. Hoss signed on at 9:45, and after Don's 10:00 newscast, Hoss took it on himself to school Don in "the wicked ways of the world."[5]

"I found out he was the devil, so I used to sneak out with him all the time," Don said.[6] At first, Don was starstruck. Being on the town with Hoss was like living inside a girlie magazine. Hoss's life was a never-ending party of beautiful women, alcohol, music, musicians, sports, and gambling.

The first time Don followed Hoss into the New Era, Hoss pointed to Sou Bridgeforth's table. "Always look there when you enter," Hoss said. "If Sou's there, acknowledge him. For me, it's me saying, 'I see you and I know your rules.'"

Don quickly learned there was another reason Hoss advised him to look to Sou's table. Sou was rarely there alone. He might be entertaining musicians like James Brown, Little Richard, Joe Tex, Aretha Franklin, or sports stars like Satchel, Joe Gilliam, Joe Lewis, or Ali.

Before long, Don and Hoss's evenings fell into a pattern. Don would give his last newscast at 10:00, after which Hoss would send him to buy booze. After Hoss signed off at midnight, they'd head to the nightclubs. The New Era was always Hoss's first choice.

On Wednesday night, November 5, Don Whitehead delivered the news that Frank Clement had died in a car accident: "The former governor was taken to General Hospital, where he was pronounced dead from massive chest injuries."

Hoss heard the broadcast and rushed to the booth. "When'd that happen?" he asked.

"Couple hours ago. He crashed on Franklin Road at Tyne Boulevard."

"He was drunk, no doubt," Hoss said.

"Why would you say that?" Don asked.

"Cause Frank's a terrible alcoholic and that's right by Doc Duff's, where he'd go to get sober."

"What kinda fool drives drunk on Franklin Road?"

5. Smith, *Pied Pipers*, 102.
6. Smith, 101.

"I've done it many times," Hoss said.

"Well, you'd better stop. Blackie's been ridin' my ass about your drinking. Just the other day, he played the tape for me over and over again, trying to get me to say that you sounded drunk. It was like being brainwashed. He'd pick at me and pick at me and pick at me. I said, 'Blackie, I just don't think he sounds drunk.' Even though you were high as a bird."[7]

"I can handle my booze."

"Yeah, bet that's what Clement said."

Johnny Bragg learned of Frank Clement's death when he heard Don announce it over WLAC. Johnny was devastated. The man who had been his "friend, his guiding angel, and had given him direction and hope" was gone.[8]

Three days later, Johnny went to the funeral. The pastor's eulogy told the mourners that Frank Clement "was a man friendly and compassionate to other people. He truly earned the esteem now given him . . . he was truly a political prodigy . . . a living legend."[9]

Following the eulogy, Johnny sang "Take My Hand, Precious Lord."

When Sou received official notification that his building was being taken by eminent domain to make way for the new highway, he nearly threw in the towel.

"You gonna close the Era for good?" Shorty asked.

"No, but I'll never buy another commercial property. Bought three and the city took 'em all. Bottom line, they don't want coloreds owning property near downtown. It's like B.B. says, the thrill is gone. I'm renting from now on 'cause whatever I buy, they'll take."

Sou moved the Era a block down Charlotte to Eleventh. The new location was much smaller, with only enough space for a stage, a dance floor, and tiny tables that could hold a few drink glasses or hamburgers.

Downsizing the Era felt similar to the waning days of Negro League

7. Smith, 103.
8. Warner, *Just Walkin'*, 222.
9. Frank Sutherland, "Dickson Takes Her Son Back," *Tennessean*, November 7, 1969, 19.

baseball when he hadn't sold enough tickets to cover the cost of the baseballs. He hadn't gone into baseball for the money; he'd done it for love of the game. And so it was with the Era. As small as his new location was, he knew he couldn't collect enough at the door to hire the great musicians the Era was known for. He'd continue running numbers so he could keep the club afloat. At least this way, folks who lost their dimes playing numbers could still have a good time at the Era, so it all evened out. Many of the musicians who'd started at the Era—James Brown, Aretha, Etta, Richard, and Ray—could now fill the ten thousand seats of the Municipal Auditorium.

On April 27, James Brown came to town on his Learjet to play the auditorium and to receive three awards: the National Association of Record Merchandisers' "bestselling Rhythm & Blues male vocalist of 1969, a certificate of merit from Governor Buford Ellington for his work with youth against the drug problem, and a humanitarian award from Nashville's Kingsmen Social Club for his services to Nashville."[10]

After John Richbourg presented Brown with the awards, he was supposed to perform. Brown's band was set up and ready to play when Brown asked the auditorium manager for the money. He handed Brown a cashier's check.

"Cash!" Brown said. "Contract says *cash* in advance."

"That's a cashier's check. It's same as cash."

"No. It ain't. Until there's dead presidents in my pocket I'm not singin' a note!" Brown turned to head back to his dressing room.

"Where am I supposed to get that much cash on Saturday night?" the manager yelled.

Kat brought a phone to Sou's table. "Emergency call for ya."

"Somebody needs bailing out?"

"Yeah. The city," Kat said.

Sou listened as John Richbourg explained the situation.

"So let me get this straight," Sou said. "The folks who condemned my two properties right there need $10,000 from me so they can pay James Brown? That's what you're asking?"

"It's what James Brown is asking," John clarified.

---

10. Jack Hurst, "James Brown May Join Nashville Super Star List," *Tennessean*, April 27, 1970.

Sou sighed. "Well, the city was smart to have you ask. I'll send the cash right over. Come by sometime, John. The musicians you manage are here all the time."

A few weeks later, Joe Simon, one of John's musicians, was booked at the Era. John took his wife, Margaret, and her son, Barry, to see Joe and Bob Wilson, John's Sound Stage 7 bandleader, perform. Wilson had recently completed work as a studio musician on Bob Dylan's *Nashville Skyline* album. At the Era, Joe performed his popular hit, "You Keep Me Hangin' On," and his most recent number, which was climbing the charts, "Chokin' Kind."

Sou asked John, Margaret, and Barry to join him at his table. They were the only white people in the club and they received some suspicious looks until Simon introduced John. Most of the Era's audience was shocked to discover that John Richbourg was a white man.

When the band took a break, Wilson and Simon came to Sou's table. Wilson told Sou how he'd listened to John on WLAC since he was a kid in Detroit. Later, when he became a professional musician, he learned "all the musicians in the Midwest listened to WLAC."[11] Wilson continued, "When I got here my aim was to get to WLAC and promote my record to John R."

"I've heard that many times," Sou said. "The Era and WLAC. We're the chicken and the egg."

"Get up on the stage and do the baby chick spiel, Dad," Barry teased.

"Oh, hell no!" John replied. "These folks'll bring those nasty things back and demand a refund! I'm not selling any chicks to anyone who knows how to find me."

Later, Hoss stumbled into the club with Don Whitehead in tow.

"Y'all just missed John R," Kat told Hoss.

"Good," Don said. "All I need's word getting back to the boss how wasted Hoss is."

"Look, Sou don't like drunks here, 'specially white ones. You need to take Hoss home. The man needs help."

A year later, Don regretted not following Kat's advice or coming clean to Gab about how out of control Hoss's drinking had become.

---

11. Randy Fox, *Shake Your Hips*: *The Excello Records Story* (Nashville: BMG, 2018), 123.

On May 1, 1970, Don was at the station when Hoss arrived wearing a tuxedo that was covered in blood.

"What the hell happened?" Don asked.

"You wouldn't believe the night I've had," Hoss said, slurring his words. "I was in a car accident. Six, actually, according to police."

"Six! How could you be in six accidents?"

"It gets worse."

"Worse? How?"

"I think I might have killed somebody."

"What?"

In the wee hours of the morning, Gab was jolted awake by the phone.

Gab listened to Don for a few moments. "Oh my God!" Gab said.

Christine sat up in bed and turned on the light. Gab's tone of voice told her something horrible had happened. She'd only heard him like this twice before—when Buddy died and, later, when he had to break the news to Joe Warren's daughter that Joe had killed himself.

"What is it, Galbreath?" Christine said, alarmed. "What happened?"

"Damn him!" Gab said into the phone. "I'll be in shortly."

Christine saw the tears in his eyes. "You gonna tell me the bad news?"

"Hoss got drunk at an event he emceed. He was en route to the station and may have killed someone with his car."

Gab pulled a pair of pants and a sweater from his closet.

"Oh my goodness. Poor Nancy. What's gonna happen now?"

"To Hoss? Nothing good. I gotta break the news to Dudley and Mountcastle before they read it in the paper. The way they'll see it, Hoss was on the clock when it happened. Emceeing events is a part of his job. And it'll be my fault for letting him come back and not sacking him as soon as I suspected he was drinking again."

"Hoss's drinking is on him, Gab. It's not your fault."

Gab sighed. If only that were true. At some level, Gab had always known alcohol was the magic elixir that turned well-bred Vandy Bill into the wild-ass Hossman. Bill was like a son to Gab, while Hoss was his problem child, albeit one that laid golden eggs and had made Gab a wealthy man. Unfortunately, those eggs hatched into chicks that now had come home to roost.

The police reported that Hoss had "hit a car at Eighth Avenue South and Demonbreun, another at Fifth Avenue South, before slamming broadside into a car at Fourth Avenue, which may have killed a woman, before finally hitting two parked cars at a service station. He was arrested for "driving under the influence plus three cases of reckless driving."[12]

Gab had left by the time the *Tennessean* was delivered. Christine sipped her coffee as she read about the woman who had been killed when "a car in which she was riding was struck by a car which police said had just sideswiped two other vehicles."[13]

The *Tennessean* reported on June 3, 1970:

William Trousdale Allen, III, 47, of 424 Page Road, was charged with second degree murder yesterday in connection with the traffic death May 1, of an Old Hickory woman, police said. Metro traffic officer Charles Hay said Allen also has been charged with driving under the influence and three cases of reckless driving as a result of a multiple accident in which six cars were involved.

On March 23, 1971, Judge Allen R. Cornelius nulled the criminal charges against Hoss. By coincidence, Allen Cornelius's law offices, prior to his judgeship, were one floor below WLAC's in the Third National Bank building during the heyday of the 50,000-watt peepers.

Meanwhile, a few blocks to the north along Jefferson Street, block by block, a mass of concrete and steel laid waste to the Black business district where an exciting, robust culture had flourished for a hundred years. Nary a historical marker was left behind to commemorate its passing.

Shortly thereafter, the Bourbons in the Tennessee senate passed, by an overwhelming margin, a resolution calling for a bust of Nathan Bedford Forrest, former slave trader turned Confederate general turned first Grand Wizard of the Ku Klux Klan, to be created and installed in the Tennessee State Capitol.

Or, to quote Sou, the Bourbons had once again danced on the graves of his ancestors.

---

12. "Woman Dies in Collision," *Tennessean*, May 2, 1970, 11.
13. "Wreck Leads To Murder Charge Here," *Tennessean*, June 3, 1970, 42.

EPILOGUE

"SENTIMENTAL JOURNEY" (VERSE TWO)

To be ignorant of what occurred before you were born is to remain always a child. For what is the worth of a human life if it is not woven into the life of our ancestors by record of history?

—MARCUS TULLIUS CICERO

When I decided to write this book, I enlisted the assistance of my father and my Aunt Gayle. I was surprised when my dad said, "No one could write that story but you."

At the time, I thought he was referring to my keen recall ability, a gift my father and I shared. Yet he meant that, as with most things in life, it was all in the timing. I had been born at the right time, in the right place, and had spent the first three summers of the '70s pestering the right people with my annoying curiosity.

After Hoss's drunk-driving incident, WLAC was in crisis. I happened to be at my grandparents' home on June 10 when Hoss was indicted by a grand jury. My grandmother and I were sitting at the breakfast bar when my grandfather called with the news. I remember Tee's distress and her refusal to share any of the details. Having overheard her side of the conversation, I was aware a tragedy had occurred involving Hoss. When I pestered Tee, she ran out of patience with me, something that I'd never before experienced. Frustrated, she insisted I take a nap. At thirteen, I was well past the nap stage, but on that day, I napped. For that reason alone, the day was permanently imprinted in my memory.

Later that afternoon, a Friday, my grandfather arrived home early. We packed up to head for higher, cooler ground.

During summer weekends, WLAC broadcast a "Lake and Land Report." This little news brief provided weekend weather in addition to fishing and boating information. The reports collected information via a helicopter, a houseboat, and a speedboat. The houseboat, which slept eight people, was called the *Nauta Line*.

My grandfather and other station execs used the *Nauta Line* to entertain family, friends, and clients. In July of 1969, Pop and Tee had hosted my family as well as my Aunt Gayle's family on the *Nauta Line*. My younger cousin Kim and I, being the only girl cousins, were bunked together in the crew quarters below the captain's cabin. One day, we discovered our cabin underwater. We swam in the room a bit, then went up the steps to inform Pop there was a swimming pool in our cabin. Aunt Gayle claimed she'd never seen her father move so fast.

That was our final trip on the *Nauta Line*. And it nixed the idea of Pop buying a houseboat when he retired. Especially since Tee thought she couldn't swim. She would tie a rope to her wrist and attach it to the dock so she could reel herself back to shore. My mischievous brother Brett and I occasionally untied the rope and set her adrift. Once Tee was quite a distance from the dock, we'd hold up the loose end of the rope and tell her not to drown. When she panicked, we'd remind her she'd been treading water just fine for hours. We found this hilarious. She didn't.

After the fiasco on the *Nauta Line*, Pop decided to purchase an Airstream trailer instead. He also bought two campsite lots on the Cumberland Plateau at Lake Tansi Village. We'd go to Lake Tansi on the weekends to escape

Nashville's heat and humidity. Occasionally, my grandmother, my cousins, and I would go to Tansi a few days before my grandfather. We'd stop at the Cracker Barrel for lunch, which at the time was just one small restaurant and gift shop at a gas station. Now they're everywhere.

When Pop arrived a few days later, he'd fill Tee in on what had happened at work. Kim and I slept in the trailer with my grandparents, while our brothers slept in a pop-up camper on the adjacent lot. As a result, we eavesdropped on a lot of whispered conversations our grandparents hadn't intended us to hear. Most seemed to involve Hoss. Despite Hoss having been indicted for second-degree murder, and Gab having made sobriety a condition of Hoss's employment, Gab refused to abandon him. He confided that he felt partly to blame for Hoss's condition. It wasn't possible for someone to live as two completely different people, as Hoss had been doing, without suffering the consequences. Hoss received treatment for his addiction at Cumberland Heights, a rehabilitation facility. His radio shows were taped and replayed so the listening audience would be unaware of his absence. And because most people knew him as Hoss, the news reports of William Trousdale Allen III's indictment didn't necessarily register with his listeners.

With the country in the worst recession since the thirties, Jimmy Ward felt that WLAC needed to appeal to a younger, wealthier, whiter audience. A new programming director was hired to implement a change in format to Top 40. Gab, John, and Gene protested. They were the trio that had birthed rhythm and blues programming. "Thus their rebellion—explicit in their loud, rude, on-air style and implicit in their love for forbidden black culture—had become an essential component of rock and roll."[1] By the early 1950s, their entire nighttime schedule had sold out. But with Ward in charge and the change blessed by Dudley and Mountcastle, the three pioneers of rhythm and blues programming were overruled.

In September 1972, Ward issued a press release announcing WLAC would become a contemporary Top 40 station. I suspect the winding down of R & B was the reason my grandfather had been compelled to share his stories with me

---

1. Eric Rothenbuhler, "Rock and Roll Format," in *Encyclopedia of Radio*, vol. 3, ed. Christopher H. Sterling (New York: FitzRoy Dearborn, 2004), 1220.

during that summer. He was able to relive some of his fondest moments with someone who was truly interested.

In April 1973, the station dropped their long affiliation with CBS news. Gab told Don Whitehead he would now have to concentrate on local news. One of Don's favorite activities at WLAC had been sharing the national news updates with WVOL, the Black station where my father had worked. WVOL employed a former Miss Black Nashville, Oprah Winfrey, who at the time was a speech major at TSU and, like Don, participated in theater productions. Because Don had so much in common with the bright young woman, he enjoyed mentoring and interacting with her. Within a year, Oprah was hired as a reporter for WLAC-TV.

The summer of '73 was the last one I spent with my grandparents. It was also the last summer Gene, John, and Gab worked at WLAC. They didn't agree with the station's programming change and left in protest. They were like foster parents who'd raised a child and when that child left, abandoned the calling. Together, they had introduced "cotton field" blues to the nation, cross-fertilized the airwaves, and given the genre commercial legitimacy. The bad luck, bad love, bad whiskey, loneliness, and despair that fueled the lyrics of the blues and gave witness to the inequity of the Jim Crow South had become their collective calling card. When John and Gene had been allowed to select their own music, the broadcasts had meaning. The bland repetition of Top 40, without theme or purpose, seemed to tranquilize listeners rather than enlighten them. The new format was as different from the old as a washboard was from a violin.

Gene retired for the second time that spring. On August 1, after thirty-one years at the station, John delivered his final broadcast. The man music historians now consider the granddaddy of R & B bought an Airstream trailer to at last spend quality time with the extended family he'd worked so long and hard to support.

On March 26, 1985, when John was terminally ill with emphysema and three different cancers, Wolfman Jack emceed a benefit concert for John, featuring performances by James Brown, B.B. King, Ella Washington, Jackie Beavers, Hank Ballard, the Neville Brothers, Joe Simon, Ruth Brown, the Coasters, Carla Thomas, Charlie Daniels, Rufus Thomas, and others. The

"Roots of Rhythm & Rock" tribute at the Ryman Auditorium was said to be one of James Brown's best performances.

John died a year later. Of him, the *Tennessean*'s editor wrote:

> Mr. Richbourg was a man of great kindness, compassion and generosity. He saw good in almost everyone including a few who were at least mean-spirited. He certainly was never that. He was a loving person, dedicated to family and church. He would like being remembered as that and not a legend. But a legend he was.[2]

After years of trying to get the board to let him hire a Black deejay, Gab's final act was to hire Spider Harrison, a Black man from New York who had been broadcasting in Indianapolis. Gab had spent twenty-eight years defending his deejays, advertisers, and revolutionary programming. With race music now established as R & B and its country hybrid by-product, rock and roll, dominating the charts, Gab felt his work was done.

Hoss was the only member of the "Three Kings of Late Night" to stay at the station after the change. After he was released from the Cumberland Heights rehab facility in June 1971, he switched his program to feature gospel music. He couldn't be the wild-ass Hossman without liquor, and his R & B broadcasts had fueled that lifestyle. Full of remorse for his misbehavior and with a steely determination to remain sober, Hoss reoriented his life.

"If I'd stayed with blues and pop, I'd have had to broadcast live at night from the studio. I knew if I stayed up [there] to do a show from one to three in the morning I was a dead duck. There was no way I could do it and stay dry."[3]

Rather than live as a blues musician, he lived as a gospel musician. He kept a letter on the wall beside him that read, "I listened to you for two nights last week when I could not sleep. Your program helped me make it through the night."[4]

Along with the gospel music he played, Hoss brought solace and inspiration

---

2. "Mr. Richbourgh Influenced Many," *Tennessean*, February 19, 1986, 10.
3. John L. Landes, "WLAC, the Hossman, and Their Influence on Black Gospel," *Black Music Research Journal* 7 (1987), 76.
4. Landes, 76.

to his listeners. To his credit, Hoss remained sober for the rest of his life and he went out of his way to make amends. He remarried Nancy. Together they helped raise Rogan's daughter.

Reminiscing about his life, Hoss said:

> When I was playing the blues, I've often said, I was living the blues. I lived the lyrics and it brought a lot of pain to me and my family and to a lot of other people. I drank too much. In fact, I was an alcoholic. But it went hand-in-hand with the kind of music I was playing and the kind of life I was leading. It all went together. I used to drink a pint or more on air every night. But it never seemed to affect my delivery. I don't think anyone out there ever knew except maybe my boss. But it was a way of life with me; the music was exciting and I was trying to get up every night to be on top of the records.[5]

Hoss retired in 1992. On May 5, his long career was celebrated with a roast and benefit concert for Cumberland Heights, where he'd been treated for his alcohol addiction. "A Night for the Hossman" featured performances by Rev. Al Green and Shirley Cesar. Gab spoke during the roast. The index cards Gab used to outline his speech included these words: "We were not only co-workers but good friends. . . . Oh Hoss, we've had lots of laughs, a few tears, and some wonderful times together. Thank you for sharing them with me but thank you most for sharing yourself. Your friendship is one of the things I treasure most in this world."[6]

They stayed close friends for life.

It was during that summer when I first heard my grandfather mention Sou's name. I'd nearly forgotten about this until I started researching Black night-clubs. Sou's name stayed with me because in Hendersonville, we'd frequently cruise the boat by Johnny Cash's place. When my grandfather mentioned Sou, I asked if he'd inspired Cash's song, "A Boy Named Sue." He said he hadn't; the lyrics were penned by Shel Silverstein, who had been inspired to write a story about his childhood friend, a boy named Jean. Yet, knowing Silverstein lived

---

5. Landes, 76
6. E. G. Blackman, personal correspondence, April 27, 1992.

in Nashville and frequented the New Era Club, I'd like to imagine Silverstein chose to name this mythical Sue after Sou Bridgeforth.

I continued to try to visit my grandparents for a few days each summer. In August 1992, I took my daughters, Christy and Leanne, with me to Hendersonville. While there, Pop told me how he'd organized a foursome of eighty-year-old golfers, who could each shoot their age, at Bluegrass Country Club. They advertised in national golf magazines for a like-aged foursome. Each golfer was required to be over eighty with individual handicaps that confirmed they could shoot their age. Gab had received no response. The following year, he tried again, this time advertising for twosomes. Still no response. Then one day, when Gab was at Bluegrass, a longtime Black caddy, Sammy Watkins, told Gab someone had asked about the ad. The interested golfer wanted to know if the person advertising for a twosome was Gab Blackman, formerly of WLAC radio. Sammy confirmed it was and told the golfer to call Gab. That golfer was Sou.

They set a date to play, and Gab intentionally scheduled the match after September 17, as on that day he turned eighty-four, and at that level of play one stroke can determine who wins.

Sou and Gab scheduled a tee time at Two Rivers, so neither had a home-course advantage. On the day they played, they were both eighty-four and had the same handicap. As I wrote this story, the thought occurred to me that Sou and Gab were like doppelgangers of a different race. They had so much in common, even their daughters, who were most commonly addressed by their middle names—Gab's daughter, Susan Gayle, and Sou's daughter, Harriett Gail, who was called Baby at home and Gail by her extended family. Had Gab and Sou been born in another place, or at another time, they may have been as close as brothers. Yet for most of their lives, friendships between Black men and white men in the South weren't just unusual, they were virtually illegal. Jim Crow wouldn't have allowed them to play a golf match or even share a meal.

I regret never having followed up with my grandfather about that golf game. Harriett and I can only imagine what they must have discussed. We agreed that Sou likely won and Gab probably did most of the talking. In fact, Gab probably came home with a sunburned tongue.

Sou still owned and operated the New Era Club when he and Gab played golf, which must have provided a lot of fodder for interesting conversations. Sou sold the club in 1996.

Sou and Gab were also each lifelong baseball fans. Sou spent many long afternoons at the Old Negro League Sports Shop, entertaining curious customers with stories of what once transpired at Sulphur Dell, where nothing now remains but a historical marker. Three years before Sou passed away in 2004, he wrote a brief biography, which included the following:

> I entered the world with a purpose . . . to be the very best I could be . . . I am blessed and thankful, and I give much credit to my grandparents, Henry and Mary Stuart . . . they made me what I am today . . . a self-supporting, giving person who gives an honest day's work for honest pay, and one who tries to treat others as I want to be treated. . . . The Nashville community has been good to me, and I had tried to be good to them! I am proud of my heritage, my family, my friends, and the contributions I have been able to give to the communities in which I have lived. If I had my life to live over, I don't believe I would change a thing. I have been truly blessed to be . . . A boy named Sou.[7]

A few days after Gab retired from WLAC, my grandparents planned to come visit us in Omaha. The morning before they were scheduled to leave, my grandfather suffered a heart attack. En route to the hospital, Gab said, "Christine, the Lord has always been so good to us. Isn't it good this happened today instead of after we had already gotten on the road to Omaha?"

After Jimmy Ward heard of Gab's heart attack and what he'd said to Christine on the way to the hospital, Jimmy wrote Gab. In part, his letter of January 7, 1974, reads:

> That epitomizes the Blackmans' spirit of optimism—the ability to see the good that comes from our challenges, rather than just the bleak and discouraging. In fact, as I look back over the years, most of the things that I have learned from you have come from seeing an example rather than from

---

7. Bridgeforth personal pamphlet, July 2001.

preachment. That is the way He taught us to live. "Let your light so shine that by their works, you shall know them."[8]

Gab was listening to an Atlanta Braves baseball game when he died of a heart attack in November 1997. Gayle and her husband, Lance, found him at his antique desk with cookies and milk and a baseball score pad. With his final instructions, Gab left us these words of wisdom:

"I had more than a sixty-five-year love affair with Christine and our family. Christine taught me that the most important word during a lifetime is LOVE. . . . Remember that an act of love, no matter how great or small, is never forgotten. I learned from 'Tee' that a smile, a 'How are you?' . . . and a warm, close, caring hug always gives Love, Faith and Hope."

Jimmy Ward was quoted in the *Tennessean*: "Gab was instrumental in making WLAC an advertising force throughout the South."[9]

The *Hendersonville Star News* reported, "Gab was a man of impeccable integrity and a very caring individual. He really cared for his fellow human beings, rich or poor, and with that there was such love that grew out of Gab."

This is what made Gab and Sou such similar men. They were fair-minded and truly cared about other people. They each went out of their way to help others and to be a champion for those less fortunate.

As with Dr. Ulmer, who advised me on the Black church and how the broadcasts were received by the audience, and Greg Howard, who honed my storytelling skills, I found a kindred spirit in Harriett Bridgeforth Jordon. I cherish every moment I spend with her. Each time we're together we think how unfortunate it was that Sou and Gab were in their mid-eighties before they had the opportunity to enjoy each other's company. There is wisdom in the old adage that "variety is the spice of life," which certainly applies to one's friendships.

At the time Harriett and I started working together, a movement was underway to remove the bust of Nathan Bedford Forrest from the Tennessee State Capitol. Tennessee's governor Bill Lee had campaigned on the promise that he wouldn't allow Confederate monuments to be removed or destroyed;

8. Personal correspondence, James Ward to Gab Blackman, January 1973.
9. Katrina Creekmore, *Tennessean*, November 16, 1997, 31.

however, over the two years Harriett and I worked on these pages, Governor Lee's opinion evolved.

On July 23, 2021, we celebrated the relocation of Forrest's bust from the State Capitol to the Tennessee State Museum, where it belongs. And while it seemed long overdue, to quote Helen—that ain't nuthin'!

The removal of the Forrest bust came a year after Nashville renamed Fifth Avenue North—where the student protests had occurred—John Lewis Way. Charlotte Avenue, where each of the four incarnations of the New Era Club were located, is now Martin Luther King Jr. Blvd. We were also able to tour the newly opened National Museum of African American Music together. It was one of the most enjoyable days of my life.

At long last, Nashville finally lived up to its reputation as "the Athens of the South." The city you visit today is not the city described in these pages. If one considers Nashville a character in this book, it's the character with the most profound story arc.

And our two protagonists, Gab and Sou? I like to imagine they're dancing in heaven, Sou in his baseball cleats and Gab in his two-tone, leather dance shoes, metal plates and all.

ACKNOWLEDGMENTS

While my name alone is on the cover, the narrative and stories contained within these pages were made possible by the generous assistance of:

Harriett Bridgeforth Jordan, whose contribution was invaluable. Her enthusiastic encouragement and delightful sense of humor made a tedious writing process fun; and Dr. Kenneth Ulmer, whose spiritual guidance motivated me throughout this long journey.

My brother and sister-in-law, Cris and Tina Blackman, provided both encouragement and a downtown Nashville writer's haven. The sunset view from the towering balcony was the perfect antidote to long days spent staring at blurry microfilm.

The mentors: author (The) Wes Smith, who first documented this story and then encouraged me to write it; Gregory Allen Howard, who helped structure the pages and helped with the interviews; and Carole Greene, who suggested the creative nonfiction format and became my first editor; I am forever indebted.

Thank you to those who generously provided information, documents, and photographs: Ed Blackman, Don Whitehead, Nikki Nobles, Spider Harrison, Barry Kirby, Chris Zowarka, Ellen Baldassarre, Gayle and Lance McMinn, Kaye and Steve George, Barbara Young, Kim and Jerry Lumpkins, Wade McMinn, Ronnie Yates, Eugene Brown, Wendell Melvin, Rev. James Lawson, Libby Battle, Billy Cox, Lucious Talley, James Watkins, Buddy Burke, Michael Gray, Karen Russell, Barry Maddox, John Wood, Lorenzo Washington, Bebe Evans, as well as the late James Ward, Lelaine Richbourg Cleaves, Little Richard, and B.B. King.

My enthusiastic assistant, best friend, and dependable girl Friday, Tess Chiodo; bookkeeper/Jill-of-all-trades, Ruth Lowther; and tech-savvy right-hand-man, Patrick De Mare; without y'all, the mountains of research would still be thousands of random pages in three-ring binders.

To my agent, Shannon Marven at Dupree Miller, as well as the team at Harper Horizon (past and present): Andrea and Amanda, Matt, Austin, Andrew, Sicily, Kevin, and Belinda—thank you for giving me the opportunity to share these historic events with the world.

And finally, none of this would have been possible without the loving support of my daughters, Christy Thrasher and Leanne Thrasher Chang; and my husband, Michael Iacampo; who provided both financial and emotional support. Thank you for always believing in me.

Paula Hope Blackman Iacampo

January 2023

ABOUT THE AUTHOR

A retired gemologist, Paula Blackman—granddaughter of E. Gab Blackman—turned her lifelong storytelling hobby into a second career, becoming an author, screenwriter, and playwright. She is a sixth-generation Tennessee native who divides her time between Nashville and Southwest Florida, where she lives with her husband, Michael Iacampo.